FOB AND OTHER PLAYS
by David Henry Hwang

FOB—this deeply moving, at times wildly funny play explores the conflicts and similarities between two Chinese-Americans and a Chinese exchange student who is "fresh-off-the-boat."

The Dance and the Railroad—explores the inhuman working conditions that led up to the 1867 strike of Chinese railway workers.

Family Devotions—a complicated and disturbing play described by the playwright himself: "It's about the myths that grow up around a family history and how legends of past family members affect the lives of the living."

The House of Sleeping Beauties—a fantasy based on a Japanese short story about a bizarre brothel.

The Sound of a Voice—tells of the extraordinary chance encounter of a medieval wandering Samurai with a seductive woman living in solitude.

1000 Airplanes on the Roof—the result of Hwang's collaboration with Philip Glass, this is a uniquely fascinating science fiction music-drama about a man who has been abducted by space aliens.

Individually brilliant, these six plays combine to reflect the extraordinary scope and range of an important new voice in the American theater.

DAVID HENRY HWANG was born in 1957 of Chinese immigrant parents. Acknowledged as one of the brightest young American playwrights at work today, Hwang is the author of the Tony award-winning play *M. Butterfly,* available in a Plume edition.

D0448543

FOB
and Other Plays

David Henry Hwang

with a Foreword by Maxine Hong Kingston

A PLUME BOOK

PLUME
Published by the Penguin Group
Penguin Books USA Inc., 375 Hudson Street, New York, New York 10014,
U.S.A.
Penguin Books Ltd, 27 Wrights Lane, London W8 5TZ, England
Penguin Books Australia Ltd, Ringwood, Victoria, Australia
Penguin Books Canada Ltd, 10 Alcorn Ave., Suite 300, Toronto, Canada M4V
3B2
Penguin Books (N.Z.) Ltd, 182-190 Wairau Road, Auckland 10, New Zealand
Penguin Books Ltd, Registered Offices: Harmondsworth, Middlesex, England

Published by Plume, an imprint of New American Library, a division of
Penguin Books USA Inc.

REGISTERED TRADEMARK—MARCA REGISTRADA

LIBRARY OF CONGRESS CATALOGING-IN-PUBLICATION DATA

Hwang, David Henry, 1957–
    FOB and other plays / by David Henry Hwang ;
    with a foreword by Maxine Hong Kingston.
        p.   cm.
    ISBN 0-452-26323-9
    I. Title.
    PS 3558.W83F6 1990
    812'.54—dc20   89-13319
                                                      CIP

First Printing, March, 1990
2   3   4   5   6   7   8   9   10   11

PRINTED IN THE UNITED STATES OF AMERICA

Contents

Foreword

by Maxine Hong Kingston

"Look here," says a long-lost relative in David Henry Hwang's latest play. "At your face. Study your face and you will see—the shape of your face is the shape of faces back many generations. . . ." Not only I but many other Chinese Americans could not hold back tears. There—on the stage, in public—were our gestures, our voices, our accents, our own faces. It isn't sad scenes that bring the tears, but a realization of how isolated we've been and a wonder that our private Chinese lives and secret language can be communally understood. To see even one other person indicate "myself" by pointing to his nose makes me know I am not alone; there are two of us. But to be among an audience at a play—here are many of us. Here is a community. We become proud to the bones.

One of the happiest moments I have ever had at the theater was watching the young men in *FOB* pour hot sauce on their food and gulp it down in an eating contest. I myself had just written a scene about an eating race. To have a fellow writer who works an ocean and a continent away meet me at an intersection reassures me that there is a place called Chinese America and that I am seeing it with an authentic vision.

In fact, *Family Devotions*, the most complicated and disturbing of the plays, has a humor that is utterly familiar. Let me savor some of it again by quoting a few lines:

AMA: . . . You remember Twa-Ling? Before we leave China, before Communist come, she say, "I will send you a picture. If Communists are good, I will stand—if bad, I will sit."

POPO: That does not mean anything!

AMA: In picture she sent, she was lying down!

Yes, in the picture my grandmother sent, she was lying down! We make up stories about the people far away.

The characters in David Hwang's plays speak idioms and make sounds that go straight to the heart and the guts: "Ai-ya." "Suffer, good for you." "Junk stuffs." That wonderful scene where Popo "translates" Jenny's speech and comes up with all the wrong meanings. And here exactly is our view of the Japanese from World War II movies: "Kill and laugh. Kill and laugh." "Torture and laugh." David Hwang has an ear for Chinatown English, the language of childhood and the subconscious, the language of emotion, the language of home.

Telling true stories to one another is very important for those whose histories and literature have been left out of textbooks. Writers will find these plays appealing because their author deals with some troublesome basic questions: How to tell stories and what stories to tell? *The Dance and the Railroad* and *Family Devotions,* two plays quite different from each other in their moods and powers, both tell about people who are shut out of mainstream cultures and how they manage to create their own rites. In the former play, the dance turns out to be beautiful, but in the latter, the "devotions" become grotesque and deadly. "You don't remember," accuses a character in *Family Devotions.* "Your stories do not remember."

David Hwang writes stories that do remember. Especially in *FOB*, he draws from Chinese mythology and asks what good those myths do us in America. *The Dance and the*

Railroad reminds us that when our pioneer ancestors built the railroad through the Sierras, they struck against inhuman "coolie" labor. This play is also about artists who have to support art with hard labor. After work, they practice their art on their own time. Finally, their new art praises the working man.

A good playwright also "remembers" true stories that haven't happened. David Hwang's plays are not just about what is familiar; they take us far imaginatively. In *Family Devotions*, the humor turns black. These are no family devotions I ever participated in. The two most beguiling characters die suddenly and nightmarishly. Is this a warning? Is this what happens to a family that is warped by isolation? Is it time to stop hanging on to shreds of strange traditions somebody brought from China?

Chinese American actors are given too few dignified parts to play. If no playwrights like David Hwang came along, a generation of actors who speak our accents would be lost. A novelist can only invent an approximate orthography. For voices, the play's the thing. Chinese American theater, which started out with a bang—firecrackers, drums—keeps dying out. David Henry Hwang gives it life once again.

Introduction

While in London recently preparing the West End production of *M. Butterfly*, I wrote an article for *The Guardian* about Orientalism, defined by the scholar Edward Seyd as a view of the East as mysterious, inscrutable, and ultimately inferior. Several weeks later, I met an Anglo-Indian gentleman who complimented me on the piece and made a telling observation: He was surprised that I had referred to American history as "*our* history." In England, he felt, minorities had not yet come to regard British history as their own, nor were they encouraged to do so.

This highlighted to me again the difference between Old World countries and the American experiment. Though it is often observed in the breach, America—at least in principle—subscribes to the notion that whoever takes residence on these shores may call them home. This is a relatively new concept in the history of ideas, and I think people of color grapple with it in a particularly vital fashion. As an Asian American, one of the particular burdens of my minority is that we are never completely accepted as Americans; we are perpetual foreigners. Hence, acquaintances may assume I possess a knowledge of Chinese where they would never presume the native language proficiency of an American of, say, Swedish descent. On a more frightening level, Japanese Americans were interned in concentration camps during World War II, while the loyalty of German- and Italian-Americans went rightfully unchallenged.

In attempting to define my place in America, I have evolved through several different phases, and I imagine that many more lay ahead of me. Initially, we tend to be motivated by that most childlike of needs: to be accepted, to belong. This leads to an assimilationist phase, the desire to "out-white the whites." The Asian child sees America defined as predominantly of one color. Wanting to be part of this land, he attempts to become the same. The difficulty is, of course, that this is not possible; our inability to become white at will can produce terrible self-loathing. My first play, *FOB*, dealt largely with this dilemma. Certainly the American-born character Dale loathes the "Fresh-Off-the-Boat" Steve precisely because the latter represents all the identifications Dale has spent a lifetime attempting to avoid.

I discovered in college that the assimilationist model was dangerous and self-defeating. I attended Stanford in the late-1970s and, while many would consider the primary cultural focus of this era to be "Saturday Night Fever," it was also a time of budding Asian American consciousness. The Black Power movements which had begun on campuses in the late-1960s erupted in our communities a few years later. Living in an Asian American dorm, becoming involved with theater and musical groups of similar focus, I entered what might be considered an "isolationist-nationalist" phase. I became interested in working with and writing primarily for other Asian Americans.

Out of this period came *The Dance and the Railroad* and *Family Devotions*. The former is a history play, and the reclaiming of our American past is certainly a priority for Asians. An actual incident, the Chinese railroad workers' strike of 1867, provides the background of this piece. So often "coolie" laborers have been characterized in America as passive and subservient, two stereotypes often attached to Asians. The strike is important because it reminds us that in historical fact these were assertive men who stood up for their rights in the face of great adversity. *Family Devotions* is clearly autobiographical. I was raised as a born-again Christian, and the rejection of this Western mythology is, among other things, a casting off of the brainwashing white missionaries have consistently attempted to impose on "heathen" Asian cultures.

Having completed what amounts to a trilogy on Chinese America, I found myself in a curious position. Essentially, I had said everything I wanted to about my immediate background for the time being. As an artist, I now desired to explore different areas, while remaining committed to working within the Asian community. The result was two plays about tragic love set in Japan. I had long been fascinated by Japanese literature and film, and these seemed a logical extension of my interest. *The House of Sleeping Beauties* is based on a novella by the Nobel Prize-winning author Yasunari Kawabata. My piece is a fantasy about how the story may have come to be written, with Kawabata himself as a major character. (Subsequent to the play's composition, however, several people who knew the author during his lifetime confided to me that the bizarre brothel described in the novella does actually exist, so perhaps my speculations are not so fantastic.) *The Sound of a Voice* is inspired by Japanese ghost stories, although it has occurred to me that, with only minor alterations, it could be set in a mysterious forest on any continent.

After the production of these plays, I went through a two-year period of inactivity. The isolationist-nationalist model became less appealing to me. I continue to believe that such a phase is useful. To the extent that one's own self-esteem has been damaged by racism in the larger society, it is good and often necessary to become whole by interacting with members of one's own group. This having been achieved, however, it is self-defeating for individuals of any nationality to define their circle of acquaintances primarily by race. I cannot help but compare those who do so to the person who spends too many years loitering about his old high school.

Furthermore, isolationism runs the risk of reinforcing a dangerous prejudice of the larger society: namely, that minorities are defined first and foremost by race. If we are all equally Americans, then we should be equally able to write about many different types of characters. In tracing the history of ideas, it is interesting to observe how a notion which is progressive in one era calcifies and becomes reactionary in another. The idea that people of color, women, gays should define their own identities was radical and important in the 1950s. Going into the 1990s, however, we see how Hollywood, for example, has turned this into a kind of literary segregation; as illustration, Black writers are rarely hired except for projects involving Black topics. I am quick to stress here that the freedom to write on *any* subject must certainly extend as well to those who *choose* to address only, say, Asian Americans. These fall within a great American tradition of writers such as Tennessee Williams or F. Scott Fitzgerald who concentrated primarily on one group of people. America, however, must not restrict its "ethnic" writers to "ethnic" material, while assuming that white males can master any topic they so desire.

The immediate result of these musings was *Rich Relations*, my first play without characters specified as Asian. Though not without its detractors, this work remains important to me as the piece which reestablished my commitment to writing. A play about the possibility of resurrection, it did indeed resurrect my own love for work and point the way toward the non-Asian characters that were to follow in such works as *M. Butterfly*.

1000 Airplanes on the Roof sprang initially from an idea by Philip Glass and evolved into a three-way collaboration between myself, Mr. Glass, and the designer Jerome Sirlin.

Printed in this volume is one element of this multimedia music drama, a monologue delivered by the character M. about his possible encounter with beings from other worlds. While researching the topic of UFO abductions, I was moved by the plight of individuals who believe they have encountered this phenomenon. They seem to be caught in an insoluble dilemma: To the extent that they admit this has happened, they are, by definition, crazy; if they try to deny the experience, however, they create a dysjunction with their own past which then drives them crazy. In an odd way, this seemed not so far removed from the discomfort of Dale in *FOB*, as he attempted to deny his Asian past in order to assimilate into present-day America.

As the eighties draw to a close, my preoccupation with identity continues to evolve. I now believe that racial and ethnic distinctions in this country are useful only to a point. Certainly, as we identify ourselves as Irish American or Black American or Italian American or Mexican American, we are proclaiming the right of all these traditions to be incorporated into the multicultural landscape that is the American ideal. Our pride is a statement that we will never feel inferior because of our heritage. Yet it is important not to stray across a fine line and lapse into the chauvinism that would hold one culture somehow superior over any other. To do so would be to tragically ape the racism which has often manifested itself in American history.

I have also come full circle on the issue of tradition. Tradition is useful primarily as a reference point; isolation from the past makes for foolish decisions in the present. Yet the past provides so very few examples of societies worthy of emulation—societies which eschewed racism, sexism, imperialism, which provided for their poor, accepted alternative lifestyles, and renounced violence. How much more productive than a glorification of the past is an attempt to build a new model for the future.

Over the next decades, as Caucasians become increasingly a plurality rather than a majority in this country, we will struggle to evolve a truly progressive nation, one in which different ethnic, political, and social groups co-exist in a state of equality. Though America has often advertised itself as such, its actual history has more often been one of hypocrisy and prejudice. Though Misters Bush and Reagan may preach otherwise, the greatness of America lies not in a return to the past. In both my life and my work I will continue to grapple with an American dream for the future.

—DAVID HENRY HWANG

New York City, July 1989

FOB

For the warriors of my family

Playwright's Note

The roots of *FOB* are thoroughly American. The play began when a sketch I was writing about a limousine trip through Westwood, California, was invaded by two figures from American literature. Fa Mu Lan, the girl who takes her father's place in battle, from Maxine Hong Kingston's *The Woman Warrior*, and Gwan Gung, the god of fighters and writers, from Frank Chin's *Gee, Pop!*

This fact testifies to the existence of an Asian American literary tradition. Japanese Americans, for instance, wrote plays in American concentration camps during World War II. Earlier, with the emergence of the railroads, came regular performances of Cantonese operas, featuring Gwan Gung, the adopted god of Chinese America.

FOB was first produced by Nancy Takahashi for the Stanford Asian American Theatre Project. It was performed at Okada House on March 2, 1979, with the following cast:

DALE........................ Loren Fong
GRACE........................ Hope Nakamura
STEVE........................ David Pating

Directed by the author; lights by Roger Tang; sets by George Prince; costumes by Kathy Ko; Randall Tong, assistant director.

The play was then developed at the 1979 O'Neill National Playwrights Conference in Waterford, Connecticut, with the cast of Ernest Abuba, Calvin Jung, and Ginny Yang, directed by Robert Alan Ackerman.

FOB was produced in New York by Joseph Papp at the New York Shakespeare Festival Public Theater, where it opened on June 8, 1980, with the following cast:

DALE........................ Calvin Jung
GRACE........................ Ginny Yang
STEVE........................ John Lone

On-stage Stage
Managers................ Willy Corpus
                         Tzi Ma
On-stage Musician ...... Lucia Hwong

Directed by Mako; lighting by Victor En Yu Tan; sets by Akira Yoshimura and James E. Mayo; costumes by Susan Hom; choreography by John Lone; music by Lucia Hwong; David Oyama, assistant director.

CHARACTERS
(all in early twenties)

DALE, a second-generation American of Chinese descent.
GRACE, his cousin, a first-generation Chinese American.
STEVE, her friend, a Chinese newcomer.

PLACE

The back room of a small Chinese restaurant in Torrance, California.

TIME

The year 1980.

[handwritten: Gives definitions & things → represents culture!]

SYNOPSIS OF SCENES

Act one, Scene 1. Late afternoon.
Act one, Scene 2. A few minutes later.
Act two. After Dinner.

DEFINITIONS

chong you bing is a type of Chinese pancake, a Northern Chinese appetizer often made with dough and scallions, with a consistency similar to that of *pita* bread.
Gung Gung means "grandfather."
Mei Guo means "beautiful country," a Chinese term for America.
da dao and *mao* are two swords, the traditional weapons of Gwan Gung and Fa Mu Lan, respectively.

5

PROLOGUE

LIGHTS UP *on a blackboard. Enter* DALE *dressed preppie. The blackboard is the type which can flip around so both sides can be used. He lectures like a university professor, using the board to illustrate his points.*

DALE: F–O–B. Fresh Off the Boat. FOB. What words can you think of that characterize the FOB? Clumsy, ugly, greasy FOB. Loud, stupid, four-eyed FOB. Big feet. Horny. Like Lenny in *Of Mice and Men.* Very good. A literary reference. High-water pants. Floods, to be exact. Someone you wouldn't want your sister to marry. If you are a sister, someone you wouldn't want to marry. That assumes we're talking about boy FOBs, of course. But girl FOBs aren't really as . . . FOBish. Boy FOBs are the worst, the . . . pits. They are the sworn enemies of all ABC—oh, that's "American Born Chinese"—of all ABC girls. Before an ABC girl will be seen on Friday night with a boy FOB in Westwood, she would rather burn off her face.

(He flips around the board. On the other side is written: "1. Where to find FOBs. 2. How to spot a FOB")

FOBs can be found in great numbers almost anyplace you happen to be, but there are some locations where they

6

cluster in particularly large swarms. Community Colleges, Chinese club discos, Asian sororities, Asian fraternities, Oriental churches, shopping malls, and, of course, Bee Gee concerts. How can you spot a FOB? Look out! If you can't answer that, you might be one. (*He flips back the board, reviews*) F-O-B. Fresh Off the Boat. FOB. Clumsy, ugly, greasy FOB. Loud, stupid, four-eyed FOB. Big feet. Horny. Like Lenny in *Of Mice and Men*. Floods. Like Lenny in *Of Mice and Men*. F-O-B. Fresh Off the Boat. FOB.

(LIGHTS FADE *to black. We hear American pop music, preferably in the funk—R&B—disco area*)

Conflict: between FOB's and ABC's

ACT ONE

Scene 1

The back room of a small Chinese restaurant in Torrance, California. Single table, with tablecloth; various chairs, supplies. One door leads outside, a back exit, another leads to the kitchen. Lights up on GRACE, *at the table. The music is coming from a small radio. On the table is a small, partially wrapped box, and a huge blob of discarded Scotch tape. As* GRACE *tries to wrap the box, we see what has been happening: The tape she's using is stuck; so, in order to pull it out, she must tug so hard that an unusable quantity of tape is dispensed. Enter* STEVE, *from the back door, unnoticed by* GRACE. *He stands, waiting to catch her eye, tries to speak, but his voice is drowned out by the music. He is dressed in a stylish summer outfit.*

GRACE: Aaaai-ya!

STEVE: Hey!

(No response; he turns off the music)

GRACE: Huh? Look. Out of tape.

STEVE: *(In Chinese)* Yeah.

GRACE: One whole roll. You know how much of it got on here? Look. That much. That's all.

STEVE: *(In Chinese)* Yeah. Do you serve *chong you bing* today?

GRACE: *(Picking up box)* Could've skipped the wrapping paper, just covered it with tape.

STEVE: *(In Chinese)* Excuse me!

8

GRACE: Yeah? *(Pause)* You wouldn't have any on you, would
ya?

STEVE: *(English from now onward)* Sorry? No. I don't have
bing. I want to buy *bing.*

GRACE: Not *bing!* Tape. Have you got any tape?

STEVE: Tape? Of course I don't have tape.

GRACE: Just checking.

STEVE: Do you have any *bing?*

(Pause)

GRACE: Look, we're closed till five . . .

STEVE: Idiot girl.

GRACE: Why don't you take a menu?

STEVE: I want you to tell me!

(Pause)

GRACE: *(Ignoring* STEVE*)* Working in a Chinese restaurant,
you learn to deal with obnoxious customers.

STEVE: Hey! You!

GRACE: If the customer's Chinese, you insult them by giving forks.

STEVE: I said I want you to tell me!

GRACE: If the customer's Anglo, you starve them by not
giving forks.

STEVE: You serve *bing* or not?

GRACE: But it's always easy just to dump whatever happens
to be in your hands at the moment.

(She sticks the tape blob on STEVE*'s face)*

STEVE: I suggest you answer my question at once!

GRACE: And I suggest you grab a menu and start doing
things for yourself. Look, I'll get you one, even. How's
that?

STEVE: I want it from your mouth!

GRACE: Sorry. We don't keep 'em there.

STEVE: If I say they are there, they are there.

(He grabs her box)

GRACE: What— What're you doing? Give that back to me!
(They parry around the table)

STEVE: Aaaah! Now it's different, isn't it? Now you're listening to me.

GRACE: 'Scuse me, but you really are an asshole, you know that? Who do you think you are?

STEVE: What are you asking me? Who I am?

GRACE: Yes. You take it easy with that, hear?

STEVE: You ask who *I* am?

GRACE: One more second and I'm gonna call the cops.

STEVE: Very well, I will tell you.
(She picks up the phone. He slams it down)

STEVE: I said, I'll tell you.

GRACE: If this is how you go around meeting people, I think it's pretty screwed.

STEVE: Silence! I am Gwan Gung! God of warriors, writers, and prostitutes!
(Pause)

GRACE: Bullshit!

STEVE: What?

GRACE: Bullshit! Bull-shit! You are not Gwan Gung. And gimme back my box.

STEVE: I am Gwan Gung. Perhaps we should see what you have in here.

GRACE: Don't open that! *(Beat)* You don't look like Gwan Gung. Gwan Gung is a warrior.

STEVE: I am a warrior!

GRACE: Yeah? Why are you so scrawny, then? You wouldn't last a day in battle.

STEVE: My credit! Many a larger man has been humiliated by the strength in one of my size.

GRACE: Tell me, then. Tell me, if you are Gwan Gung. Tell me of your battles. Of one battle. Of Gwan Gung's favorite battle.

STEVE: Very well. Here is a living memory: One day, Gwan

Gung woke up and saw the ring of fire around the sun and decided, "This is a good day to slay villagers." So he got up, washed himself, and looked over a map of the Three Kingdoms to decide where first to go. For those were days of rebellion and falling empires, so opportunity to slay was abundant. But planned slaughter required an order and restraint which soon became tedious. So Gwan Gung decided a change was in order. He called for his tailor, who he asked to make a beautiful blindfold of layered silk, fine enough to be weightless, yet thick enough to blind the wearer completely. The tailor complied, and soon produced a perfect piece of red silk, exactly suited to Gwan Gung's demands. In gratitude, Gwan Gung stayed the tailor's execution sentence. He then put on his blindfold, pulled out his sword, and began passing over the land, swiping at whatever got in his path. You see, Gwan Gung figured there was so much revenge and so much evil in those days that he could slay at random and still stand a good chance of fulfilling justice. This worked very well until his sword, in its blind fury, hit upon an old and irritable atom bomb.

(GRACE *catches* STEVE, *takes back the box*)

GRACE: Ha! Some Gwan Gung you are! Some warrior you are! You can't even protect a tiny box from the grasp of a woman! How could you have shielded your big head in battle?

STEVE: Shield! Shield! I still go to battle!

GRACE: Only your head goes to battle, 'cause only your head is Gwan Gung.

(Pause)

STEVE: You made me think of you as a quiet listener. A good trick. What is your name?

GRACE: You can call me "The Woman Who Has Defeated Gwan Gung," if that's really who you are.

STEVE: Very well. But that name will change before long.

GRACE: That story you told—that wasn't a Gwan Gung story.

STEVE: What—you think you know all of my adventures through stories? All the books in the world couldn't record the life of one man, let alone a god. Now—do you serve *bing*?

GRACE: I won the battle; you go look yourself. There.

STEVE: You working here?

GRACE: Part time. It's my father's place. I'm also in school.

STEVE: School? University?

GRACE: Yeah. UCLA.

STEVE: Excellent. I have also come to America for school.

GRACE: Well, what use would Gwan Gung have for school?

STEVE: Wisdom. Wisdom makes a warrior stronger.

GRACE: Pretty good. If you are Gwan Gung, you're not the dumb jock I was expecting. Got a lot to learn about school, though.

STEVE: Expecting? You were expecting me?

GRACE: *(Quickly)* No, no. I meant, what I expected from the stories.

STEVE: Tell me, how do people think of Gwan Gung in America? Do they shout my name while rushing into battle, or is it too sacred to be used in such ostentatious display?

GRACE: Uh—no.

STEVE: No—what? I didn't ask a "no" question.

GRACE: What I mean is, neither. They don't do either of those.

STEVE: Not good. The name of Gwan Gung has been restricted for the use of leaders only?

GRACE: Uh—no. I think you better sit down.

STEVE: This is very scandalous. How are the people to take my strength? Gwan Gung might as well not exist, for all they know.

GRACE: You got it.

STEVE: I got what? You seem to be having trouble making your answers fit my questions.

GRACE: No, I think you're having trouble making your questions fit my answers.

STEVE: What is this nonsense? Speak clearly, or don't speak at all.

GRACE: Speak clearly?

STEVE: Yes. Like a warrior.

GRACE: Well, you see, Gwan Gung, god of warriors, writers, and prostitutes, no one gives a wipe about you 'round here. You're dead.

(Pause)

STEVE: You . . . you make me laugh.

GRACE: You died way back . . . hell, no one even noticed when you died—that's how bad off your PR was. You died and no one even missed a burp.

STEVE: You lie! The name of Gwan Gung must be feared around the world—you jeopardize your health with such remarks. *(Pause)* You—you have heard of me, I see. How can you say—?

GRACE: Oh, I just study it a lot—Chinese American history, I mean.

STEVE: Ah. In the schools, in the universities, where new leaders are born, they study my ways.

GRACE: Well, fifteen of us do.

STEVE: Fifteen. Fifteen of the brightest, of the most promising?

GRACE: One wants to be a dental technician.

STEVE: A man studies Gwan Gung in order to clean teeth?

GRACE: There's also a middle-aged woman that's kinda bored with her kids.

STEVE: I refuse—I don't believe you—your stories. You're just angry at me for treating you like a servant. You're trying to sap my faith. The people—the people outside—they know me—they know the deeds of Gwan Gung.

GRACE: Check it out yourself.

STEVE: Very well. You will learn—learn not to test the spirit of Gwan Gung.

(STEVE exits. GRACE *picks up the box. She studies it)*

GRACE: Fa Mu Lan sits and waits. She learns to be still while the emperors, the dynasties, the foreign lands flow past, unaware of her slender form, thinking it a tree in the woods, a statue to a goddess long abandoned by her people. But Fa Mu Lan, the Woman Warrior, is not ashamed. She knows that the one who can exist without movement while the ages pass is the one to whom no victory can be denied. It is training, to wait. And Fa Mu Lan, the Woman Warrior, must train, for she is no goddess, but girl—girl who takes her father's place in battle. No goddess, but woman—warrior-woman *(She breaks through the wrapping, reaches in, and pulls out another box, beautifully wrapped and ribboned)*—and ghost. *(She puts the new box on the shelf, goes to the phone, dials)* Hi, Dale? Hi, this is Grace . . . Pretty good. How 'bout you? . . . Good, good. Hey, listen, I'm sorry to ask you at the last minute and everything, but are you doing anything tonight? . . . Are you sure? . . . Oh, good. Would you like to go out with me and some of my friends? . . . Just out to dinner, then maybe we were thinking of going to a movie or something . . . Oh, good . . . Are you sure? . . . Yeah, okay. Um, we're all going to meet at the restaurant . . . No, *our* restaurant . . . right—as soon as possible. Okay, good . . . I'm really glad that you're coming. Sorry it's such short notice. Okay. Bye, now . . . Huh? Frank? Oh, okay. *(Pause)* Hi, Frank . . . Pretty good . . . Yeah? . . . No, I don't think so . . . Yeah . . . No, I'm sorry, I'd still rather not . . . I don't want to, okay? Do I have to be any clearer than that? . . . You are not! . . . You don't even know when they come—you'd have to lie on those tracks for hours . . . Forget it, okay? . . . Look, I'll get you a schedule so you can time it

properly . . . It's not a favor, damn it. Now goodbye! *(She hangs up) Jesus!*
(STEVE enters)

STEVE: Buncha weak boys, what do they know? One man—ChinaMan—wearing a leisure suit—green! I ask him, "You know Gwan Gung?" He says, "Hong Kong?" I say, "No, no. Gwan Gung." He says, "Yeah. They got sixty thousand people living on four acres. Went there last year." I say, "No, no. Gwan Gung." He says, "Ooooh! Gwan Gung?" I say, "Yes, yes, Gwan Gung." He says, "I never been there before."

GRACE: See? Even if you didn't die—who cares?

STEVE: Another kid—blue jeans and a T-shirt—I ask him, does he know Gwan Gung? He says, he doesn't need it, he knows Jesus Christ. What city is this now?

GRACE: Los Angeles.

STEVE: This isn't the only place where a new ChinaMan can land, is it?

GRACE: I guess a lot go to San Francisco.

STEVE: Good. This place got a bunch of weirdos around here.

GRACE: Yeah.

STEVE: They could never be followers of Gwan Gung. All who follow me must be loyal and righteous.

GRACE: Maybe you should try some other state.

STEVE: Huh? What you say?

GRACE: Never mind. You'll get used to it—like the rest of us.
(Pause. STEVE begins laughing)

STEVE: You are a very clever woman.

GRACE: Just average.

STEVE: No. You do a good job to make it seem like Gwan Gung has no followers here. At the university, what do you study?

GRACE: Journalism.

STEVE: Journalism—you are a writer, then?

GRACE: Of a sort.

STEVE: Very good. You are close to Gwan Gung's heart.

GRACE: As close as I'm gonna get.

STEVE: I would like to go out tonight with you.

GRACE: I knew it. Look, I've heard a lot of lines before, and yours is very creative, but . . .

STEVE: I will take you out.

GRACE: You will, huh?

STEVE: I do so because I find you worthy to be favored.

GRACE: You're starting to sound like any other guy now.

STEVE: I'm sorry?

GRACE: Look—if you're going to have any kinds of relationships with women in this country, you better learn to give us some respect.

STEVE: Respect? I give respect.

GRACE: The pushy, aggressive type is out, understand?

STEVE: Taking you out is among my highest tokens of respect.

GRACE: Oh, c'mon—they don't even say that in Hong Kong.

STEVE: You are being asked out by Gwan Gung!

GRACE: I told you, you're too wimpy to be Gwan Gung. And even if you were, you'd have to wait your turn in line.

STEVE: What?

GRACE: I already have something for tonight. My cousin and I are having dinner.

STEVE: You would turn down Gwan Gung for your cousin?

GRACE: Well, he has an X-1/9.

(Pause)

STEVE: What has happened?

GRACE: Look—I tell you what. If you take both of us out, then it'll be okay, all right?

STEVE: I don't want to go out with your cousin!

GRACE: Well, sorry. It's part of the deal.

STEVE: Deal? What deals? Why am I made part of these deals?

GRACE: 'Cause you're in the U.S. in 1980, just like the rest of us. Now quit complaining. Will you take it or not?

(Pause)

STEVE: Gwan Gung . . . bows to no one's terms but his own.

GRACE: Fine. Why don't you go down the street to Imperial Dragon Restaurant and see if they have *bing*?

STEVE: Do you have *bing*?

GRACE: See for yourself.

(She hands him a menu. He exits. GRACE *moves with the box)*

GRACE: Fa Mu Lan stood in the center of the village and turned round and round as the bits of fingers, the tips of tongues, the arms, the legs, the peeled skulls, the torn maidenheads, all whirled by. She pulled the loose gown closer to her body, stepped over the torsos, in search of the one of her family who might still be alive. Reaching the house that was once her home, crushing bones in her haste, only to find the doorway covered with the stretched and dried skin of that which was once her father. Climbing through an open window, noticing the shiny black thousand-day-old egg still floating in the shiny black sauce. Finding her sister tied spread-eagle on the mat, finding her mother in the basket in pieces, finding her brother nowhere. The Woman Warrior went to the mirror, which had stayed unbroken, and let her gown come loose and drop to the ground. She turned and studied the ideographs that had long ago been carved into the flesh of her young back . . . Carved by her mother, who lay carved in the basket.

*(*DALE *enters, approaches* GRACE)*

She ran her fingers over the skin and felt the ridges where there had been pain.

(DALE *is behind* GRACE)

GRACE: But now they were firm and hard.

(DALE *touches* GRACE, *who reacts by swinging around and knocking him to the ground. Only after he is down does she see his face*)

GRACE: Dale! Shit! I'm sorry. I didn't . . . !

DALE: *(Groggy)* Am I late?

GRACE: I didn't know it was you, Dale.

DALE: Yeah. Well, I didn't announce myself.

GRACE: You shouldn't just come in here like that.

DALE: You're right. Never again.

GRACE: I mean, you should've yelled from the dining room.

DALE: Dangerous neighborhood, huh?

GRACE: I'm so sorry. Really.

DALE: Yeah. Uh—where're your other friends? They on the floor around here too?

GRACE: No. Uh—this is really bad, Dale. I'm really sorry.

DALE: What?—you can't make it after all?

GRACE: No, I can make it. It's just that . . .

DALE: They can't make it? Okay, so it'll just be us. That's cool.

GRACE: Well, not quite us.

DALE: Oh.

GRACE: See, what happened is— You know my friend Judy?

DALE: Uh—no.

GRACE: Well, she was gonna come with us—with me and this guy I know—his name is . . . Steve.

DALE: Oh, he's with you, right?

GRACE: Well, sort of. So since she was gonna come, I thought you should come too.

DALE: To even out the couples?

GRACE: But now my friend Judy, she decided she had too much work to do, so . . . oh, it's all messed up.

DALE: Well, that's okay. I can go home—or I can go with you, if this guy Steve doesn't mind. Where is he, anyway?

GRACE: I guess he's late. You know, he just came to this country.

DALE: Oh yeah? How'd you meet him?

GRACE: At a Chinese dance at UCLA.

DALE: Hmmmm. Some of those FOBs get moving pretty fast.

(GRACE glares)

DALE: Oh. Is he . . . nice?

GRACE: He's okay. I don't know him that well. You know, I'm really sorry.

DALE: Hey, I said it was okay. Jesus, it's not like you hurt me or anything.

GRACE: For that, too.

DALE: Look— *(He hits himself)* No pain!

GRACE: What I meant was, I'm sorry tonight's got so messed up.

DALE: Oh, it's okay. I wasn't doing anything anyway.

GRACE: I know, but still . . .

(Silence)

DALE: Hey, that Frank is a joke, huh?

GRACE: Yeah. He's kind of a pain.

DALE: Yeah. What an asshole to call my friend.

GRACE: Did you hear him on the phone?

DALE: Yeah, all that railroad stuff?

GRACE: It was real dumb.

DALE: Dumb? He's dumb. He's doing it right now.

GRACE: Huh? Are you serious?

DALE: Yeah. I'm tempted to tie him down so, for once in his life, he won't screw something up.

GRACE: You're kidding!

DALE: Huh? Yeah, sure I'm kidding. Who would I go bowling with?

GRACE: No, I mean about him actually going out there—is that true?

DALE: Yeah—he's lying there. You know, right on Torrance Boulevard?

GRACE: No!

DALE: Yeah!

GRACE: But what if a train really comes?

DALE: I dunno. I guess he'll get up.

GRACE: I don't believe it!

DALE: Unless he's fallen asleep by that time or something.

GRACE: He's crazy.

DALE: Which is a real possibility for Frank, he's such a bore anyway.

GRACE: He's weird.

DALE: No, he just thinks he's in love with you.

GRACE: Is he?

DALE: I dunno. We'll see when the train comes.

GRACE: Do you think we should do something?

DALE: What?—You're not gonna fall for the twerp, are you?

GRACE: Well, no, but . . .

DALE: He's stupid—and ugly, to boot.

GRACE: . . . but staying on the tracks is kinda dangerous.

DALE: Let him. Teach him a lesson.

GRACE: You serious?

DALE: *(Moving closer to* GRACE*)* Not to fool with my cousin. *(He strokes her hair. They freeze in place, but his arm continues to stroke.* STEVE *enters, oblivious of* DALE *and* GRACE, *who do not respond to him. He speaks to the audience as if it were a panel of judges)*

STEVE: No! Please! Listen to me! This is fifth time I come here. I tell you both my parents, I tell you their parents, I tell you their parents' parents and who was adopted great-granduncle. I tell you how many beggars in home town and name of their blind dogs. I tell you number of steps from my front door to temple, to well, to governor house, to fields, to whorehouse, to fifth cousin inn, to eighth neighbor toilet—you ask only: What for am I in whorehouse? I tell north, south, northeast, southwest, west, east, north-northeast, south-southwest, east eastsouth—Why will you not let me enter in America? I come here five times—I raise lifetime fortune five times. Five times, I first come here, you say to me I am illegal, you return me on boat to fathers and uncles with no gold, no treasure, no fortune, no rice. I only want to come to America—come to "Mountain of Gold." And I hate Mountain and I hate America and I hate you! *(Pause)* But this year you call 1914—very bad for China.

(Pause; light shift. GRACE *and* DALE *become mobile and aware of* STEVE*'s presence)*

GRACE: Oh! Steve, this is Dale, my cousin. Dale, Steve.

DALE: Hey, nice to meet . . .

STEVE: *(Now speaking with Chinese accent)* Hello. Thank you. I am fine.

(Pause)

DALE: Uh, yeah. Me too. So, you just got here, huh? What'cha think?

*(*STEVE *smiles and nods,* DALE *smiles and nods;* STEVE *laughs,* DALE *laughs;* STEVE *hits* DALE *on the shoulder. They laugh some more. They stop laughing)*

DALE: Oh. Uh—good. *(Pause)* Well, it looks like it's just gonna be the three of us, right? *(To* GRACE*)* Where you wanna go?

GRACE: I think Steve's already taken care of that. Right, Steve?

STEVE: Excuse?

GRACE: You made reservations at a restaurant?

STEVE: Oh, reservations. Yes, yes.

DALE: Oh, okay. That limits the possibilities. Guess we're going to Chinatown or something, right?

GRACE: *(To* STEVE*)* Where is the restaurant?

STEVE: Oh. The restaurant is a French restaurant. Los Angeles downtown.

DALE: Oh, we're going to a Western place? *(To* GRACE*)* Are
you sure he made reservations?

GRACE: We'll see.

DALE: Well, I'll get my car.

GRACE: Okay.

STEVE: No!

DALE: Huh?

STEVE: Please—allow me to provide car.

DALE: Oh. You wanna drive.

STEVE: Yes. I have car.

DALE: Look—why don't you let me drive? You've got enough
to do without worrying about—you know—how to get
around L.A., read the stop signs, all that.

STEVE: Please—allow me to provide car. No problem.

DALE: Well, let's ask Grace, okay? *(To* GRACE*)* Grace, who
do you think should drive?

GRACE: I don't really care. Why don't you two figure it out?
But let's hurry, okay? We open pretty soon.

DALE: *(To* STEVE*)* Look—you had to pick the restaurant
we're going to, so the least I can do is drive.

STEVE: Uh, your car—how many people sit in it?

DALE: Well, it depends. Right now, none.

GRACE: *(To* DALE*)* He's got a point. Your car only seats two.

DALE: He can sit in the back. There's space there. I've fit
luggage in it before.

GRACE: *(To* STEVE*)* You want to sit in back?

STEVE: I sit—where?

DALE: Really big suitcases.

GRACE: Back of his car.

STEVE: X-1/9? Aaaai-ya!

DALE: X-1/9?

STEVE: No deal!

DALE: How'd he know that? How'd he know what I drive?

STEVE: Please. Use my car. Is . . . big.

DALE: Yeah? Well, how much room you got? *(Pause; slower)* How-big-your-car-is?

STEVE: Huh?

DALE: Your car—how is big?

GRACE: How big is your car?

STEVE: Oh! You go see.

DALE: 'Cause if it's, like, a Pinto or something, it's not that much of a difference.

STEVE: Big and black. Outside.

GRACE: Let's hurry.

DALE: Sure, sure.

(Exits)

GRACE: What you up to, anyway?

STEVE: *(Dropping accent)* Gwan Gung will not go into battle without equipment worthy of his position.

GRACE: Position? You came back, didn't you? What does that make you?

DALE: *(Entering)* Okay. There's only one black car out there—

STEVE: Black car is mine.

DALE: —and that's a Fleetwood limo. Now, you're not gonna tell me that's his.

STEVE: Cadillac. Cadillac is mine.

DALE: Limousine . . . Limousine is yours?

STEVE: Yes, yes. Limousine.

(Pause)

DALE: *(To GRACE)* You wanna ride in that black thing? People will think we're dead.

GRACE: It does have more room.

DALE: Well, it has to. It's built for passengers who can't bend.

GRACE: And the driver *is* expensive.

DALE: He could go home—save all that money.

GRACE: Well, I don't know. You decide.

DALE: *(To STEVE)* Look, we take my car, savvy?

STEVE: Please—drive my car.

DALE: I'm not trying to be unreasonable or anything.

STEVE: My car—just outside.

DALE: I know where it is, I just don't know why it is.

GRACE: Steve's father manufactures souvenirs in Hong Kong.

DALE: *(To* STEVE*)* Oh, and that's how you manage that out there, huh?—from thousands of aluminum Buddhas and striptease pens.

GRACE: Well, he can't drive and he has the money—

DALE: *(To* GRACE*)* I mean, wouldn't you just feel filthy?

GRACE: —so it's easier for him.

DALE: Getting out of a limo in the middle of Westwood? People staring, thinking we're from 'SC? Wouldn't you feel like dirt?

GRACE: It doesn't matter either way to me.

(Pause)

DALE: Where's your social conscience?

GRACE: Look—I have an idea. Why don't we just stay here.

STEVE: We stay here to eat?

GRACE: No one from the restaurant will bother us, and we can bring stuff in from the kitchen.

STEVE: I ask you to go out.

DALE: Look, Grace, I can't put ya out like that.

GRACE: *(To* DALE*)* It's no problem, really. It should be fun. *(To* STEVE*)* Since there are three of us—

DALE: Fun?

GRACE: *(To* STEVE*)* —it is easier to eat here.

DALE: How can it be fun? It's cheaper.

STEVE: Does not seem right.

GRACE: I mean, unless our restaurant isn't nice enough.

DALE: No, no—that's not it.

STEVE: *(Watching* DALE*)* No—this place, very nice.

GRACE: Are you sure?

DALE: Yeah. Sure.

STEVE: *(Ditto)* Yeah. Sure.

DALE: Do you have . . . uh—those *burrito* things?

GRACE: *Moo-shoo?*

DALE: Yeah, that.

GRACE: Yeah.

DALE: And black mushrooms.

GRACE: Sure.

DALE: And sea cucumber?

STEVE: Do you have *bing*?

(Pause)

GRACE: Look, Dad and Russ and some of the others are gonna be setting up pretty soon, so let's get our place ready, okay?

DALE: Okay. Need any help?

GRACE: Well, yeah. That's what I just said.

DALE: Oh, right. I thought maybe you were just being polite.

GRACE: Yeah. Meet me in the kitchen.

DALE: Are you sure your dad won't mind?

GRACE: What?

DALE: Cooking for us.

GRACE: Oh, it's okay. He'll cook for anybody.

(Exits. Silence)

DALE: So, how do you like America?

STEVE: Very nice.

DALE: "Very nice." Good, colorful Hong Kong English. English—how much of it you got down, anyway?

STEVE: Please repeat?

DALE: English—you speak how much?

STEVE: Oh—very little.

DALE: Honest. *(Pause)* You feel like you're an American? Don't tell me. Lemme guess. Your father. *(He switches into a mock Hong Kong accent.)* Your fad-dah tink he sending you here so you get yo' M.B.A., den go back and covuh da world wit' trinkets and beads. Diversify. Franchise. Sell—ah—Hong Kong X-Ray glasses at tourist shop at Buckingham Palace. You know—ah—"See da Queen"? *(Switches back)* He's hoping your American education's gonna create an empire of defective goods and breakable merchandise. Like those little cameras with the slides inside? I bought one at Disneyland once and it ended up having pictures of Hong Kong in it. You know how shitty it is to expect the Magic Kingdom and wind up with the skyline of Kowloon? Part of your dad's plan, I'm sure. But you're gonna double-cross him. Coming to America, you're gonna jump the boat. You're gonna decide you like us. Yeah—you're gonna like having fifteen theaters in three blocks, you're gonna like West Hollywood and Newport Beach. You're gonna decide to become an American. Yeah, don't deny it—it happens to the best of us. You can't hold out—you're no different. You won't even know it's coming before it has you. Before you're trying real hard to be just like the rest of us—go dinner, go movie, go motel, bang-bang. And when your father writes you that do-it-yourself acupuncture sales are down, you'll throw that letter in the basket and burn it in your brain. And you'll write that you're gonna live in Monterey Park a few years before going back home—and you'll get your green card—and you'll build up a nice little stockbroker's business and have a few American kids before your dad realizes what's happened and dies, his hopes reduced to a few chattering teeth and a pack of pornographic playing cards. Yeah—great things come to the U.S. out of Hong Kong.

STEVE: *(Lights a cigarette, blows smoke, stands)* Such as your parents?

(STEVE turns on the music, exits. BLACKOUT)

Scene 2

LIGHTS UP *on* DALE *and* STEVE *eating. It is a few minutes later and food is on the table.* DALE *eats Chinese style, vigorously shoveling food into his mouth.* STEVE *picks.* GRACE *enters carrying a jar of hot sauce.* STEVE *sees her.*

STEVE: *(To* GRACE*)* After eating, you like to go dance?

DALE: *(Face in bowl)* No, thanks. I think we'd be conspicuous.

STEVE: *(To* GRACE*)* Like to go dance?

GRACE: Perhaps. We will see.

DALE: *(To* STEVE*)* Wait a minute. Hold on. How can you just . . . ? I'm here, too, you know. Don't forget I exist just 'cuz you can't understand me.

STEVE: Please repeat?

DALE: I get better communication from my fish. Look, we go see movie. Three here, see? One, two, three. Three can see movie. Only two can dance.

STEVE: *(To* GRACE*)* I ask you to go dance.

GRACE: True, but . . .

DALE: *(To* GRACE*)* That would really be a screw, you know? You invite me down here, you don't have anyone for me to go out with, but you decide to go dancing.

GRACE: Dale, I understand.

DALE: Understand? That would really be a screw. *(To* STEVE*)* Look, if you wanna dance, go find yourself some nice FOB partner.

STEVE: "FOB"? Has what meaning?

GRACE: Dale . . .

DALE: F—O—B. Fresh Off the Boat. FOB.

GRACE: Dale, I agree.

DALE: See, we both agree. *(To* GRACE*)* He's a pretty prime example, isn't he? All those foreign students—

GRACE: I mean, I agree about going dancing.

DALE: —go swimming in their underwear and everything— What?

GRACE: *(To* STEVE*)* Please understand. This is not the right time for dancing.

STEVE: Okay.

DALE: "Okay." It's okay when *she* says it's okay.

STEVE: *(To* DALE*)* "Fresh Off Boat" has what meaning?

(Pause)

DALE: *(To* GRACE*)* Did you ever hear about Dad his first year in the U.S.?

GRACE: Dale, he wants to know . . .

DALE: Well, Gung Gung was pretty rich back then, so Dad must've been a pretty disgusting . . . one, too. You know, his first year here, he spent, like, thirteen thousand dollars. And that was back 'round 1950.

GRACE: Well, Mom never got anything.

STEVE: FOB means what?

DALE: That's probably 'cause women didn't get anything back then. Anyway, he bought himself a new car—all kinds of stuff, I guess. But then Gung Gung went bankrupt, so Dad had to work.

GRACE: And Mom starved.

DALE: Couldn't hold down a job. Wasn't used to taking orders from anyone.

GRACE: Mom was used to taking orders from everyone.

STEVE: Please explain this meaning.

DALE: Got fired from job after job. Something like fifteen in a year. He'd just walk in the front door and out the back, practically.

GRACE: Well, at least he had a choice of doors. At least he was educated.

STEVE: *(To* DALE*)* Excuse!

DALE: Huh?

GRACE: He was educated. Here. In America. When Mom came over, she couldn't quit just 'cause she was mad at her employer. It was work or starve.

DALE: Well, Dad had some pretty lousy jobs, too.

STEVE: *(To* DALE*)* Explain, please!

GRACE: Do you know what it's like to work eighty hours a week just to feed yourself?

DALE: Do you?

STEVE: Dale!

DALE: *(To* STEVE*)* It means you. You know how, if you go to a fish store or something, they have the stuff that just came in that day? Well, so have you.

STEVE: I do not understand.

DALE: Forget it. That's part of what makes you one.
(Pause)

STEVE: *(Picking up hot sauce, to* DALE*)* Hot. You want some?
(Pause)

DALE: Well, yeah. Okay. Sure.
*(*STEVE *puts hot sauce on* DALE*'s food)*

DALE: Hey, isn't that kinda a lot?

GRACE: See, Steve's family comes from Shanghai.

DALE: Hmmmm. Well, I'll try it.
(He takes a gulp, puts down his food)

GRACE: I think perhaps that was too much for him.

DALE: No.

GRACE: Want some water?

DALE: Yes.
*(*GRACE *exits)*

DALE: You like hot sauce? You like your food hot? All right—here. *(He dumps the contents of the jar on* STEVE*'s plate, stirs)* Fucking savage. Don't you ever worry about your intestines falling out?
*(*GRACE *enters, gives water to* DALE. STEVE *sits shocked)*

DALE: Thanks. FOBs can eat anything, huh? They're specially trained. Helps maintain the characteristic greasy look.

(STEVE, cautiously, begins to eat his food) .

DALE: What—? Look, Grace, he's eating that! He's amazing! A freak! What a cannibal!

GRACE: *(Taking DALE's plate)* Want me to throw yours out?

DALE: *(Snatching it back)* Huh? No. No, I can eat it.

(DALE and STEVE stare at each other across the table. In unison, they pick up as large a glob of food as possible, stuff it into their mouths. They cough and choke. They rest, repeat the face-off a second time. They continue in silent pain. GRACE, who has been watching this, speaks to us)

GRACE: Yeah. It's tough trying to live in Chinatown. But it's tough trying to live in Torrance, too. It's true. I don't like being alone. You know, when Mom could finally bring me to the U.S., I was already ten. But I never studied my English very hard in Taiwan, so I got moved back to the second grade. There were a few Chinese girls in the fourth grade, but they were American-born, so they wouldn't even talk to me. They'd just stay with themselves and compare how much clothes they all had, and make fun of the way we all talked. I figured I had a better chance of getting in with the white kids than with them, so in junior high I started bleaching my hair and hanging out at the beach—you know, Chinese hair looks pretty lousy when you bleach it. After a while, I knew what beach was gonna be good on any given day, and I could tell who was coming just by his van. But the American-born Chinese, it didn't matter to them. They just giggled and went to their own dances. Until my senior year in high school—that's how long it took for me to get over this whole thing. One night I took Dad's car and drove on Hollywood Boulevard, all the way from downtown to Beverly Hills, then back on Sunset. I was looking and listening—all the time with the window down, just so I'd feel like I was part of the city. And that Friday, it was—I guess—I said, "I'm lonely. And I don't like it. I don't like being alone." And that was all. As soon as I said it, I felt all of the breeze—it was really cool on my face—and I heard all of the radio—and the music sounded really good, you know? So I drove home.

(Pause. DALE *bursts out coughing)*

GRACE: Oh, I'm sorry. Want some more water, Dale?

DALE: It's okay. I'll get it myself.

(He exits)

STEVE: *(Looks at* GRACE*)* Good, huh?

*(*STEVE *and* GRACE *stare at each other, as* LIGHTS FADE TO BLACK*)*

END OF ACT ONE

ACT TWO

In BLACKOUT.

DALE: I am much better now. *(Single spot on* DALE*)* I go out now. Lots. I can, anyway. Sometimes I don't ask anyone, so I don't go out. But I could. *(Pause)* I am much better now. I have friends now. Lots. They drive Porsche Carreras. Well, one does. He has a house up in the Holly-wood Hills where I can stand and look down on the lights of L.A. I guess I haven't really been there yet. But I could easily go. I'd just have to ask. *(Pause)* My parents—they don't know nothing about the world, about watching Benson at the Roxy, about ordering *hors d'oeuvres* at Scandia's, downshifting onto the Ventura Freeway at midnight. They're yellow ghosts and they've tried to cage me up with Chinese-ness when all the time we were in America. *(Pause)* So, I've had to work real hard—real hard—to be myself. To not be a Chinese, a yellow, a slant, a gook. To be just a human being, like everyone else, *(Pause)* I've paid my dues. And that's why I am much better now. I'm making it, you know? I'm making it in America.

(A napkin is thrown in front of DALE's *face from right. As it passes, the lights go up. The napkin falls on what we recognize as the dinner table from the last scene. We are in the back room. Dinner is over.* STEVE *has thrown the napkin from where he is sitting in his chair.* DALE *is standing upstage of the table and had been talking to* STEVE*)*

32

DALE: So, look, will you just not be so . . . Couldn't you just be a little more . . . ? I mean, we don't have to do all this . . . You know what's gonna happen to us tomorrow morning? *(He burps)* What kinda diarrhea . . . ? Look, maybe if you could just be a little more . . . *(He gropes)* normal. Here—stand up.

(STEVE does)

DALE: Don't smile like that. Okay. You ever see *Saturday Night Fever*?

STEVE: Oh. *Saturday* . . .

DALE: Yeah.

STEVE: Oh. *Saturday Night Fever*. Disco.

DALE: That's it. Okay. You know . . .

STEVE: John Travolta.

DALE: Right. John Travolta. Now, maybe if you could be a little more like him.

STEVE: Uh—Bee Gees?

DALE: Yeah, right. Bee Gees. But what I mean is . . .

STEVE: You like Bee Gees?

DALE: I dunno. They're okay. Just stand a little more like him, you know, his walk?

(DALE tries to demonstrate)

STEVE: I believe Bee Gees very good.

DALE: Yeah. Listen.

STEVE: You see movie name of . . .

DALE: Will you listen for a sec?

STEVE: . . . *Grease?*

DALE: Hold on!

STEVE: Also Bee Gees.

DALE: I'm trying to help you!

STEVE: Also John Travolta?

DALE: I'm trying to get you normal!

STEVE: And—Oliver John-Newton.

DALE: WILL YOU SHUT UP? I'M TRYING TO HELP YOU! I'M TRYING . . .

STEVE: Very good!

DALE: . . . TO MAKE YOU LIKE JOHN TRAVOLTA!

(DALE grabs STEVE by the arm. Pause. STEVE coldly knocks DALE's hands away. DALE picks up the last of the dirty dishes on the table and backs into the kitchen. GRACE enters from the kitchen with the box wrapped in Act I. She sits in a chair and goes over the wrapping, her back to STEVE. He gets up and begins to go for the box, almost reaching her. She turns around suddenly, though, at which point he drops to the floor and pretends to be looking for something. She then turns back front, and he resumes his attempt. Just as he reaches the kitchen door, DALE enters with a wet sponge)

DALE: *(To STEVE)* Oh, you finally willing to help? I already brought in all the dishes, you know. Here—wipe the table.

(DALE gives sponge to STEVE, returns to kitchen. STEVE throws the sponge on the floor, sits back at table. GRACE turns around, sees sponge on the floor, picks it up, and goes to wipe the table. She brings the box with her and holds it in one hand)

GRACE: Look—you've been wanting this for some time now. Okay. Here. I'll give it to you. *(She puts it on the table)* A welcome to this country. You don't have to fight for it—I'll give it to you instead.

(Pause; STEVE pushes the box off the table)

GRACE: Okay. Your choice.

(GRACE wipes the table)

DALE: *(Entering from kitchen; sees GRACE)* What—you doing this?

GRACE: Don't worry, Dale.

DALE: I asked him to do it.

GRACE: I'll do it.

DALE: I asked him to do it. He's useless! *(DALE takes the sponge)* Look, I don't know how much English you know, but look-ee! *(He uses a mock Chinese accent)*

GRACE: Dale, don't do that.

DALE: *(Using sponge)* Look—makes table all clean, see?

GRACE: You have to understand . . .

DALE: Ooooh! Nice and clean!

GRACE: . . . he's not used to this.

DALE: Look! I can see myself!

GRACE: Look, I can do this. Really.

DALE: Here—now you do. *(DALE forces STEVE's hand onto the sponge)* Good. Very good. Now, move it around. *(DALE leads STEVE's hand)* Oh, you learn so fast. Get green card, no time flat, buddy.

(DALE removes his hand; STEVE stops)

DALE: Uh-uh-uh. You must do it yourself. Come. There—now doesn't that make you feel proud? *(He takes his hand off; STEVE stops. DALE gives up, crosses downstage. STEVE remains at the table, still)*

DALE: Jesus! I'd trade him in for a vacuum cleaner any day.

GRACE: You shouldn't humiliate him like that.

DALE: What humiliate? I asked him to wipe the table, that's all.

GRACE: See, he's different. He probably has a lot of servants at home.

DALE: Big deal. He's in America, now. He'd better learn to work.

GRACE: He's rich, you know.

DALE: So what? They all are. Rich FOBs.

GRACE: Does that include me?

DALE: Huh?

GRACE: Does that include me? Am I one of your "rich FOBs"?

DALE: What? Grace, c'mon, that's ridiculous. You're not rich. I mean, you're not poor, but you're not rich either. I mean, you're not a FOB. FOBs are different. You've been over here most of your life. You've had time to thaw out. You've thawed out really well, and, besides—you're my cousin.

(DALE strokes GRACE's hair, and they freeze as before. STEVE, meanwhile, has almost imperceptibly begun to clean with his sponge. He speaks to the audience as if speaking with his family)

STEVE: Yes. I will go to America. "Mei Guo." *(Pause. He begins working)* The white ghosts came into the harbor today. They promised that they would bring us to America, and that in America we would never want for anything. One white ghost told how the streets are paved with diamonds, how the land is so rich that pieces of gold lie on the road, and the worker-devils consider them too insignificant even to bend down for. They told of a land where there are no storms, no snow, but sunshine and warmth all year round, where a man could live out in the open and feel not even discomfort from the nature around him—a worker's paradise. A land of gold, a mountain of wealth, a land in which a man can make his fortune and grow without wrinkles into an old age. And the white ghosts are providing free passage both ways. *(Pause)* All we need to do is sign a worker's contract. *(Pause)* Yes, I am going to America.

(At this point, GRACE and DALE become mobile, but still fail to hear STEVE. GRACE picks up the box)

DALE: What's that?

STEVE: *(His wiping becomes increasingly frenzied)* I am going to America because of its promises. I am going to follow the white ghosts because of their promises.

DALE: Is this for me?

STEVE: Because they promised! They promised! AND LOOK! YOU PROMISED! THIS IS SHIT! IT'S NOT TRUE.

DALE: *(Taking the box)* Let's see what's inside, is that okay?

STEVE: *(Shoves DALE to the ground and takes the box)* IT IS NOT! *(With accent)* THIS IS MINE!

DALE: Well, what kind of shit is that?

STEVE: She gave this to me.

DALE: What kind of . . . we're not at your place. We're not in Hong Kong, you know. Look—look all around you—you see shit on the sidewalks?

STEVE: This is mine!

DALE: You see armies of rice-bowl haircuts?

STEVE: She gave this to me!

DALE: People here have their flies zipped up—see?

STEVE: You should not look in it.

DALE: So we're not in Hong Kong. And I'm not one of your servant boys that you can knock around—that you got by trading in a pack of pornographic playing cards—that you probably deal out to your friends. You're in America, understand?

STEVE: Quiet! Do you know who I am?

DALE: Yeah—you're a FOB. You're a rich FOB in the U.S. But you better watch yourself. 'Cause you can be sent back.

STEVE: Shut up! Do you know who I am?

DALE: You can be sent back, you know—just like that. 'Cause you're a guest here, understand?

STEVE: *(To* GRACE*)* Tell him who I am.

DALE: I know who he is—heir to a fortune in junk merchandise. Big deal. Like being heir to Captain Crunch.

STEVE: Tell him!

(Silence)

GRACE: You know it's not like that.

STEVE: Tell him!

DALE: Huh?

GRACE: All the stuff about rice bowls and—zippers—have you ever been there, Dale?

DALE: Well, yeah. Once. When I was ten.

GRACE: Well, it's changed a lot.

DALE: Remember getting heat rashes.

GRACE: People are dressing really well now—and the whole place has become really stylish—well, certainly not everybody, but the people who are well-off enough to send their kids to American colleges—they're really kinda classy.

DALE: Yeah.

GRACE: Sort of.

DALE: You mean, like him. So what? It's easy to be classy when you're rich.

GRACE: All I'm saying is . . .

DALE: Hell, I could do that.

GRACE: Huh?

DALE: I could be classy, too, if I was rich.

GRACE: You *are* rich.

DALE: No. Just upper-middle. Maybe.

GRACE: Compared to us, you're rich.

DALE: No, not really. And especially not compared to him. Besides, when I was born we were still poor.

GRACE: Well, you're rich now.

DALE: Used to get one Life Saver a day.

GRACE: That's all? One Life Saver?

DALE: Well, I mean, that's not all I lived on. We got normal food, too.

GRACE: I know, but . . .

DALE: Not like we were living in cardboard boxes or anything.

GRACE: All I'm saying is that the people who are coming in now—a lot of them are different—they're already real Westernized. They don't act like they're fresh off the boat.

DALE: Maybe. But they're still FOBs.

STEVE: Tell him who I am!

DALE: Anyway, real nice dinner, Grace. I really enjoyed it.

GRACE: Thank you.

STEVE: Okay! I will tell myself.

DALE: Go tell yourself—just don't bother us.

GRACE: *(Standing, to* STEVE*)* What would you like to do now?

STEVE: Huh?

GRACE: You wanted to go out after dinner?

STEVE: Yes, yes. We go out.

DALE: I'll drive. You sent the hearse home.

STEVE: I tell driver—return car after dinner.

DALE: How could you . . . ? What time did you . . . ? When did you tell him to return? What time?

STEVE: *(Looks at his watch)* Seven-five.

DALE: No—not what time is it. What time you tell him to return?

STEVE: Seven-five. Go see.

(DALE exits through kitchen)

STEVE: *(No accent)* Why wouldn't you tell him who I am?

GRACE: Can Gwan Gung die?

(Pause)

STEVE: No warrior can defeat Gwan Gung.

GRACE: Does Gwan Gung fear ghosts?

STEVE: Gwan Gung fears no ghosts.

GRACE: Ghosts of warriors?

STEVE: No warrior ghosts.

GRACE: Ghosts that avenge?

STEVE: No avenging ghosts.

GRACE: Ghosts forced into exile?

STEVE: No exiled ghosts.

GRACE: Ghosts that wait?

(Pause)

STEVE: *(Quietly)* May I . . . take you out tonight? Maybe not tonight, but some other time? Another time? *(He strokes her hair)* What has happened?

DALE: *(Entering)* I cannot believe it . . . *(He sees them)* What do you think you're doing? *(He grabs STEVE's hand. To STEVE)* What . . . I step out for one second and you just go and—hell, you FOBs are sneaky. No wonder they check you so close at Immigration.

GRACE: Dale, I can really take care of myself.

DALE: Yeah? What was his hand doing, then?

GRACE: Stroking my hair.

DALE: Well, yeah. I could see that. I mean, what was it doing stroking your hair? *(Pause)* Uh, never mind. All I'm saying is . . . *(He gropes)* Jesus! If you want to be alone, why don't you just say so, huh? If that's what you really want, just say it, okay?

(Pause)

DALE: Okay. Time's up.

GRACE: Was the car out there?

DALE: Huh? Yeah. Yeah, it was. I could not believe it. I go outside and—thank God—there's no limousine. Just as I'm about to come back, I hear this sound like the roar of death and this big black shadow scrapes up beside me. I could not believe it!

STEVE: Car return—seven-five.

DALE: And when I asked him—I asked the driver, what time he'd been told to return. And he just looks at me and says, "Now."

STEVE: We go out?

DALE: What's going on here? What is this?

STEVE: Time to go.

DALE: No! Not till you explain what's going on.

STEVE: *(To GRACE)* You now want to dance?

DALE: *(To GRACE)* Do you understand this? Was this coincidence?

STEVE: *(Ditto)* I am told good things of American discos.

DALE: *(Ditto)* You and him just wanna go off by yourselves?

STEVE: I hear of Dillon's.

DALE: Is that it?

STEVE: You hear of Dillon's?

DALE: It's okay, you know.

STEVE: In Westwood.

DALE: I don't mind.

STEVE: Three—four stories.

DALE: Really.

STEVE: Live band.

DALE: Cousin.

STEVE: We go.

(He takes GRACE's *hand)*

DALE: He's just out to snake you, you know.

(He takes the other hand. From this point on, almost unnoticeably, the LIGHTS BEGIN TO DIM*)*

GRACE: Okay! That's enough! *(She pulls away)* That's enough! I have to make all the decisions around here, don't I? When I leave it up to you two, the only place we go is in circles.

DALE: Well . . .

STEVE: No, I am suggesting place to go.

GRACE: Look, Dale, when I asked you here, what did I say we were going to do?

DALE: Uh—dinner and a movie—or something. But it was a different "we," then.

GRACE: It doesn't matter. That's what we're going to do.

DALE: I'll drive.

STEVE: My car can take us to movie.

GRACE: I think we better not drive at all. We'll stay right here. *(She removes* STEVE's *tie)* Do you remember this?

DALE: What—you think I borrow clothes or something? Hell, I don't even wear ties.

*(*GRACE *takes the tie, wraps it around* DALE's *face like a blindfold)*

DALE: Grace, what are you . . . ?

GRACE: *(To* STEVE*)* Do you remember this?

DALE: I already told you. I don't need a closer look or nothing.

STEVE: Yes.

GRACE: *(Ties the blindfold, releases it)* Let's sit down.

DALE: Wait.

STEVE: You want me to sit here?

DALE: Grace, is he understanding you?

GRACE: Have you ever played Group Story?

STEVE: Yes, I have played that.

DALE: There—there he goes again! Grace, I'm gonna take . . .
   (He starts to remove the blindfold)

GRACE: *(Stopping him)* Dale, listen or you won't understand.

DALE: But how come *he's* understanding?

GRACE: Because he's listening.

DALE: But . . .

GRACE: Now, let's play Group Story.

DALE: Not again. Grace, that's only good when you're
   stoned.

GRACE: Who wants to start? Steve, you know the rules?

STEVE: Yes—I understand.

DALE: See, we're talking normal speed—and he still understood.

GRACE: Dale, would you like to start?
   (Pause)

DALE: All right.
   *(By this time, the LIGHTS HAVE DIMMED, throwing shadows
   on the stage. GRACE will strike two pots together to indicate
   each speaker change and the ritual will gradually take on ele-
   ments of Chinese opera)*
   Uh, once upon a time . . . there were . . . three bears—
   Grace, this is ridiculous!

GRACE: Tell a story.

DALE: . . . three bears and they each had . . . cancer of the
   lymph nodes. Uh—and they were very sad. So the baby
   bear said, "I'll go to the new Cedar Sinai Hospital, where
   they may have a cure for this fatal illness."

GRACE: But the new Cedar Sinai Hospital happened to be
   two thousand miles away—across the ocean.

STEVE: *(Gradually losing his accent)* That is very far.

DALE: How did—? So, the bear tried to swim over, but his
   leg got chewed off by alligators—are there alligators in
   the Pacific Ocean?—Oh, well. So he ended up having to

go for a leg *and* a cure for malignant cancer of the lymph nodes.

GRACE: When he arrived there, he came face to face with—

STEVE: With Gwan Gung, god of warriors, writers, and prostitutes.

DALE: And Gwan Gung looked at the bear and said . . .

GRACE: . . . strongly and with spirit . . .

STEVE: "One-legged bear, what are you doing on my land? You are from America, are you not?"

DALE: And the bear said, "Yes. Yes."

GRACE: And Gwan Gung replied . . .

STEVE: *(Getting up)* By stepping forward, sword drawn, ready to wound, not kill, not end it so soon. To draw it out, play it, taunt it, make it feel like a dog.

DALE: Which is probably rather closely related to the bear.

GRACE: Gwan Gung said—

STEVE: "When I came to America, did you lick my wounds? When I came to America, did you cure my sickness?"

DALE: And just as Gwan Gung was about to strike—

GRACE: There arrived Fa Mu Lan, the Woman Warrior. *(She stands, faces* STEVE. *From here on in, striking pots together is not needed)* "Gwan Gung."

STEVE: "What do you want? Don't interfere! Don't forget, I have gone before you into battle many times."

DALE: But Fa Mu Lan seemed not to hear Gwan Gung's warning. She stood between him and the bear, drawing out her own sword.

GRACE: "You will learn I cannot forget. I don't forget, Gwan Gung. Spare the bear and I will present gifts."

STEVE: "Very well. He is hardly worth killing."

DALE: And the bear hopped off. Fa Mu Lan pulled a parcel from beneath her gown.

(She removes DALE's *blindfold)*

DALE: She pulled out two items.

GRACE: "This is for you."
(She hands blindfold to STEVE*)*

STEVE: "What is that?"

DALE: She showed him a beautiful piece of red silk, thick enough to be opaque, yet so light he barely felt it in his hands.

GRACE: "Do you remember this?"

STEVE: "Why, yes. I used this silk for sport one day. How did you get hold of it?"

DALE: Then she presented him with a second item. It was a fabric—thick and dried and brittle.

GRACE: "Do you remember this?"

STEVE: *(Turning away)* "No, no. I've never seen this before in my life. This has nothing to do with me. What is it—a dragon skin?"

DALE: Fa Mu Lan handed it to Gwan Gung.

GRACE: "Never mind. Use it—as a tablecloth. As a favor to me."

STEVE: "It's much too hard and brittle. But, to show you my graciousness in receiving—I will use it tonight!"

DALE: That night, Gwan Gung had a large banquet, at which there was plenty, even for the slaves. But Fa Mu Lan ate nothing. She waited until midnight, till Gwan Gung and the gods were full of wine and empty of sense. Sneaking behind him, she pulled out the tablecloth, waving it above her head.

GRACE: *(Ripping the tablecloth from the table)* "Gwan Gung, you foolish boy. This thing you have used tonight as a tablecloth—it is the stretched and dried skins of my fathers. My fathers, whom you slew—for sport! And you have been eating the sins—you ate them!"

STEVE: "No. I was blindfolded. I did not know."

DALE: Fa Mu Lan waved the skin before Gwan Gung's face. It smelled suddenly of death.

GRACE: "Remember the day you played? Remember? Well, eat that day, Gwan Gung."

STEVE: "I am not responsible. No. No."

(GRACE throws one end of the tablecloth to DALE, who catches it. Together, they become like STEVE's parents. They chase him about the stage, waving the tablecloth like a net)

DALE: Yes!

GRACE: Yes!

STEVE: No!

DALE: You must!

GRACE: Go!

STEVE: Where?

DALE: To America!

GRACE: To work!

STEVE: Why?

DALE: Because!

GRACE: We need!

STEVE: No!

DALE: Why?

GRACE: Go.

STEVE: Hard!

DALE: So?

GRACE: Need.

STEVE: Far!

DALE: So?

GRACE: Need!

STEVE: Safe!

DALE: Here?

GRACE: No!

STEVE: Why?

DALE: Them.
  (Points)

GRACE: Them.
  (Points)

STEVE: Won't!

DALE: Must!

GRACE: Must!

STEVE: Won't!

DALE: Go!

GRACE: Go!

STEVE: Won't!

DALE: Bye!

GRACE: Bye!

STEVE: Won't!

DALE: Fare!

GRACE: Well!

(DALE *and* GRACE *drop the tablecloth over* STEVE, *who sinks to the floor.* GRACE *then moves offstage, into the bathroom–storage room, while* DALE *goes upstage and stands with his back to the audience. Silence*)

STEVE: *(Begins pounding the ground)* Noooo! *(He throws off the tablecloth, standing up full.* LIGHTS UP FULL, *blindingly)* I am GWAN GUNG!

DALE: *(Turning downstage suddenly)* What . . . ?

STEVE: I HAVE COME TO THIS LAND TO STUDY!

DALE: Grace . . .

STEVE: TO STUDY THE ARTS OF WAR, OF LITERA-TURE, OF RIGHTEOUSNESS!

DALE: A movie's fine.

STEVE: I FOUGHT THE WARS OF THE THREE KINGDOMS!

DALE: An ordinary movie, let's go.

STEVE: I FOUGHT WITH THE FIRST PIONEERS, THE FIRST WARRIORS THAT CHOSE TO FOLLOW THE WHITE GHOSTS TO THIS LAND!

DALE: You can pick, okay?

STEVE: I WAS THEIR HERO, THEIR LEADER, THEIR FIRE!

DALE: I'll even let him drive, how's that?

STEVE: AND THIS LAND IS MINE! IT HAS NO RIGHT TO TREAT ME THIS WAY!

GRACE: No. Gwan Gung, *you* have no rights.

STEVE: Who's speaking?

GRACE: *(Enters with* a da dao *and* mao, *two swords)* It is Fa Mu Lan. You are in a new land, Gwan Gung.

STEVE: Not new—I have been here before, many times. This time, I said I will have it easy. I will come as no ChinaMan before—on a plane, with money and rank.

GRACE: And?

STEVE: And—there is no change. I am still treated like this! This land... has no right. I AM GWAN GUNG!

GRACE: And I am Fa Mu Lan.

DALE: I'll be Chiang Kai-shek, how's that?

STEVE: *(To* DALE*)* You! How can you—? I came over with your parents.

GRACE: *(Turning to* STEVE*)* We are in America. And we have a battle to fight.

(She tosses the da dao *to* STEVE. *They square off)*

STEVE: I don't want to fight you.

GRACE: You killed my family.

STEVE: You were revenged—I ate your father's sins.

GRACE: That's not revenge!

(Swords strike)

GRACE: That was only the tease.

(Strike)

GRACE: What's the point in dying if you don't know the cause of your death?

(Series of strikes. STEVE *falls)*

DALE: Okay! That's it!

(GRACE stands over STEVE, *her sword pointed at his heart.* DALE *snatches the sword from her hands. She does not move)*

DALE: Jesus! Enough is enough!

(DALE takes STEVE's *sword; he also does not react)*

DALE: What the hell kind of movie was that?

(DALE turns his back on the couple, heads for the bathroom— storage room. GRACE *uses her now-invisible sword to thrust in and out of* STEVE's *heart once)*

DALE: That's it. Game's over. Now just sit down here. Breathe. One. Two. One. Two. Air. Good stuff. Glad they made it. Right, cousin?

(DALE strokes GRACE's hair. They freeze. STEVE rises slowly to his knees and delivers a monologue to the audience)

STEVE: Ssssh! Please, miss! Please—quiet! I will not hurt you, I promise. All I want is . . . food . . . anything. You look full of plenty. I have not eaten almost one week now, but four days past when I found one egg and I ate every piece of it—including shell. Every piece, I ate. Please. Don't you have anything extra? *(Pause)* I want to. Now. This land does not want us any more than China. But I cannot. All work was done, then the bosses said they could not send us back. And I am running, running from Eureka, running from San Francisco, running from Los Angeles. And I been eating very little. One egg, only. *(Pause)* All America wants ChinaMen go home, but no one want it bad enough to pay our way. Now, please, can't you give even little? *(Pause)* I ask you, what you hate most? What work most awful for white woman? *(Pause)* Good. I will do that thing for you—you can give me food. *(Pause)* Think—you relax, you are given those things, clean, dry, press. No scrub, no dry. It is wonderful thing I offer you. *(Pause)* Good. Give me those and please bring food, or I be done before these things.

(GRACE steps away from DALE with box)

GRACE: Here—I've brought you something. *(She hands him the box)* Open it.

(He hesitates, then does, and takes out a small chong you bing)

GRACE: Eat it.

(He does, slowly at first, then ravenously)

GRACE: Good. Eat it all down. It's just food. Really. Feel better now? Good. Eat the *bing*. Hold it in your hands. Your hands . . . are beautiful. Lift it to your mouth. Your

mouth . . . is beautiful. Bite it with your teeth. Your
teeth . . . are beautiful. Crush it with your tongue.
Your tongue . . . is beautiful. Slide it down your throat.
Your throat . . . is beautiful.

STEVE: Our hands are beautiful.

(She holds hers next to his)

GRACE: What do you see?

STEVE: I see . . . I see the hands of warriors.

GRACE: Warriors? What of gods, then?

STEVE: There are no gods that travel. Only warriors travel.
(Silence) Would you like go dance?

GRACE: Yeah. Okay. Sure.

(They start to leave. DALE *speaks softly)*

DALE: Well, if you want to be alone . . .

GRACE: I think we would, Dale. Is that okay? *(Pause)* Thanks
for coming over. I'm sorry things got so screwed up.

DALE: Oh—uh—that's okay. The evening was real . . . different, anyway.

GRACE: Yeah. Maybe you can take Frank off the tracks
now?

DALE: *(Laughing softly)* Yeah. Maybe I will.

STEVE: *(To* DALE*)* Very nice meeting you. *(Extends his hand)*

DALE: *(Does not take it)* Yeah. Same here.

*(*STEVE *and* GRACE *start to leave)*

DALE: You know . . . I think you picked up English faster
than anyone I've ever met.

(Pause)

STEVE: Thank you.

GRACE: See you.

STEVE: Good-bye.

DALE: Bye.

*(*GRACE *and* STEVE *exit)*

END OF ACT TWO

CODA

DALE *alone in the back room. He examines the swords, the tablecloth, the box. He sits down.*

DALE: F-O-B. Fresh Off the Boat, FOB. Clumsy, ugly, greasy FOB. Loud, stupid, four-eyed FOB. Big feet. Horny. Like Lenny in *Of Mice and Men*. F-O-B. Fresh Off the Boat. FOB.

(SLOW FADE TO BLACK)

CURTAIN

THE DANCE AND THE RAILROAD

For John and Tzi

This play was commissioned by the New Federal Theater under a grant from the U.S. Department of Education. Special thanks to Jack Tchen and the New York Chinatown History Project, and Genny Chomori of the UCLA Asian American Studies Center.

The Dance and the Railroad was first produced by the Henry Street Settlement's New Federal Theater, Woodie King, Jr., and Steve Tennen, producers. It opened on March 25, 1981, with the following cast:

LONE .... John Lone
MA .... Tzi Ma
Alternate Actor .... Glenn Kubota

Directed by John Lone; sculpture by Andrea Zakin; lights by Grant Ornstein; costumes by Judy Dearing; Alice Jankowiak was production stage manager; music and choreography by John Lone. It was then produced by Joseph Papp at the New York Shakespeare Festival Public Theater, where it opened at the Anspacher Theater on July 16, 1981, with the following cast:

LONE .... John Lone
MA .... Tzi Ma
Alternate Actor .... Toshi Toda

Directed by John Lone; set by Karen Schulz; lighting by Victor En Yu Tan; costumes by Judy Dearing; music and choreography by John Lone. Alice Jankowiak was production stage manager.

CHARACTERS

LONE, twenty years old, ChinaMan railroad worker.
MA, eighteen years old, ChinaMan railroad worker.

PLACE

A mountaintop near the transcontinental railroad.

TIME

June, 1867.

SYNOPSIS OF SCENES

Scene 1. Afternoon.
Scene 2. Afternoon, a day later.
Scene 3. Late afternoon, four days later.
Scene 4. Late that night.
Scene 5. Just before the following dawn.

Scene 1

A mountaintop. LONE *is practicing opera steps. He swings his pigtail around like a fan.* MA *enters, cautiously, watches from a hidden spot.* MA *approaches* LONE.

LONE: So, there are insects hiding in the bushes.

MA: Hey, listen, we haven't met, but—

LONE: I don't spend time with insects.

(LONE *whips his hair into* MA's *face;* MA *backs off;* LONE *pursues him, swiping at* MA *with his hair)*

MA: What the—? Cut it out!

(MA *pushes* LONE *away)*

LONE: Don't push me.

MA: What was that for?

LONE: Don't ever push me again.

MA: You mess like that, you're gonna get pushed.

LONE: Don't push me.

MA: You started it. I just wanted to watch.

LONE: You "just wanted to watch." Did you ask my permission?

MA: What?

LONE: Did you?

MA: C'mon.

LONE: You can't expect to get in for free.

MA: Listen. I got some stuff you'll wanna hear.

LONE: You think so?

MA: Yeah. Some advice.

LONE: Advice? How old are you, anyway?

MA: Eighteen.

LONE: A child.

MA: Yeah. Right. A child. But listen—

LONE: A child who tries to advise a grown man—

MA: Listen, you got this kind of attitude.

LONE: —is a child who will never grow up.

MA: You know, the ChinaMen down at camp, they can't stand it.

LONE: Oh?

MA: Yeah. You gotta watch yourself. You know what they say? They call you "Prince of the Mountain." Like you're too good to spend time with them.

LONE: Perceptive of them.

MA: After all, you never sing songs, never tell stories. They say you act like your spit is too clean for them, and they got ways to fix that.

LONE: Is that so?

MA: Like they're gonna bury you in the shit buckets, so you'll have more to clean than your nails.

LONE: But I don't shit.

MA: Or they're gonna cut out your tongue, since you never speak to them.

LONE: There's no one here worth talking to.

MA: Cut it out, Lone. Look, I'm trying to help you, all right? I got a solution.

LONE: So young yet so clever.

MA: That stuff you're doing—it's beautiful. Why don't you do it for the guys at camp? Help us celebrate?

LONE: What will "this stuff" help celebrate?

MA: C'mon. The strike, of course. Guys on a railroad gang, we gotta stick together, you know.

LONE: This is something to celebrate?

MA: Yeah. Yesterday, the weak-kneed ChinaMen, they were

running around like chickens without a head: "The white devils are sending their soldiers! Shoot us all!" But now, look—day four, see? Still in one piece. Those soldiers— we've never seen a gun or a bullet.

LONE: So you're all warrior-spirits, huh?

MA: They're scared of us, Lone—that's what it means.

LONE: I appreciate your advice. Tell you what—you go down—

MA: Yeah?

LONE: Down to the camp—

MA: Okay.

LONE: To where the men are—

MA: Yeah?

LONE: Sit there—

MA: Yeah?

LONE: And wait for me.

MA: Okay. *(Pause)* That's it? What do you think I am?

LONE: I think you're an insect interrupting my practice. So fly away. Go home.

MA: Look, I didn't come here to get laughed at.

LONE: No, I suppose you didn't.

MA: So just stay up here. By yourself. You deserve it.

LONE: I do.

MA: And don't expect any more help from me.

LONE: I haven't gotten any yet.

MA: If one day, you wake up and your head is buried in the shit can—

LONE: Yes?

MA: You can't find your body, your tongue is cut out—

LONE: Yes.

MA: Don't worry, 'cuz I'll be there.

LONE: Oh.

MA: To make sure your mother's head is sitting right next to yours.

(MA exits)

LONE: His head is too big for this mountain.
  (Returns to practicing)

Scene 2

Mountaintop. Next day. LONE *is practicing.* MA *enters.*

MA: Hey.
LONE: You? Again?
MA: I forgive you.
LONE: You . . . what?
MA: For making fun of me yesterday. I forgive you.
LONE: You can't—
MA: No. Don't thank me.
LONE: You can't forgive me.
MA: No. Don't mention it.
LONE: You—! I never asked for your forgiveness.
MA: I know. That's just the kinda guy I am.
LONE: This is ridiculous. Why don't you leave? Go down to
  your friends and play soldiers, sing songs, tell stories.
MA: Ah! See? That's just it. I got other ways I wanna spend
  my time. Will you teach me the opera?
LONE: What?
MA: I wanna learn it. I dreamt about it all last night.
LONE: No.
MA: The dance, the opera—I can do it.
LONE: You think so?
MA: Yeah. When I get outa here, I wanna go back to China
  and perform.
LONE: You want to become an actor?
MA: Well, I wanna perform.

LONE: Don't you remember the story about the three sons whose parents send them away to learn a trade? After three years, they return. The first one says, "I have become a coppersmith." The parents say, "Good. Second son, what have you become?" "I've become a silversmith." "Good—and youngest son, what about you?" "I have become an actor." When the parents hear that their son has become only an actor, they are very sad. The mother beats her head against the ground until the ground, out of pity, opens up and swallows her. The father is so angry he can't even speak, and the anger builds up inside him until it blows his body to pieces—little bits of his skin are found hanging from trees days later. You don't know how you endanger your relatives by becoming an actor.

MA: Well, I don't wanna become an "actor." That sounds terrible. I just wanna perform. Look, I'll be rich by the time I get out of here, right?

LONE: Oh?

MA: Sure. By the time I go back to China, I'll ride in gold sedan chairs, with twenty wives fanning me all around.

LONE: Twenty wives? This boy is ambitious.

MA: I'll give out pigs on New Year's and keep a stable of small birds to give to any woman who pleases me. And in my spare time, I'll perform.

LONE: Between your twenty wives and your birds, where will you find a free moment?

MA: I'll play Gwan Gung and tell stories of what life was like on the Gold Mountain.

LONE: Ma, just how long have you been in "America"?

MA: Huh? About four weeks.

LONE: You are a big dreamer.

MA: Well, all us ChinaMen here are—right? Men with little dreams—have little brains to match. They walk with their eyes down, trying to find extra grains of rice on the ground.

LONE: So, you know all about "America"? Tell me, what kind of stories will you tell?

MA: I'll say, "We laid tracks like soldiers. Mountains? We hung from cliffs in baskets and the winds blew us like birds. Snow? We lived underground like moles for days at a time. Deserts? We—"

LONE: Wait. Wait. How do you know these things after only four weeks?

MA: They told me—the other ChinaMen on the gang. We've been telling stories ever since the strike began.

LONE: They make it sound like it's very enjoyable.

MA: They said it is.

LONE: Oh? And you believe them?

MA: They're my friends. Living underground in winter— sounds exciting, huh?

LONE: Did they say anything about the cold?

MA: Oh, I already know about that. They told me about the mild winters and the warm snow.

LONE: Warm snow?

MA: When I go home, I'll bring some back to show my brothers.

LONE: Bring some—? On the boat?

MA: They'll be shocked—they never seen American snow before.

LONE: You can't. By the time you get snow to the boat, it'll have melted, evaporated, and returned as rain already.

MA: No.

LONE: No?

MA: Stupid.

LONE: Me?

MA: You been here awhile, haven't you?

LONE: Yes. Two years.

MA: Then how come you're so stupid? This is the Gold Mountain. The snow here doesn't melt. It's not wet.

LONE: That's what they told you?

MA: Yeah. It's true.

LONE: Did anyone show you any of this snow?

MA: No. It's not winter.

LONE: So where does it go?

MA: Huh?

LONE: Where does it go, if it doesn't melt? What happens to it?

MA: The snow? I dunno. I guess it just stays around.

LONE: So where is it? Do you see any?

MA: Here? Well, no, but . . . *(Pause)* This is probably one of those places where it doesn't snow—even in winter.

LONE: Oh.

MA: Anyway, what's the use of me telling you what you already know? Hey, c'mon—teach me some of that stuff. Look—I've been practicing the walk—how's this? *(Demonstrates)*

LONE: You look like a duck in heat.

MA: Hey—it's a start, isn't it?

LONE: Tell you what—you want to play some *die siu*?

MA: *Die siu*? Sure.

LONE: You know, I'm pretty good.

MA: Hey, I play with the guys at camp. You can't be any better than Lee—he's really got it down.

(LONE pulls out a case with two dice)

LONE: I used to play till morning.

MA: Hey, us too. We see the sun start to rise, and say, "Hey, if we got to sleep now, we'll never get up for work." So we just keep playing.

LONE: *(Holding out dice) Die* or *siu*?

MA: *Siu*.

LONE: You sure?

MA: Yeah!

LONE: All right. *(He rolls) Die!*

MA: *Siu!*

(They see the result)

MA: Not bad.
(They continue taking turns rolling through the following section; MA *always loses)*
LONE: I haven't touched these in two years.
MA: I gotta practice more.
LONE: Have you lost much money?
MA: Huh? So what?
LONE: Oh, you have gold hidden in all your shirt linings, huh?
MA: Here in "America"—losing is no problem. You know— End of the Year Bonus?
LONE: Oh, right.
MA: After I get that, I'll laugh at what I lost.
LONE: Lee told you there was a bonus, right?
MA: How'd you know?
LONE: When I arrived here, Lee told me there was a bonus, too.
MA: Lee teach you how to play?
LONE: Him? He talked to me a lot.
MA: Look, why don't you come down and start playing with the guys again?
LONE: "The guys."
MA: Before we start playing, Lee uses a stick to write "Kill!" in the dirt.
LONE: You seem to live for your nights with "the guys."
MA: What's life without friends, huh?
LONE: Well, why do *you* think I stopped playing?
MA: Hey, maybe you were the one getting killed, huh?
LONE: What?
MA: Hey, just kidding.
LONE: Who's getting killed here?
MA: Just a joke.
LONE: That's not a joke, it's blasphemy.
MA: Look, obviously you stopped playing 'cause you wanted to practice the opera.

LONE: Do you understand that discipline?

MA: But, I mean, you don't have to overdo it either. You don't have to treat 'em like dirt. I mean, who are you trying to impress?

(Pause. LONE throws dice into the bushes)

LONE: Oooops. Better go see who won.

MA: Hey! C'mon! Help me look!

LONE: If you find them, they are yours.

MA: You serious?

LONE: Yes.

MA: Here.

(Finds the dice)

LONE: Who won?

MA: I didn't check.

LONE: Well, no matter. Keep the dice. Take them and go play with your friends.

MA: Here. *(He offers them to LONE)* A present.

LONE: A present? This isn't a present!

MA: They're mine, aren't they? You gave them to me, right?

LONE: Well, yes, but—

MA: So now I'm giving them to you.

LONE: You can't give me a present. I don't want them.

MA: You wanted them enough to keep them two years.

LONE: I'd forgotten I had them.

MA: See, I know, Lone. You wanna get rid of me. But you can't. I'm paying for lessons.

LONE: With my dice.

MA: Mine now. *(He offers them again)* Here.

(Pause. LONE runs MA's hand across his forehead)

LONE: Feel this.

MA: Hey!

LONE: Pretty wet, huh?

MA: Big deal.

LONE: Well, it's not from playing *die siu*.

MA: I know how to sweat. I wouldn't be here if I didn't.

LONE: Yes, but are you willing to sweat after you've finished sweating? Are you willing to come up after you've spent the whole day chipping half an inch off a rock, and punish your body some more?

MA: Yeah. Even after work, I still—

LONE: No, you don't. You want to gamble, and tell dirty stories, and dress up like women to do shows.

MA: Hey, I never did that.

LONE: You've only been here a month. *(Pause)* And what about "the guys"? They're not going to treat you so well once you stop playing with them. Are you willing to work all day listening to them whisper, "That one— let's put spiders in his soup"?

MA: They won't do that to me. With you, it's different.

LONE: Is it?

MA: You don't have to act that way.

LONE: What way?

MA: Like you're so much better than them.

LONE: No. You haven't even begun to understand. To practice every day, you must have a fear to force you up here.

MA: A fear? No—it's 'cause what you're doing is beautiful.

LONE: No.

MA: I've seen it.

MA: It's ugly to practice when the mountain has turned your muscles to ice. When my body hurts too much to come here, I look at the other ChinaMen and think, "They are dead. Their muscles work only because the white man forces them. I live because I can still force my muscles to work for me." Say it. "They are dead."

MA: No. They're my friends.

LONE: Well, then, take your dice down to your friends.

MA: But I want to learn—

LONE: This is your first lesson.

MA: Look, it shouldn't matter—

LONE: It does.

MA: It shouldn't matter what I think.

LONE: Attitude is everything.

MA: But as long as I come up, do the exercises—

LONE: I'm not going to waste time on a quitter.

MA: I'm not!

LONE: Then say it.—"They are dead men."

MA: I can't.

LONE: Then you will never have the dedication.

MA: That doesn't prove anything.

LONE: I will not teach a dead man.

MA: What?

LONE: If you can't see it, then you're dead too.

MA: Don't start pinning—

LONE: Say it!

MA: All right.

LONE: What?

MA: All right. I'm one of them. I'm a dead man too.

(Pause)

LONE: I thought as much. So, go. You have your friends.

MA: But I don't have a teacher.

LONE: I don't think you need both.

MA: Are you sure?

LONE: I'm being questioned by a child.

(LONE returns to practicing. Silence)

MA: Look, Lone, I'll come up here every night—after work—I'll spend my time practicing, okay? *(Pause)* But I'm not gonna say that they're dead. Look at them. They're on strike; dead men don't go on strike, Lone. The white devils—they try and stick us with a ten-hour day. We want a return to eight hours and also a fourteen-dollar-a-month raise. I learned the demon English—listen: "Eight hour a day good for white man, all same good for ChinaMan." These are the demands of live ChinaMen, Lone. Dead men don't complain.

LONE: All right, this is something new. No one can judge the ChinaMen till after the strike.

MA: They say we'll hold out for months if we have to. The smart men will live on what we've hoarded.

LONE: A ChinaMan's mouth can swallow the earth. *(He takes the dice)* While the strike is on, I'll teach you.

MA: And afterwards?

LONE: Afterwards—we'll decide then whether these are dead or live men.

MA: When can we start?

LONE: We've already begun. Give me your hand.

Scene 3

LONE *and* MA *are doing physical exercises.*

MA: How long will it be before I can play Gwan Gung?

LONE: How long before a dog can play the violin?

MA: Old Ah Hong—have you heard him play the violin?

LONE: Yes. Now, he should take his violin and give it to a dog.

MA: I think he sounds okay.

LONE: I think he caused that avalanche last winter.

MA: He used to play for weddings back home.

LONE: Ah Hong?

MA: That's what he said.

LONE: You probably heard wrong.

MA: No.

LONE: He probably said he played for funerals.

MA: He's been playing for the guys down at camp.

LONE: He should play for the white devils—that will end this stupid strike.

MA: Yang told me for sure—it'll be over by tomorrow.

LONE: Eight days already. And Yang doesn't know anything.

MA: He said they're already down to an eight-hour day and five-dollar raise at the bargaining sessions.

LONE: Yang eats too much opium.

MA: That doesn't mean he's wrong about this.

LONE: You can't trust him. One time—last year—he went around camp looking in everybody's eyes and saying, "Your nails are too long. They're hurting my eyes." This went on for a week. Finally, all the men clipped their nails, made a big pile, which they wrapped in leaves and gave to him. Yang used the nails to season his food—he put it in his soup, sprinkled it on his rice, and never said a word about it again. Now tell me—are you going to trust a man who eats other men's fingernails?

MA: Well, all I know is we won't go back to work until they meet all our demands. Listen, teach me some Gwan Gung steps.

LONE: I should have expected this. A boy who wants to have twenty wives is the type who demands more than he can handle.

MA: Just a few.

LONE: It takes years before an actor can play Gwan Gung.

MA: I can do it. I spend a lot of time watching the opera when it comes around. Every time I see Gwan Gung, I say, "Yeah. That's me. The god of fighters. The god of adventurers. We have the same kind of spirit."

LONE: I tell you, if you work very hard, when you return to China, you can perhaps be the Second Clown.

MA: Second Clown?

LONE: If you work hard.

MA: What's the Second Clown?

LONE: You can play the *p'i p'a,* and dance and jump all over.

MA: I'll buy them.

LONE: Excuse me?

MA: I'm going to be rich, remember? I'll buy a troupe and force them to let me play Gwan Gung.

LONE: I hope you have enough money, then, to pay audiences to sit through your show.

MA: You mean, I'm going to have to practice here every night—and in return, all I can play is the Second Clown?

LONE: If you work hard.

MA: Am I that bad? Maybe I shouldn't even try to do this. Maybe I should just go down.

LONE: It's not you. Everyone must earn the right to play Gwan Gung. I entered opera school when I was ten years old. My parents decided to sell me for ten years to this opera company. I lived with eighty other boys and we slept in bunks four beds high and hid our candy and rice cakes from each other. After eight years, I was studying to play Gwan Gung.

MA: Eight years?

LONE: I was one of the best in my class. One day, I was summoned by my master, who told me I was to go home for two days because my mother had fallen very ill and was dying. When I arrived home, Mother was standing at the door waiting, not sick at all. Her first words to me, the son away for eight years, were, "You've been playing while your village has starved. You must go to the Gold Mountain and work."

MA: And you never returned to school?

LONE: I went from a room with eighty boys to a ship with three hundred men. So, you see, it does not come easily to play Gwan Gung.

MA: Did you want to play Gwan Gung?

LONE: What a foolish question!

MA: Well, you're better off this way.

LONE: What?

MA: Actors—they don't make much money. Here, you make a bundle, then go back and be an actor again. Best of both worlds.

LONE: "Best of both worlds."

MA: Yeah!

(LONE *drops to the ground, begins imitating a duck, waddling and quacking*)

MA: Lone? What are you doing? (LONE *quacks*) You're a duck? (LONE *quacks*) I can see that. (LONE *quacks*) Is this an exercise? Am I supposed to do this? (LONE *quacks*) This is dumb. I never seen Gwan Gung waddle. (LONE *quacks*) Okay. All right. I'll do it. (MA *and* LONE *quack and waddle*) You know, I never realized before how uncomfortable a duck's life is. And you have to listen to yourself quacking all day. Go crazy! (LONE *stands up straight*) Now, what was that all about?

LONE: No, no. Stay down there, duck.

MA: What's the—

LONE: *(Prompting)* Quack, quack, quack.

MA: I don't—

LONE: Act your species!

MA: I'm not a duck!

LONE: Nothing worse than a duck that doesn't know his place.

MA: All right. *(Mechanically)* Quack, quack.

LONE: More.

MA: Quack.

LONE: More!

MA: Quack, quack, quack!

(MA *now continues quacking, as* LONE *gives commands*)

LONE: Louder! It's your mating call! Think of your twenty duck wives! Good! Louder! Project! More! Don't slow down! Put your tail feathers into it! They can't hear you!

(MA *is now quacking up a storm.* LONE *exits, unnoticed by* MA)

MA: Quack! Quack! Quack! Quack. Quack . . . quack.

(He looks around) Quack . . . quack . . . Lone? . . . Lone? *(He waddles around the stage looking)* Lone, where are you? Where'd you go? *(He stops, scratches his left leg with his right*

foot) C'mon—stop playing around. What is this? *(LONE enters as a tiger, unseen by* MA*)* Look, let's call it a day, okay? I'm getting hungry. *(MA turns around, notices* LONE *right before* LONE *is to bite him)* Aaaaah! Quack, quack, quack!

*(They face off, in character as animals. Duck-*MA *is terrified)*

LONE: Grrrr!

MA: *(As a cry for help)* Quack, quack, quack!

(LONE pounces on MA. *They struggle, in character.* MA *is quacking madly, eyes tightly closed.* LONE *stands up straight.* MA *continues to quack)*

LONE: Stand up.

MA: *(Eyes still closed)* Quack, quack, quack!

LONE: *(Louder)* Stand up!

MA: *(Opening his eyes)* Oh.

LONE: What are you?

MA: Huh?

LONE: A ChinaMan or a duck?

MA: Huh? Gimme a second to remember.

LONE: You like being a duck?

MA: My feet fell asleep.

LONE: You change forms so easily.

MA: You said to.

LONE: What else could you turn into?

MA: Well, you scared me—sneaking up like that.

LONE: Perhaps a rock. That would be useful. When the men need to rest, they can sit on you.

MA: I got carried away.

LONE: Let's try . . . a locust. Can you become a locust?

MA: No. Let's cut this, okay?

LONE: Here. It's easy. You just have to know how to hop.

MA: You're not gonna get me—

LONE: Like this.

(He demonstrates)

MA: Forget it, Lone.

LONE: I'm a locust.

(He begins jumping toward MA*)*

MA: Hey! Get away!

LONE: I devour whole fields.

MA: Stop it.

LONE: I starve babies before they are born.

MA: Hey, look, stop it!

LONE: I cause famines and destroy villages.

MA: I'm warning you! Get away!

LONE: What are you going to do? You can't kill a locust.

MA: You're not a locust.

LONE: You kill one, and another sits on your hand.

MA: Stop following me.

LONE: Locusts always trouble people, If not, we'd feel useless. Now, if you became a locust, too . . .

MA: I'm not going to become a locust.

LONE: Just stick your teeth out!

MA: I'm not gonna be a bug! It's stupid!

LONE: No man who's just been a duck has the right to call
anything stupid.

MA: I thought you were trying to teach me something.

LONE: I am. Go ahead.

MA: All right. There. That look right?

LONE: Your legs should be a little lower. Lower! There.
That's adequate. So how does it feel to be a locust?

*(*LONE *gets up)*

MA: I dunno. How long do I have to do this?

LONE: Could you do it for three years?

MA: Three years? Don't be—

LONE: You couldn't, could you? Could you be a duck for
that long?

MA: Look, I wasn't born to be either of those.

LONE: Exactly. Well, I wasn't born to work on a railroad, either.
"Best of both worlds." How can you be such an insect!

(Pause)

MA: Lone . . .

LONE: Stay down there! Don't move! I've never told anyone my story—the story of my parents' kidnapping me from school. All the time we were crossing the ocean, the last two years here—I've kept my mouth shut. To you, I finally tell it. And all you can say is, "Best of both worlds." You're a bug to me, a locust. You think you understand the dedication one must have to be in the opera? You think it's the same as working on a railroad.

MA: Lone, all I was saying is that you'll go back too, and—

LONE: You're no longer a student of mine.

MA: What?

LONE: You have no dedication.

MA: Lone, I'm sorry.

LONE: Get up.

MA: I'm honored that you told me that.

LONE: Get up.

MA: No.

LONE: No?

MA: I don't want to. I want to talk.

LONE: Well, I've learned from the past. You're stubborn. You don't go. All right. Stay there. If you want to prove to me that you're dedicated, be a locust till morning. I'll go.

MA: Lone, I'm really honored that you told me.

LONE: I'll return in the morning.

(Exits)

MA: Lone? Lone, that's ridiculous. You think I'm gonna stay like this? If you do, you're crazy. Lone? Come back here.

Place on the "fear of the yellow tide"
→ taps into their psycho-sexual myths/anxieties

Scene 4

What is pt. of long things @ locusts?

Night. MA, *alone, as a locust.*

MA: Locusts travel in huge swarms, so large that when they cross the sky, they block out the sun, like a storm. Second Uncle—back home—when he was a young man, his whole crop got wiped out by locusts one year. In the famine that followed, Second Uncle lost his eldest son and his second wife—the one he married for love. Even to this day, we look around before saying the word "locust," to make sure Second Uncle is out of hearing range. About eight years ago, my brother and I discovered Second Uncle's cave in back of the stream near our house. We saw him come out of it one day around noon. Later, just before the sun went down, we sneaked in. We only looked once. Inside, there must have been hundreds—maybe five hundred or more—grasshoppers in huge bamboo cages—and around them—stacks of grasshopper legs, grasshopper heads, grasshopper antennae, grasshoppers with one leg, still trying to hop but toppling like trees coughing, grasshoppers wrapped around sharp branches rolling from side to side, grasshoppers legs cut off grasshopper bodies, then tied around grasshoppers and tightened till grasshoppers died. Every conceivable kind of grasshopper in every conceivable stage of life and death, subject to every conceivable grasshopper torture. We ran out quickly, my brother and I—we knew an evil place by the thickness of the air. Now, I think of Second Uncle. How sad that the locusts forced him to take out his agony on innocent grasshoppers. What if Second Uncle could see me now? Would he cut off my legs? He might as well. I can barely feel them. But then again, Second Uncle never tortured actual locusts, just weak grasshoppers.

grasshopper/locust identification

Scene 5

Night. MA *still as a locust.*

LONE: *(Off, singing)*
> Hit your hardest
> Pound out your tears
> The more you try
> The more you'll cry
> At how little I've moved
> And how large I loom
> By the time the sun goes down

MA: You look rested.

LONE: Me?

MA: Well, you sound rested.

LONE: No, not at all.

MA: Maybe I'm just comparing you to me.

LONE: I didn't even close my eyes all last night.

MA: Aw, Lone, you didn't have to stay up for me. You coulda just come up here and—

LONE: For you?

MA: —apologized and everything woulda been—

LONE: I didn't stay up for you.

MA: Huh? You didn't?

LONE: No.

MA: Oh. You sure?

LONE: Positive. I was thinking, that's all.

MA: About me?

LONE: Well . . .

MA: Even a little?

LONE: I was thinking about the ChinaMen—and you. Get up, Ma.

MA: Aw, do I have to? I've gotten to know these grasshoppers real well.

LONE: Get up. I have a lot to tell you.

MA: What'll they think? They take me in, even though I'm a little large, then they find out I'm a human being. I stepped on their kids. No trust. Gimme a hand, will you? *(LONE helps MA up, but MA's legs can't support him)* Aw, shit. My legs are coming off.

(He lies down and tries to straighten them out)

LONE: I have many surprises. First, you will play Gwan Gung.

MA: My legs will be sent home without me. What'll my family think? Come to port to meet me and all they get is two legs.

LONE: Did you hear me?

MA: Hold on. I can't be in agony and listen to Chinese at the same time.

LONE: Did you hear my first surprise?

MA: No. I'm too busy screaming.

LONE: I said, you'll play Gwan Gung.

MA: Gwan Gung?

LONE: Yes.

MA: Me?

LONE: Yes.

MA: Without legs?

LONE: What?

MA: That might be good.

LONE: Stop that!

MA: I'll become a legend. Like the blind man who defended Amoy.

LONE: Did you hear?

MA: "The legless man who played Gwan Gung."

LONE: Isn't this what you want? To play Gwan Gung?

MA: No, I just wanna sleep.

LONE: No, you don't. Look. Here. I brought you something.

MA: Food?

LONE: Here. Some rice

MA: Thanks, Lone. And duck?

LONE: Just a little.

MA: Where'd you get the duck?

LONE: Just bones and skin.

MA: We don't have duck. And the white devils have been blockading the food.

LONE: Sing—he had some left over.

MA: Sing? That thief?

LONE: And something to go with it.

MA: What? Lone, where did you find whiskey?

LONE: You know, Sing—he has almost anything.

MA: Yeah. For a price.

LONE: Once, even some thousand-day-old eggs.

MA: He's a thief. That's what they told me.

LONE: Not if you're his friend.

MA: Sing don't have any real friends. Everyone talks about him bein' tied in to the head of the klan in San Francisco. Lone, you didn't have to do this. Here. Have some.

LONE: I had plenty.

MA: Don't gimme that. This cost you plenty, Lone.

LONE: Well, I thought if we were going to celebrate, we should do it as well as we would at home.

MA: Celebrate? What for? Wait.

LONE: Ma, the strike is over.

MA: Shit, I knew it. And we won, right?

LONE: Yes, the ChinaMen have won. They can do more than just talk.

MA: I told you. Didn't I tell you?

LONE: Yes. Yes, you did.

MA: Yang told me it was gonna be done. He said—

LONE: Yes, I remember.

MA: Didn't I tell you? Huh?

LONE: Ma, eat your duck.

MA: Nine days, we civilized the white devils. I knew it. I knew we'd hold out till their ears started twitching. So that's where you got the duck, right? At the celebration?

LONE: No, there wasn't a celebration.

MA: Huh? You sure? ChinaMen—they look for any excuse to party.

LONE: But I thought *we* should celebrate.

MA: Well, that's for sure.

LONE: So you will play Gwan Gung.

MA: God, nine days. Shit, it's finally done. Well, we'll show them how to party. Make noise. Jump off rocks. Make the mountain shake.

LONE: We'll wash your body, to prepare you for the role.

MA: What role?

LONE: Gwan Gung. I've been telling you.

MA: I don't wanna play Gwan Gung.

LONE: You've shown the dedication required to become my student, so—

MA: Lone, you think I stayed up last night 'cause I wanted to play Gwan Gung?

LONE: You said you were like him.

MA: I am. Gwan Gung stayed up all night once to prove his loyalty. Well, now I have too. Lone, I'm honored that you told me your story.

LONE: Yes . . . That is like Gwan Gung.

MA: Good. So let's do an opera about *me.*

LONE: What?

MA: You wanna party or what?

LONE: About you?

MA: You said I was like Gwan Gung, didn't you?

LONE: Yes, but—

MA: Well, look at the operas he's got. I ain't even got one.

LONE: Still, you can't—

MA: You tell me, is that fair?

LONE: You can't do an opera about yourself.

MA: I just won a victory, didn't I? I deserve an opera in my honor.

LONE: But it's not traditional.

MA: Traditional? Lone, you gotta figure any way I could do Gwan Gung wasn't gonna be traditional anyway. I may be as good a guy as him, but he's a better dancer. *(Sings)*

Old Gwan Gung, just sits about
Till the dime-store fighters have had it out
Then he pitches his peach pit
Combs his beard
Draws his sword
And they scatter in fear   *Chinese Opera style Provides*

LONE: What are you talking about?

MA: I just won a great victory. I get—whatcha call it?—poetic license. C'mon. Hit the gongs. I'll immortalize my story.

LONE: I refuse. This goes against all my training. I try and give you your wish and—

MA: Do it. Gimme my wish. Hit the gongs.

LONE: I never—I can't.

MA: Can't what? Don't think I'm worth an opera? No, I guess not. I forgot—you think I'm just one of those dead men.

(Silence. LONE *pulls out a gong.* MA *gets into position.* LONE *hits the gong. They do the following in a mock-Chinese-opera style)*

MA: I am Ma. Yesterday, I was kicked out of my house by my three elder brothers, calling me the lazy dreamer of the family. I am sitting here in front of the temple trying to decide how I will avenge this indignity. Here comes the poorest beggar in this village. *(He cues* LONE*)* He is called Fleaman because his body is the most popular meeting place for fleas from around the province.

LONE: *(Singing)*
> Fleas in love,
> Find your happiness
> In the gray scraps of my suit

MA: Hello, Flea—
LONE: *(Continuing)*
> Fleas in need,
> Shield your families
> In the gray hairs of my beard

MA: Hello, Flea—
(LONE cuts MA off, continues an extended improvised aria)
MA: Hello, Fleaman.
LONE: Hello, Ma. Are you interested in providing a home for these fleas?
MA: No!
LONE: This couple here—seeking to start a new home. Housing today is so hard to find. How about your left arm?
MA: I may have plenty of my own fleas in time. I have been thrown out by my elder brothers.
LONE: Are you seeking revenge? A flea epidemic on your house? *(To a flea)* Get back there. You should be asleep. Your mother will worry.
MA: Nothing would make my brothers angrier than seeing me rich.
LONE: Rich? After the bad crops of the last three years, even the fleas are thinking of moving north.
MA: I heard a white devil talk yesterday.
LONE: Oh—with hair the color of a sick chicken and eyes round as eggs? The fleas and I call him Chicken-Laying-an-Egg.
MA: He said we can make our fortunes on the Gold Mountain, where work is play and the sun scares off snow.
LONE: Don't listen to chicken-brains.
MA: Why not? He said gold grows like weeds.
LONE: I have heard that it is slavery.

MA: Slavery? What do you know, Fleaman? Who told you? The fleas? Yes, I will go to Gold Mountain.

(Gongs. MA *strikes a submissive pose to* LONE)

LONE: "The one hundred twenty-five dollars passage money is to be paid to the said head of said Hong, who will make arrangements with the coolies, that their wages shall be deducted until the debt is absorbed."

*(*MA *bows to* LONE. *Gongs. They pick up fighting sticks and do a water-crossing dance. Dance ends. They stoop next to each other and rock)*

MA: I have been in the bottom of this boat for thirty-six days now. Tang, how many have died?

LONE: Not me. I'll live through this ride.

MA: I didn't ask how you are.

LONE: But why's the Gold Mountain so far?

MA: We left with three hundred and three.

LONE: My family's depending on me.

MA: So tell me, how many have died?

LONE: I'll be the last one alive.

MA: That's not what I wanted to know.

LONE: I'll find some fresh air in this hole.

MA: I asked, how many have died.

LONE: Is that a crack in the side?

MA: Are you listening to me?

LONE: If I had some air—

MA: I asked, don't you see—?

LONE: The crack—over there—

MA: Will you answer me, please?

LONE: I need to get out.

MA: The rest here agree—

LONE: I can't stand the smell.

MA: That a hundred eighty—

LONE: I can't see the air—

MA: Of us will not see—

LONE: And I can't die.

MA: Our Gold Mountain dream.

(LONE/TANG *dies;* MA *throws his body overboard. The boat docks.* MA *exits, walks through the streets. He picks up one of the fighting sticks, while* LONE *becomes the mountain)*

MA: I have been given my pickax. Now I will attack the mountain.

(MA *does a dance of labor.* LONE *sings)*

LONE:

> Hit your hardest
> Pound out your tears
> The more you try
> The more you'll cry
> At how little I've moved
> And how large I loom
> By the time the sun goes down

(Dance stops)

MA: This mountain is clever. But why shouldn't it be? It's fighting for its life, like we fight for ours.

(*The* MOUNTAIN *picks up a stick.* MA *and the* MOUNTAIN *do a battle dance. Dance ends)*

MA: This mountain not only defends itself—it also attacks. It turns our strength against us.

(LONE *does* MA's *labor dance, while* MA *plants explosives in midair. Dance ends)*

MA: This mountain has survived for millions of years. Its wisdom is immense.

(LONE *and* MA *begin a second battle dance. This one ends with them working the battle sticks together.* LONE *breaks away, does a warrior strut)*

LONE: I am a white devil! Listen to my stupid language: "Wha che doo doo blah blah." Look at my wide eyes— like I have drunk seventy-two pots of tea. Look at my funny hair—twisting, turning, like a snake telling lies. *(To* MA) Bla bla doo doo tee tee.

MA: We don't understand English.

LONE: *(Angry)* Bla bla doo doo tee tee!

MA: *(With Chinese accent)* Please you-ah speak-ah Chinese?

LONE: Oh. Work—uh—one—two—more—work—two—

MA: Two hours more? Stupid demons. As confused as your hair. We will strike!

(Gongs. MA *is on strike)*

MA: *(In broken English)* Eight hours day good for white man, all same good for ChinaMan.

LONE: The strike is over! We've won!

MA: I knew we would.

LONE: We forced the white devil to act civilized.

MA: Tamed the barbarians!

LONE: Did you think—

MA: Who woulda thought?

LONE: —it could be done?

MA: Who?

LONE: But who?

MA: Who could tame them?

MA *and* LONE: Only a ChinaMan!

(They laugh)

LONE: Well, c'mon.

MA: Let's celebrate!

LONE: We have.

MA: Oh.

LONE: Back to work.

MA: But we've won the strike.

LONE: I know. Congratulations! And now—

MA: —back to work?

LONE: Right.

MA: No.

LONE: But the strike is over.

(LONE tosses MA *a stick. They resume their stick battle as before, but* MA *is heard over* LONE'*s singing)*

LONE:	MA:
Hit your hardest	Wait.
Pound out your	I'm tired of this!
tears	How do we end it?
The more you try	Let's stop now, all
The more you'll cry	right?
At how little I've	Look, I said enough!
moved	
And how large I	
loom	
By the time the	
sun goes down.	

(MA *tosses his stick away, but* LONE *is already aiming a blow toward it, so that* LONE *hits* MA *instead and knocks him down*)

MA: Oh! Shit . . .

LONE: I'm sorry! Are you all right?

MA: Yeah. I guess.

LONE: Why'd you let go? You can't just do that.

MA: I'm bleeding.

LONE: That was stupid—where?

MA: Here.

LONE: No.

MA: Ow!

LONE: There will probably be a bump.

MA: I dunno

LONE: What?

MA: I dunno why I let go.

LONE: It was stupid.

MA: But how were we going to end the opera?

LONE: Here. *(He applies whiskey to* MA*'s bruise)* I don't know.

MA: Why didn't we just end it with the celebration? Ow! Careful.

LONE: Sorry. But Ma, the celebration's not the end. We're returning to work. Today. At dawn.

MA: What?

LONE: We've already lost nine days of work. But we got eight hours.

MA: Today? That's terrible.

LONE: What do you think we're here for? But they listened to our demands. We're getting a raise.

MA: Right. Fourteen dollars.

LONE: No. Eight.

MA: What?

LONE: We had to compromise. We got an eight-dollar raise.

MA: But we wanted fourteen. Why didn't we get fourteen?

LONE: It was the best deal they could get. Congratulations.

MA: Congratulations? Look, Lone, I'm sick of you making fun of the ChinaMen.

LONE: Ma, I'm not. For the first time. I was wrong. We got eight dollars.

MA: We wanted fourteen.

LONE: But we got eight hours.

MA: We'll go back on strike.

LONE: Why?

MA: We could hold out for months.

LONE: And lose all that work?

MA: But we just gave in.

LONE: You're being ridiculous. We got eight hours. Besides, it's already been decided.

MA: I didn't decide. I wasn't there. You made me stay up here.

LONE: The heads of the gangs decide.

MA: And that's it?

LONE: It's done.

MA: Back to work? That's what they decided? Lone, I don't want to go back to work.

LONE: Who does?

MA: I forgot what it's like.

LONE: You'll pick up the technique again soon enough.

MA: I mean, what it's like to have them telling you what to do all the time. Using up your strength.

LONE: I thought you said even after work, you still feel good.

MA: Some days. But others . . . *(Pause)* I get so frustrated sometimes. At the rock. The rock doesn't give in. It's not human. I wanna claw it with my fingers, but that would just rip them up. I wanna throw myself head first onto it, but it'd just knock my skull open. The rock would knock my skull open, then just sit there, still, like nothing had happened, like a faceless Buddha. *(Pause)* Lone, when do I get out of here?

LONE: Well, the railroad may get finished—

MA: It'll never get finished.

LONE: —or you may get rich.

MA: Rich. Right. This is the Gold Mountain. *(Pause)* Lone, has anyone ever gone home rich from here?

LONE: Yes. Some.

MA: But most?

LONE: Most . . . do go home.

MA: Do you still have the fear?

LONE: The fear?

MA: That you'll become like them—dead men?

LONE: Maybe I was wrong about them.

MA: Well, I do. You wanted me to say it before. I can say it now: "They are dead men." Their greatest accomplishment was to win a strike that's gotten us nothing.

LONE: They're sending money home.

MA: No.

LONE: It's not much, I know, but it's something.

MA: Lone, I'm not even doing that. If I don't get rich here, I might as well die here. Let my brothers laugh in peace.

LONE: Ma, you're too soft to get rich here, naïve—you believed the snow was warm.

MA: I've got to change myself. Toughen up. Take no shit.

Count my change. Learn to gamble. Learn to win. Learn to
stare. Learn to deny. Learn to look at men with opaque eyes.

LONE: You want to do that?

MA: I will. 'Cause I've got the fear. You've given it to me.
(Pause)

LONE: Will I see you here tonight?

MA: Tonight?

LONE: I just thought I'd ask.

MA: I'm sorry, Lone. I haven't got time to be the Second Clown.

LONE: I thought you might not.

MA: Sorry.

LONE: You could have been a . . . fair actor.

MA: You coming down? I gotta get ready for work. This is
gonna be a terrible day. My legs are sore and my arms are
outa practice.

LONE: You go first. I'm going to practice some before
work. There's still time.

MA: Practice? But you said you lost your fear. And you said
that's what brings you up here.

LONE: I guess I was wrong about that, too. Today, I am
dancing for no reason at all.

MA: Do whatever you want. See you down at camp.

LONE: Could you do me a favor?

MA: A favor?

LONE: Could you take this down so I don't have to take it all?
(LONE points to a pile of props)

MA: Well, okay. *(Pause)* But this is the last time.

LONE: Of course, Ma. *(MA exits)* See you soon. The last
time. I suppose so.

*(LONE resumes practicing. He twirls his hair around as in the
beginning of the play. The sun begins to rise. It continues rising
until LONE is moving and seen only in shadow)*

CURTAIN

FAMILY
DEVOTIONS

For my Ama and Ankong,
and Sam Shepard

Family Devotions was produced by Joseph Papp at the New York Shakespeare Festival Public Theater, where it opened in the Newman Theater on October 18, 1981, with the following cast:

JOANNE .... Jodi Long
WILBUR .... Jim Ishida
JENNY .... Lauren Tom
AMA .... Tina Chen
POPO .... June Kim
HANNAH .... Helen Funai
ROBERT .... Michael Paul Chan
DI-GOU .... Victor Wong
CHESTER .... Marc Hayashi

Directed by Robert Alan Ackerman; sets by David Gropman; lights by Tom Skelton; costumes by Willa Kim.

CHARACTERS

JOANNE, late thirties, Chinese American raised in the Philippines.

WILBUR, her husband, Japanese American, <u>nisei</u> (second generation).

JENNY, their daughter, seventeen.

AMA, Joanne's mother, born in China, emigrated to the Philippines, then to America.

POPO, Ama's younger sister.

HANNAH, Popo's daughter and Joanne's cousin, 5 years older than Joanne.

ROBERT, Hannah's husband, Chinese American, first generation.

DI-GOU, Ama and Popo's younger brother, born and raised in China, still a resident of the People's Republic of China (P.R.C.).

CHESTER, Hannah and Robert's son, early twenties.

```
          AMA————————————————————POPO————————DI-GOU
           |                       |
WILBUR—m—JOANNE           HANNAH—m—ROBERT
     |                            |
  JENNY                        CHESTER
```

SYNOPSIS OF SCENES

Act One. Late afternoon, the lanai/sunroom and tennis court
   of a home in <u>Bel Air, California.</u>
Act Two. Same scene, immediately following.

DEFINITION

Jok is a Chinese rice porridge.

Di-Gou is coming from China. going to have a BarB-B-Q

ACT ONE

The sunroom and backyard of a home in Bel Air. Everywhere is glass—glass roof, glass walls. Upstage of the lanai/sunroom is a patio with a barbecue and a tennis court. The tennis court leads offstage. As the curtain rises, we see a single spotlight on an old Chinese face and hear Chinese music or chanting. Suddenly, the music becomes modern-day funk or rock 'n' roll, and the lights come up to reveal the set.

The face is that of DI-GOU, *an older Chinese man wearing a blue suit and carrying an old suitcase. He is peering into the sunroom from the tennis court, through the glass walls. Behind him, a stream of black smoke is coming from the barbecue.*

(Offstage) Wilbur! Wilbur!

*(*DI-GOU *exits off the tennis court. Enter* JOANNE, *from the house. She is a Chinese American woman, attractive, in her late-thirties. She sees the smoke coming from the barbecue)*

JOANNE: Aiii-ya! *(She heads for the barbecue, and on her way notices that the sunroom is a mess)* Jenny! *(She runs out to the barbecue, opens it up. Billows of black smoke continue to pour out)* Oh, gosh. Oh, golly. *(To offstage)* Wilbur! *(She begins pulling burnt objects out of the barbecue)* Sheee! *(She pulls out a chicken, dumps it onto the ground)* Wilbur! *(She pulls out another chicken, does the same)* Wilbur, the heat was too high on the barbecue! *(She begins pulling out burnt objects and tossing them all over the tennis court)* You should have been watching it! It could have exploded! We could all have been blown up! *(She picks up another chicken, examines it)* You think we can have some of this? *(She pauses, tosses it onto the court)* We'll get some more chickens. We'll put barbecue sauce on them and stick them into the microwave. *(She exits into the house holding a chicken on the end of her fork)* Is this okay, do you think?

(WILBUR appears on the tennis court. He is a Japanese American man, nisei, in his late thirties. His hair is permed. He wears tennis clothes)

WILBUR: Hon? *(He looks around)* What's up? *(He picks a burnt chicken off the tennis court)* Hon? *(He walks over to the barbecue)* Who—? Why's the heat off? *(He walks around the tennis court picking up chickens)* Jesus! *(He smears grease on his white tennis shirt, notices it)* Aw, shit! *(He dumps all the chickens except one, which he has forgotten to pick up, back into the barbecue. He walks into the sunroom, gets some ice, and tries to dab at the stain)* Hon? Will you come here a sec? *(He exits into the house)*

(JENNY appears on the tennis court. She is seventeen, WILBUR and JOANNE's daughter. She carries a large wire mesh box)

JENNY: Chickie! *(Looking around)* Chickie? Chickie, where the hell did you go? You know, it's embarrassing. It's embarrassing being this old and still having to chase a chicken all over the house. *(She sees the lone burnt chicken on the court. She creeps over slowly, then picks it up)* Blaagh! Who cooked this? See, Chickie, this is what happens— what happens when you're a bad chickie.

(CHESTER, a young Chinese American male in his early twenties, appears on the tennis court. He tries to sneak up on JENNY)

JENNY: *(To chicken)* Look, if you bother Popo and Ama, I'm gonna catch shit, and you know what that means for you—chicken soccer. You'll be sorry. *(CHESTER is right behind JENNY)* You'll be sorry if you mess with me. *(She turns around, catching* CHESTER) Oh, good. You have to be here, too.

CHESTER: No, I don't. I've gotta pack.

JENNY: They'll expect you to be here when that Chinese guy gets here. What's his name? Dar-gwo?

CHESTER: I dunno. Dah-gim?

JENNY: Doo-goo? Something.

CHESTER: Yeah. I'm not staying.

JENNY: So what else is new?

CHESTER: I don't have time.

JENNY: You luck out 'cause you don't live here. Me—there's no way I can get away. When you leaving?

CHESTER: Tomorrow.

JENNY: Tomorrow? And you're not packed?

CHESTER: Don't rub it in. Listen, you still have my green suitcase?

JENNY: Yeah. I wish *I* had an excuse not to be here. All I need is to meet another old relative. Another goon.

CHESTER: Yeah. Where's my suitcase?

JENNY: First you have to help me find Chickie.

CHESTER: Jesus!

AMA: *(Offstage)* Joanne!

CHESTER: *(To* JENNY) All right. I don't want them to know I'm here.

(CHESTER *and* JENNY *exit.* POPO *and* AMA *enter. They are* JOANNE's *aunt and mother, respectively)*

AMA: Joanne! Joanne! Jenny! Where is Joanne?

POPO: Probably busy.

AMA: Where is Jenny? Joanne?

POPO: Perhaps you can find, ah, Wilbur.

AMA: Joanne!

POPO: Ah, you never wish to see Wilbur.

AMA: I see him at wedding. That is enough. He was not at church again today.

POPO: Ah?

AMA: He will be bad influence when Di-gou arrive. Wilbur—holy spirit is not in him.

POPO: Not matter. He can perhaps eat in kitchen.

AMA: Outside!

POPO: This is his house.

AMA: All heart must join as one—

POPO: He may eat inside!

AMA: —only then, miracles can take place.

POPO: But in kitchen.

AMA: Wilbur—he never like family devotions.

POPO: Wilbur does not come from Christian family.

AMA: He come from Japanese family.

POPO: I mean to say, we—ah—very fortunate. Mama teach us all Christianity. Not like Wilbur family.

AMA: When Di-gou arrive, we will remind him. What Mama tells us.

POPO: Di-gou can remember himself.

AMA: No.

POPO: But we remember.

AMA: You forget—Di-gou, he lives in China.

POPO: So?

AMA: Torture. Communists. Make him work in rice fields.

POPO: I no longer think so.

AMA: In rice field, all the people wear wires in their heads—yes! Wires force them work all day and sing Communist song. Like this!

(She mimes harvesting rice and singing)

POPO: No such thing!

AMA: Yes! You remember Twa-Ling? Before we leave China, before Communist come, she say, "I will send you a picture. If Communists are good, I will stand—if bad, I will sit."

POPO: That does not mean anything!

AMA: In picture she sent, she was lying down!

POPO: Picture was not sent for ten years. Probably she forget.

AMA: You wait till Di-gou arrive. You will see.

POPO: See what?

AMA: Brainwash! You watch for little bit of wires in his hair.

(POPO notices the lone burnt chicken on the tennis court)

POPO: What's there?

AMA: Where?

POPO: There—on cement.

AMA: Cannot see well.

POPO: There. Black.

AMA: Oh. I see.

POPO: Looks like *gao sai.*

AMA: They sometimes have problem with the dog.

POPO: Ha!

AMA: Very bad dog.

POPO: At home, dog do that?—we shoot him.

AMA: Should be punish.

POPO: Shot! *(Pause)* That no *gao sai.*

AMA: No? What then?

POPO: I don't know.

AMA: Oh, I know.

POPO: What?

AMA: That is Chickie.

POPO: No. That no Chickie.

AMA: They have a chicken—"Chickie."

(They get up, head toward the chicken)

POPO: No. That one, does not move.

AMA: Maybe sick. *(They reach the chicken)* Aiii-ya! What happen to Chickie!

POPO: *(Picking it up)* This chicken very sick!

(She laughs)

AMA: Wilbur.

POPO: Huh?

AMA: Wilbur—his temper is very bad.

POPO: No!

AMA: Yes. Perhaps Chickie bother him too much.
POPO: No—this is only a chicken.
AMA: "Chickie" *is* chicken!
POPO: No—this—another chicken.
AMA: How you know?
POPO: No matter now. Like this, all chicken look same. Here. Throw away. No good.
AMA: Very bad temper. Japanese man. *(AMA sees POPO looking for a trash can)* Wait.
POPO: Huh?
AMA: Jenny—might want to keep it.
POPO: This?
AMA: Leave here until we know.
   (She takes the chicken from POPO)
POPO: No, throw away. *(She takes it back)* Stink up whole place soon.
AMA: Don't want to anger Wilbur!
POPO: You pig-head!
AMA: He do this to Chickie—think what he will do to us?
POPO: *Zin gao tza!* [Always so much trouble!]
AMA: You don't know Japanese man!
   (AMA knocks the chicken from POPO's hands; they circle around it like boxers sparring)
POPO: *Pah-di!* [Spank you!]
AMA: Remember? During war? Pictures they show us? Always—Japanese man kill Chinese!
POPO: Go away, pig-head!
AMA: In picture—Japanese always kill and laugh, kill and laugh.
POPO: If dirty, should throw away!
AMA: Sometimes—torture and laugh, too.
POPO: Wilbur not like that! Hardly even laugh!
AMA: When he kill Chickie, then he laugh!
   (They both grab the chicken; JOANNE enters, sees them)
JOANNE: Hi, Mom, Auntie. Who cleaned up the chicken?

AMA: Huh? This is not Chickie?

POPO: *(To* AMA*)* Tell you things, you never listen. *Gong-gong-ah!* [Idiot!]

JOANNE: When's Hannah getting here?

POPO: Hannah—she is at airport.

JOANNE: We had a little accident and I need help programming the microwave. Last time, I put a roast inside and it disintegrated. She should be here already.

AMA: Joanne, you prepare for family devotions?

JOANNE: Of course, Mom. I had the maid set up everything just like you said.

(She exits)

AMA: Good. Praise to God will bring Di-gou back to family. Make him rid of Communist demon.

POPO: He will speak in tongue of fire. Like he does when he is a little boy with See-goh-poh.

*(*WILBUR *enters the tennis court with an empty laundry basket. He heads for the barbecue.* JOANNE *follows him)*

JOANNE: *(To* WILBUR*)* Hon, what are you going to do with those?

WILBUR: *(Referring to the burnt chicken)* I'm just going to give them to Grizzly.

(He piles the chickens into the basket)

JOANNE: All right. *(She notices that the mess in the lanai has not been touched.)* Jenny! *(To* WILBUR*)* But be careful not to give Grizzly any bones!

*(*JOANNE *exits)*

WILBUR: *(To* AMA *and* POPO*)* How you doin', Mom, Auntie?

AMA: *(To* POPO, *sotto voce)* Kill and laugh.

WILBUR: Joanne tells me you're pretty excited about your brother's arrival—pretty understandable, after all these years— what's his name again? Di-ger, Di-gow, something . . .

AMA: Di-gou!

WILBUR: Yeah, right. Gotta remember that. Be pretty embarrassing if I said the wrong name. Di-gou.

POPO: Di-gou is not his name.

WILBUR: What? Not his—? What is it again? Di-gow? De—?

AMA: Di-gou!

WILBUR: Di-gou.

POPO: That is not his name.

WILBUR: Oh. It's the tones in Chinese, isn't it? I'm saying the wrong tone: Di-góu? Or Di-gou? Or—

POPO: Di-gou meaning is "second brother."

WILBUR: Oh, I see. It's not his name. Boy, do I feel ignorant in these situations. If only there were some way I could make sure I don't embarrass myself tonight.

AMA: Eat outside.

WILBUR: Outside?

POPO: Or in kitchen.

WILBUR: In the kitchen? That's great! You two are real jokers, you know?

AMA: No. We are not.

WILBUR: C'mon. I should bring you down to the club someday. The guys never believe it when I tell them how much I love you two.

AMA: *(To* POPO*) Gao sai.*

*(*JENNY *enters the sunroom)*

WILBUR: Right. *"Gao sai"* to you, too. *(He starts to leave, sees* JENNY*)* Wash your hands before you play with your grandmother.

JENNY: *(To* WILBUR*)* Okay, Dad. *(To* AMA*)* Do I have to, Ama?

AMA: No. Of course not.

JENNY: Can I ask you something personal?

AMA: Of course.

JENNY: Did Daddy just call you "dog shit"?

AMA: Jenny!

POPO: Yes. Very good!

JENNY: Doesn't that bother you?

POPO: *(To* AMA*)* Her Chinese is improving!

JENNY: We learned it in Chinese school.

AMA: Jenny, you should not use this American word.

JENNY: Sorry. It just slipped out.

AMA: You do not use such word at school, no?

JENNY: Oh, no. Of course not.

AMA: You should not use anyplace.

JENNY: Right.

POPO: Otherwise—no good man wants marry you.

JENNY: You mean, no rich man.

AMA: No—money is not important.

POPO: As long as he is good man.

(Pause)

AMA: Christian.

POPO: Chinese.

AMA: Good education.

POPO: Good school.

AMA: Princeton.

POPO: Harvard.

AMA: Doctor.

POPO: Surgeon.

AMA: Brain surgeon.

POPO: Surgeon general.

AMA: Otherwise—you marry anyone that you like.

JENNY: Ama, Popo—look, I'm only seventeen.

POPO: True. But you can develop the good habits now.

JENNY: I don't want to get married till I'm at least thirty or something.

POPO: Thirty! By that time we are dead!

AMA: Gone to see God!

POPO: Lie in ground, arms cross!

JENNY: Look at it this way: how can I be a good mother if I have to follow my career around?

AMA: Your career will not require this.

JENNY: Yeah, it will. What if I have to go on tour?

AMA: Dental technicians do not tour.

JENNY: Ama!

POPO: Only tour—one mouth to next mouth: "Hello. Clean your teeth?"

JENNY: Look, I'm telling you, I'm going to be a dancer.

AMA: We say—you can do both. Combine skills.

JENNY: That's ridiculous.

POPO: Be first dancing dental technician.

JENNY: I don't wanna be a dental technician!

POPO: Dancing dental technician very rare. You will be very popular.

JENNY: Why can't I be like Chester?

AMA: You cannot be like Chester.

JENNY: Why not!

POPO: You do not play violin. Chester does not dance. No hope.

JENNY: I know, but, I mean, he's a musician. Why can't I be a dancer?

AMA: Chester—his work very dangerous.

JENNY: Dangerous?

AMA: He just receive new job—play with Boston Symphony.

JENNY: Yeah. I know. He's leaving tomorrow. So? What's so bad about Boston?

AMA: Conductor—Ozawa—he is Japanese.

JENNY: Oh, no. Not this again.

AMA: Very strict. If musicians miss one note, they must kill themself!

JENNY: Don't be ridiculous. That's no reason why I can't be like Chester.

POPO: But Chester—he makes plenty money.

JENNY: Yeah. Right. Now. But he has to leave home to do it, see? I want a career, too. So what if I never get married?

AMA: Jenny! You must remember—you come from family of See-goh-poh. She was a great evangelist.

JENNY: I know about See-goh-poh. She was your aunt.

AMA: First in family to become Christian.

POPO: She make this family chosen by God.

JENNY: To do what? Clean teeth?

AMA: Jenny!

JENNY: Look, See-goh-poh never got married because of her work, right?

AMA: See-goh-poh was marry to God.

POPO: When Di-gou arrive, he will tell you his testimony. How See-goh-poh change his life.

AMA: Before, he is like you. *(To* POPO*)* You remember?

POPO: Yes. He is always so fussy.

JENNY: I'm not fussy.

AMA: Stubborn.

POPO: Complain this, complain that.

JENNY: I'm not complaining!

AMA: He will be very happy to meet you. Someone to complain with.

JENNY: I'm just telling you, there's no such thing as a danc-ing dental technician!

AMA: Good. You will be new discovery.

POPO: When Di-gou is a little boy, he never play with other children. He only read the books.
Read books—and play tricks.

AMA: He is very naughty.

POPO: He tell other children there are ghosts hide inside the tree, behind the bush, in the bathroom at night.

AMA: One day, he feed snail poison to gardener.

POPO: Then, when he turns eight year old, See-goh-poh decide she will bring him on her evangelism tour. When he return, he had the tongue of fire.

JENNY: Oh, c'mon—those kind of things only happened in China.

AMA: No—they can happen here as well.

POPO: Di-gou at eight, he goes with See-goh-poh on her first evangelism tour—they travel all around Fukien—thirty day and night, preach to all villages. Five hundred people accept Christ on these thirty day, and See-goh-poh heal many sick, restore ear to deaf, put tongue in mouth of dumb, all these thing and cast out the demon. Perhaps even one dead man—dead and wither—he rise up from his sleep. Di-gou see all this while carry See-goh-poh's bag and bring her food, ah? After thirty day, they return home. We have large banquet—perhaps twelve different dish that night—outside—underneath—ah—cloth. After we eat, See-goh-poh say, "Now is time for Family Devotions, and this time, he will lead." See-goh-poh point to Di-gou, who is still a boy, but he walk up in front of table and begin to talk and flame begin to come from his mouth, over his head. Fire. Fire, all around. His voice—so loud—praise and testify the miracle of God. Louder and louder, more and more fire, till entire sky fill with light, does not seem to be night, like middle of day, like twelve noon. When he finish talk, sun has already rise, and cloth over our head, it is all burn, gone, ashes blow away.

(JOANNE *enters, pulling* CHESTER *behind. He carries a suitcase*)

JOANNE: Look who's here!

POPO: Chester—good you decide to come.

JOANNE: He looked lost. This house isn't that big, you know.

(Exits)

AMA: *(To* CHESTER*)* You come for reunion with Di-gou. Very good.

CHESTER: Un—look, I really can't stay. I have to finish packing.

AMA: You must stay—see Di-gou!

CHESTER: But I'm leaving tomorrow.

(Doorbell.)

CHESTER: Oh, no.

JOANNE: Can someone get that?   *(Simul-*

JENNY: Too late!   *taneously)*

POPO: Di-gou!

AMA: *(To* CHESTER*)* You must! This will be Di-gou!

*(*WILBUR *crosses with basket, now full of chicken bones)*

WILBUR: I'll get it. Chester, good to see you made it.

(Exits)

JENNY: He almost didn't.

CHESTER: I'm really short on time. I gotta go. I'll see you tomorrow at the airport.

POPO: Chester! When Di-gou arrive, he must see whole family! You stay!

*(*CHESTER *pauses, decides to stay)*

CHESTER: *(To* JENNY*)* This is ridiculous. I can't stay.

JENNY: I always have to. Just grin a lot when you meet this guy. Then everyone will be happy.

CHESTER: I don't wanna meet this guy!

*(*WILBUR *enters with* HANNAH *and* ROBERT, *who are* CHES-TER's *parents.* HANNAH *is* POPO's *daughter. She is five years older than* JOANNE*)*

WILBUR: *(To* ROBERT*)* What? What do you mean?

AMA: *(Stands up on a chair; a speech)* Di-gou, thirty year have pass since we last see you—

WILBUR: *(To* AMA*)* Not now, Ma.

AMA: Do you still love God?

ROBERT: What do you mean, "What do you mean?" That's what I mean.

HANNAH: He wasn't there, Wilbur. *(To* AMA*)* Auntie! Di-gou isn't with us.

AMA: What? How can this be?

ROBERT: Those Chinese airliners—all junk stuffs—so inefficient.

AMA: Where is he?

POPO: *(To* ROBERT*)* You sure you look close?

ROBERT: What "look close"? We just waited for everyone to get off the plane.

AMA: Where is he?

HANNAH: *(To* AMA*)* We don't know, Auntie! *(To* CHESTER*)* Chester, are you packed?

AMA: Don't know?

CHESTER: *(To* HANNAH*)* No, I'm not. And I'm really in a hurry.

HANNAH: You're leaving tomorrow! Why aren't you packed?

CHESTER: I'm trying to, Mom.

(ROBERT pulls out a newspaper clipping, shows it to CHESTER*)*

ROBERT: Look, son, I called the Chinese paper, used a little of my influence—they did a story on you. Here—

CHESTER: *(Looks at clipping)* I can't read this, Dad! It's in Chinese!

ROBERT: *(Takes back clipping)* Little joke, there.

AMA: *(To anyone who will listen)* Where is he?

HANNAH: *(To* AMA*)* Auntie, ask Wilbur. *(To* CHESTER*)* Get packed!

CHESTER: All right!

WILBUR: *(Trying to explain to* AMA*)* Well, Mom, they said he wasn't at—

AMA: *(Ignoring* WILBUR *totally)* Where is he?!

(ROBERT continues to study the newspaper clipping, points a section out to CHESTER*)*

ROBERT: Here—this is where it talks about my bank.

CHESTER: I'm going to pack.

HANNAH: *(To* CHESTER*)* Going?

CHESTER: *(To* HANNAH*)* You said I should—

HANNAH: *(To* CHESTER*)* You have to stay and see Di-gou!

(WILBUR makes another attempt to explain the situation to AMA*)*

WILBUR: *(To* AMA*)* See, Mom, I guess—

AMA: *(Ignoring him again)* Where is he?

(ROBERT continues studying his clipping, oblivious)

ROBERT: *(Translating, to* CHESTER*)* It says, "Great Chinese violinist will conduct and solo with New York Philharmonic."

CHESTER: What? It says what?

HANNAH: *(To* CHESTER*)* You came without being packed? *(*AMA *decides to look for* DI-GOU *on her own, and starts searching the house.)*

AMA: Di-gou! Di-gou!

WILBUR: *(Following* AMA*)* Ma, listen. I'll explain.

HANNAH: *(To* CHESTER*)* How can you be so inefficient?

CHESTER: *(To* ROBERT*)* Dad, I just got a job playing in the violin section in Boston.

AMA: Di-gou! Di-gou!

CHESTER: *(To* ROBERT*)* I'm not conducting, and—

ROBERT: *(To* CHESTER*)* Ssssh! I know. But good publicity— for the bank.

HANNAH: *(To* CHESTER*)* Well, I'll help you pack later. But you have to stay till Di-gou arrives. Sheesh!

CHESTER: I can't believe this!

AMA: *(Continuing her search)* Di-gou! Are you already in bathroom?
(Exits)

HANNAH: *(To* AMA*)* Auntie, he wasn't at the airport! *(To* WILBUR*)* Why didn't you tell her?

WILBUR: *(Following* AMA*)* I'm trying! I'm trying!
(Exits)

ROBERT: It's those Communist airlines, I'm telling you. Inefficient.

HANNAH: We asked at the desk. They didn't have a flight list.

AMA: *(Entering)* Then where is he?

WILBUR: *(Entering, in despair)* Joanne, will you come here?

ROBERT: They probably left him in Guam.

POPO: *(To* ROBERT*)* We give you that photograph. You remember to bring it?

ROBERT: Of course I remembered.

HANNAH: *(To* POPO*)* Mom, it's not Robert's fault.

POPO: *(To* HANNAH*)* Should leave him *(Refers to* ROBERT*)* in car.

HANNAH: I tried.

ROBERT: In the car?

HANNAH: He wanted to come in.

ROBERT: It's hot in the car!

AMA: *(To* ROBERT*)* Suffer, good for you.

POPO: *(To* HANNAH*)* You cannot control your husband.

ROBERT: I suffer enough.

HANNAH: He said he could help.

POPO: He is wrong again.

AMA: What to do now?

   *(*JENNY *exits in the confusion;* JOANNE *enters)*

JOANNE: What's wrong now?

WILBUR: They lost your uncle.

JOANNE: Who lost him?

HANNAH: We didn't lose him.

AMA: *(To* ROBERT*)* You ask at airport desk?

ROBERT: I'm telling you, he's in Guam.

JOANNE: *(To* HANNAH*)* How could you lose a whole uncle?

HANNAH: We never had him to begin with!

JOANNE: So where is he?

ROBERT: Guam, I'm telling—!

POPO: *(To* ROBERT*)* Guam, Guam! Shut mouth or go there
  yourself!

HANNAH: *(A general announcement)* We don't know where he
  is!

JOANNE: Should I call the police?

WILBUR: You might have looked longer at the airport.

HANNAH: That's what I said, but he *(Refers to* ROBERT*)* said,
  "Aaah, too much trouble!"

POPO: *(To* ROBERT*)* See? You do not care about people from
  other province besides Shanghai.

ROBERT: *(To* POPO*)* Mom, I care. It's just that—

POPO: *(To* ROBERT*)* Your father trade with Japanese during
  war.

WILBUR: Huh?

ROBERT: Mom, let's not start that.

POPO: Not like our family. We die first!

WILBUR: What's all this about?

ROBERT: Hey, let's not bring up all this other junk, right?

POPO: *(To* ROBERT*)* You are ashamed.

ROBERT: The airport is a big place.

WILBUR: *(To* ROBERT*)* Still, you should've been able to spot an old Chinese man.

ROBERT: Everyone on that plane was an old Chinese man!

AMA: True. All Communist look alike.

HANNAH: Hold it, everybody! *(Pause)* Listen, Di-gou has this address, right?

AMA: No.

HANNAH: No? *(To* POPO*)* Mom, you said he did.

POPO: Yes. He does.

AMA: *(To* POPO*)* Yes? But I did not write to him.

POPO: I did.

AMA: Now, Communist—they will know this address.

POPO: Never mind.

AMA: No safety. Bomb us.

HANNAH: Okay, he has this address, and he can speak English—after all, he went to medical school here, right? So he shouldn't have any problem.

JOANNE: What an introduction to America.

HANNAH: All we can do is wait.

ROBERT: We went up to all these old Chinese men at the airport, asked them, "Are you our Di-gou?" They all said yes. What could we do? They all looked drunk, bums.

JOANNE: Maybe they're all still wandering through the metal detectors, looking for their families, and will continue till they die.

(CHESTER *wanders onto the tennis court, observes the following section from far upstage)*

JOANNE: I must have been only about seven the last time Di-gou visited us in the Philippines.

AMA: Less.

JOANNE: Maybe less.

WILBUR: Honey, I'm sure everyone here has a memory, too. You don't see them babbling about it, do you?

JOANNE: The last thing I remember about Di-gou, he was trying to convince you grown-ups to leave the Philippines and return to China. There was a terrible fight—one of the worst that ever took place in our complex. I guess he wanted you to join the Revolution. The fight was so loud that all our servants gathered around the windows to watch.

AMA: They did this?

POPO: Shoot them.

JOANNE: I guess this was just around 1949. Finally, Di-gou left, calling you all sorts of terrible names. On his way out, he set fire to one of our warehouses. All us kids sat around while the servants tried to put it out.

POPO: No. That was not a warehouse.

HANNAH: Yeah, Joanne—the warehouses were concrete, remember?

JOANNE: *(To* HANNAH*)* But don't you remember a fire?

HANNAH: Yes.

POPO: I think he burn a pile of trash.

ROBERT: *(To* WILBUR*)* I know how you feel. They're always yap-yap-yapping about their family stories—you'd think they were the only family in China. *(To* HANNAH*)* I have memories, too.

HANNAH: You don't remember anything. You have a terrible memory.

ROBERT: Look, when I was kidnapped, I didn't know—

HANNAH: Sssssh!

JOANNE: Quiet, Robert!

POPO: Like broken record—ghang, ghang, ghang.

WILBUR: *(To* ROBERT*)* I tell you what: you wanna take a look at my collection of tax shelters?

ROBERT: Same old stuff?

WILBUR: No. Some new ones.

(They exit. DI-GOU *appears on the tennis court; only* CHESTER *sees him, but* CHESTER *says nothing.* CHESTER *watches* DI-GOU *watching the women)*

JOANNE: Anyway, he set fire to something and the flames burned long into the night. One servant was even killed in it, if I remember correctly. I think Matthew's nursemaid was trying to put it out when her dress caught fire and, like a fool, she ran screaming all over the complex. All the adults were too busy to hear her, I guess, and all the kids just sat there and watched this second fire, moving in circles and screaming. By morning, both fires were out, and our tutors came as usual. But that day, nothing functioned just right—I think the water pipes broke in Sah-Zip's room, the cars wouldn't start—something—all I remember is servants running around all day with one tool or another. And that was how Di-gou left Manila for the last time. Left Manila and returned to China—in two fires—one which moved—and a great rush of handymen.

*(*DI-GOU *is now sitting in their midst in the sunroom. He puts down his suitcase. They turn and see him. He sticks his thumb out, as if for hitchhiking, but it is pointed in the wrong direction)*

DI-GOU: "Going my way?"

AMA: Di-gou!

DI-GOU: "Hey, baby, got a lift?"

POPO: You see? Our family members will always return.

JOANNE: *(To* DI-GOU*)* Are you—? Oh, you're—? Well, nice— How did you get here?

DI-GOU: *(Pulls a book out of his jacket)* Our diplomacy handbook. Very useful.

POPO: Welcome to America!

DI-GOU: *(Referring to the handbook)* It says, "When transportation is needed, put your thumb as if to plug a hole."

AMA: *(On chair)* Di-gou, thirty year have passed—

DI-GOU: *(Still reading)* "And say, 'Going my way?' "
AMA: Do you still believe in God?
DI-GOU: "Or, 'Hey, baby, got a lift?' "
AMA: Do you?
HANNAH: *(To* AMA*)* Auntie, he's explaining something.
DI-GOU: It worked! I am here!
AMA: *(Getting down off chair)* Still as stubborn as before.
DI-GOU: Hello, my sisters.
POPO: Hello, Di-gou. This is my daughter, Hannah.
HANNAH: *(To* DI-GOU*)* Were you at the airport? We were
  waiting for you.
DI-GOU: Hannah. Oh, last time, you were just a baby.
AMA: *(Introducing* JOANNE*)* And Joanne, remember?
JOANNE: Hello, Di-gou. How was your flight?
DI-GOU: Wonderful, wonderful.
POPO: Where is Chester? Chester! *(*CHESTER *enters the lanai)*
  Him—this is number one grandson.
DI-GOU: Oh, you are Chester. You are the violinist, yes?
CHESTER: You're Di-gou?
DI-GOU: Your parents are so proud of you.
HANNAH: We are not. He's just a kid who needs to pack.
AMA: Where is Jenny? Jenny!
HANNAH: *(To* DI-GOU*)* We figured you'd be able to get here
  by yourself.
DI-GOU: Oh, yes.
  (He sticks out his thumb. JENNY *enters)*
JOANNE: Jenny! Say, "Hi, Di-gou."
JENNY: Hi, Di-gou.
DI-GOU: *(To* JOANNE*)* This is your daughter?
JOANNE: Yes. Jenny. *(Pause)* Jenny, say, "Hi, Di-gou."
JENNY: Mom, I just did!
JOANNE: Oh. Right.
JENNY: Will you cool out?
DI-GOU: Jenny, the last time I saw your mother, she was
  younger than you are now.

JENNY: He's kinda cute.

JOANNE: Jenny, your grand-uncle is not cute.

DI-GOU: Thank you.

JENNY: *(To* JOANNE*)* Can I go now?

AMA: Why you always want to go?

JENNY: Sorry, Ama. Busy.

JOANNE: *(Allowing* JENNY *to leave)* All right.

DI-GOU: *(To* JENNY*)* What are you doing?

JENNY: Huh? Reading.

DI-GOU: Oh. Schoolwork.

JENNY: Nah. *Vogue.*

   (Exits.)

JOANNE: I've got to see about dinner. *(To* HANNAH*)* Can you give me a hand? I want to use my new Cuisinart.

HANNAH: All right. What do you want to make?

JOANNE: I don't know. What does a Cuisinart do?

   *(*HANNAH *and* JOANNE *exit;* DI-GOU, AMA, POPO, *and* CHES-TER *are left in the sunroom)*

AMA: Di-gou, thirty year have pass. Do you still love God?

DI-GOU: Thirty-three.

AMA: Ah?

POPO: 1949 to 1982. Thirty-three. He is correct.

AMA: Oh. But you do still love God? Like before?

DI-GOU: You know, sisters, after you left China, I learned that I never did believe in God.

   (Pause)

AMA: What!

POPO: How can you say this?

CHESTER: Ama, Popo, don't start in on that—he just got here.

POPO: You defend him?

AMA: *(Chasing* CHESTER *out to tennis court)* You both are influence by bad people.

POPO: Spend time with bums! Communist bum, musician bum, both same.

DI-GOU: Just to hear my sisters after all these years—you may speak whatever you like.

AMA: Do you still love God?

DI-GOU: I have much love.

AMA: For God?

DI-GOU: For my sisters.

(Pause)

POPO: You are being very difficult.

AMA: You remember when you first become Christian?

POPO: You travel with See-goh-poh on her first evangelism tour? Before we move to Philippines and you stay in China? Remember? You speak in tongues of fire.

DI-GOU: I was only eight years old. That evening is a blur to me.

AMA: Tonight—we have family devotions. You can speak again. Miracles. You still believe in miracles?

DI-GOU: It is a miracle that I am here again with you!

POPO: Why you always change subject? You remember Ah Hong? Your servant? How See-goh-poh cast out his opium demon?

DI-GOU: I don't think that happened.

AMA: Yes! Remember? After evangelism tour—she cast out his demon.

POPO: Ah Hong tell stories how he eats opium, then he can see everything so clear, like—uh—glass. He can see even through wall, he say, and can see—ah—all the way through floor. Yes! He say he can see through ground, all the way to hell. And he talk with Satan and demon who pretend to be Ah Hong's dead uncles. You should remember.

DI-GOU: I vaguely recall some such stories.

(DI-GOU *opens up his suitcase during* POPO's *following speech and takes out two small Chinese toys and a small Chinese flag. He shows them to* POPO, *but she tries to ignore them*)

POPO: Demon pretend to be ghost, then show himself everyplace to Ah Hong—in kitchen, in well, in barn, in street of village. Always just sit there, never talk, never move, just sit. So See-goh-poh come, call on God, say only, "Demon begone."

AMA: And from then on, no more ghost, no more opium.

POPO: You—you so happy, then. You say, you will also cast out the demon.

DI-GOU: We were all just children.

(He lines the toys up on the floor)

AMA: But you have faith of a child.

DI-GOU: Ah Hong didn't stop eating opium, though. He just needed money. That's why two years later, he was fired.

AMA: Ah Hong never fired!

POPO: I do not think so.

DI-GOU: Yes, my tenth, eleventh birthday, he was fired.

AMA: No—remember? Ah Hong die many year later—just before you come to America for college.

DI-GOU: No, he was fired before then.

POPO: No. Before you leave, go to college, you must prepare your own suitcase. *(To* AMA*)* Bad memory.

AMA: Brainwash.

(ROBERT and WILBUR enter; CHESTER *exits off the tennis court.* ROBERT *and* WILBUR *surround* DI-GOU*)*

ROBERT and WILBUR: Welcome!

WILBUR: How you doing, Di-gow?

ROBERT: *(Correcting* WILBUR*)* Di-gou!

WILBUR: Oh, right. "Di-gou."

ROBERT: *(To* DI-GOU*)* We tried to find you at the airport.

WILBUR: *(To* DI-GOU*)* That means "second brother."

ROBERT: So, you escaped the Communists, huh?

WILBUR: Robert and I were just—

ROBERT: Little joke, there.

WILBUR: —looking at my collection of tax shelters.

ROBERT: China's pretty different now, huh?

WILBUR: You care to take a look?

ROBERT: I guess there's never a dull moment—

WILBUR: Probably no tax shelters, either.

ROBERT: —waiting for the next cultural revolution.

WILBUR: Oh, Robert!

ROBERT: Little joke, there.

WILBUR: *(To* DI-GOU*)* That's how he *(Refers to* ROBERT*)* does business.

ROBERT: Of course, I respect China.

WILBUR: He says these totally outrageous things.

ROBERT: But your airlines—so inefficient.

WILBUR: And people remember him.

ROBERT: How long were you in Guam?

WILBUR: *(To* ROBERT*)* He wasn't in Guam!

ROBERT: No?

WILBUR: *(To* DI-GOU*)* Well, we're going to finish up the tour.

ROBERT: My shelters are all at my house.

WILBUR: Feel welcome to come along.

ROBERT: His *(Refers to* WILBUR*)* are kid stuff. Who wants land in Montana?

WILBUR: *(To* ROBERT*)* Hey—I told you. I need the loss.
(WILBUR *and* ROBERT *exit, leaving* DI-GOU *with* AMA *and* POPO. *There is a long silence)*

DI-GOU: Who are they?

POPO: Servants.

AMA: Don't worry. They will eat outside. In America, servants do not take over their masters' house.

DI-GOU: What are you talking about?

AMA: We know. In China now, servants beat their masters.

DI-GOU: Don't be ridiculous. I have a servant. A chauffeur.
(ROBERT *reenters)*

ROBERT: Hey, Di-gou—we didn't even introduce ourselves.

DI-GOU: Oh, my sisters explained it to me.

ROBERT: I'm Robert. Hannah's my wife. (ROBERT *puts his arm around* DI-GOU*)* When we married, I had nothing. I was working in grocery stores, fired from one job after another. But she could tell—I had a good heart.

DI-GOU: It is good to see servants marrying into the mon-
eyed ranks. We are not aware of such progress by even
the lowest classes.

(Pause)

ROBERT: Huh?

DI-GOU: To come to this—from the absolute bottom of
society.

ROBERT: Wait, wait. I mean, sure, I made progress, but "the
bottom of society"? That's stretching it some, wouldn't
you say?

DI-GOU: Did you meet Hannah while preparing her food?

ROBERT: Huh? No, we met at a foreign students' dance at
UCLA.

DI-GOU: Oh. You attended university?

ROBERT: Look, I'm not a country kid. It's not like I was that
poor. I'm from Shanghai, you know.

POPO: *(To* ROBERT*)* Ssssh! Neighbors will hear!

ROBERT: I'm cosmopolitan. So when I went to college, I just
played around at first. That's the beauty of the free-
enterprise system, Di-gou. If you wanna be a bum, it lets
you be a bum. I wasted my time, went out with all those
American girls.

POPO: One girl.

ROBERT: Well, one was more serious, a longer commitment . . .

POPO: Minor.

DI-GOU: What?

POPO: He go out with girl—only fifteen year old.

ROBERT: I didn't know!

POPO: *(To* ROBERT*)* How come you cannot ask?

ROBERT: I was just an FOB. This American girl—she talked
to me—asked me out—kissed me on first date—and I
thought, "Land of opportunity!" Anyway, I decided to
turn my back on China.

POPO: *(To* DI-GOU*)* He cannot even ask girl how old.

ROBERT: This is my home. When I wanted to stop being a bum, make money, it let me. That's America!

DI-GOU: I also attended American university. Columbia Medical School.

ROBERT: Right. My wife told me.

POPO: *(To* ROBERT*)* But he does not date the minor!

ROBERT: *(To* POPO*)* How was I supposed to know? She looked fully developed!

*(*AMA *and* POPO *leave in disgust, leaving* ROBERT *alone with* DI-GOU*)*

ROBERT: *(To* DI-GOU*)* Well, then, you must understand American ways.

DI-GOU: It has been some time since I was in America.

ROBERT: Well, it's improved a lot, lemme tell you. Look, I have a friend who's an immigration lawyer. If you want to stay here, he can arrange it.

DI-GOU: Oh, no. The thought never even—

ROBERT: I know, but listen. I did it. Never had any regrets. We might be able to get your family over, too.

DI-GOU: Robert, I cannot leave China.

ROBERT: Huh? Look, Di-gou, people risk their lives to come to America. If only you could talk to—to the boat people.

DI-GOU: Uh—the food here looks very nice.

ROBERT: Huh? Oh, help yourself, Go ahead.

DI-GOU: Thank you. I will wait.

ROBERT: No, go on!

DI-GOU: Thank you, but—

ROBERT: Look, in America, there's so much, we don't have to be polite at all!

DI-GOU: Please—I'm not yet hungry.

ROBERT: Us Chinese, we love to eat, right? Well, here in America, we can be pigs!

DI-GOU: I'm not hungry.

ROBERT: I don't see why you can't—? Look. *(He picks up a piece of food, a bao.)* See? *(He stuffs the whole thing into his mouth)* Pigs!

DI-GOU: Do you mind? I told you, I'm not—

ROBERT: I know. You're not hungry. Think I'm hungry? No, sir! What do I have to do to convince you? Here. *(He drops a tray of* guo-tieh *on the ground, begins stomping them)* This is the land of plenty!

DI-GOU: Ai! Robert!

(ROBERT continues stomping them like roaches)

ROBERT: There's one next to your foot! *(He stomps it)* Gotcha!

DI-GOU: Please! It is not right to step on food!

ROBERT: "Right?" Now, see, that's your problem in the P.R.C.—lots of justice, but you don't produce.

(WILBUR enters, catching ROBERT in the act)

WILBUR: Robert? What are you—? What's all this?

ROBERT: *(Stops stomping)* What's the big deal? You got a cleaning woman, don't you?

(JENNY enters)

JENNY: Time to eat yet? *(She sees the mess)* Blaagh.

(HANNAH enters)

HANNAH: What's all this?

JENNY: Never mind.

(JENNY exits; WILBUR points to ROBERT, indicating to HAN-NAH that ROBERT is responsible for the mess. AMA and POPO also enter at this moment and see WILBUR's indication)

DI-GOU: In China, the psychological problems of wealth are a great concern.

POPO: Ai! Who can clean up after man like this!

WILBUR: Robert, I just don't think this is proper.

AMA: Wilbur—not clean himself.

ROBERT: Quiet! You all make a big deal out of nothing!

DI-GOU: I am a doctor. I understand.

POPO: But Robert—he also has the fungus feet.

ROBERT: Shut up, everybody! Will you all just shut up? I was showing Di-gou American ways!

(WILBUR takes DI-GOU's arm)

WILBUR: *(To DI-GOU)* Uh—come out here. I'll show you some American ways.

(WILBUR and DI-GOU *go out to the tennis court)*

ROBERT: *(To* WILBUR*)* What do you know about American ways? You were born here!

POPO: *(To* AMA*)* Exercise—good for him.

ROBERT: Only us immigrants really know American ways!

POPO: *('To* AMA, *pinching her belly)* Good for here.

HANNAH: *(To* ROBERT*)* Shut up, dear. You've done enough damage today.

(WILBUR gets DI-GOU *a racket)*

AMA: *(To* POPO*)* In China, he *(Refers to* DI-GOU*)* receives plenty exercise. Whenever Communists, they come torture him.

WILBUR. *(On tennis court, to* DI-GOU*)* I'll set up the machine. *(He goes* OFF*)*

ROBERT: *(In sunroom, looking at tennis court)* What's so American about tennis?

HANNAH: *(To* ROBERT*)* Yes, dear.

ROBERT: You all ruined it!

HANNAH: You ruined the *guo-tieh*, dear.

ROBERT: What's a few *guo-tieh* in defense of America?

DI-GOU: *(To* WILBUR*)* I have not played tennis since my college days at Columbia.

ROBERT: *(To* HANNAH*)* He *(Refers to* DI-GOU*)* was being so cheap! Like this was a poor country!

HANNAH: He's lived in America before, dear.

ROBERT: That was years ago. When we couldn't even buy a house in a place like this.

HANNAH: We still can't.

ROBERT: What?

HANNAH: Let's face it. We still can't afford—

ROBERT: That's not what I mean, stupid! I mean, when we wouldn't be able to because we're Chinese! He doesn't know the new America. I was making a point and you all ruined it!

HANNAH: Yes, dear. Now let's go in and watch the Betamax.

ROBERT: No!

HANNAH: C'mon! (ROBERT *and* HANNAH *exit*)

(On the tennis court, DI-GOU *and* WILBUR *stand next to each other, facing offstage. A machine offstage begins to shoot tennis balls at them, each ball accompanied by a small explosive sound. A ball goes by;* DI-GOU *tries to hit it, but it is too high for him. Two more balls go by, but they are also out of* DI-GOU's *reach. A fourth ball is shot out, which hits* WILBUR)

WILBUR: Aaaah!

(Balls are being shot out much faster now, pummeling WILBUR *and* DI-GOU. AMA *and* POPO *continue to sit in the sunroom, staring away from the tennis court, peaceful and oblivious)*

DI-GOU: Aaah!

WILBUR: I don't—! This never happened—!

DI-GOU: Watch out!

WILBUR: I'll turn off the machine.

DI-GOU: Good luck! Persevere! Overcome! Oh! Watch—!

(A volley of balls drives WILBUR *back.* AMA *and* POPO *hear the commotion, look over to the tennis court. The balls stop shooting out)*

ROBERT: Tennis.

AMA: A fancy machine.

(They return to looking downstage. The balls begin again)

WILBUR: Oh, no!

AMA: Wilbur—he is such a bad loser.

POPO: Good exercise, huh? His age—good for here.

(She pinches her belly)

DI-GOU: I will persevere!

*(*DI-GOU *tries to get to the machine, is driven back)*

WILBUR: No! Di-gow!

DI-GOU: I am overcome!

WILBUR: Joanne!

(He begins crawling like a guerrilla toward the machine and finally makes it offstage. The balls stop, presumably because WILBUR *reached the machine.* DI-GOU *runs off the court)*

DI-GOU: *(Breathless)* Is it time yet . . . that we may cease to have . . . such enjoyment?

(WILBUR crosses back onto the tennis court and into the lanai)

WILBUR: *(To offstage)* Joanne! This machine's too fast. I don't pay good money to be attacked by my possessions! *(Exits)*

(AMA and POPO get up, exit into the house, applauding DI-GOU as they go, for his exercise)

AMA *and* POPO: *(Clapping)* Good, good, very good!

(DI-GOU is left alone on the tennis court. He is hit by a lone tennis ball. CHESTER enters, with a violin case. It is obvious that he has thrown that ball)

CHESTER: Quite a workout, there.

DI-GOU: America is full of surprises—why do all these products function so poorly?

CHESTER: Looks like "Made in U.S." is gonna become synonymous with defective workmanship. *(Pause)* You wanna see my violin?

DI-GOU: I would love to.

CHESTER: I thought you might. Here.

(He removes the violin from its case)

CHESTER: See? No "Made in U.S." label.

DI-GOU: It is beautiful.

CHESTER: Careful! The back has a lacquer which never dries—so don't touch it, or you'll leave your fingerprints in it forever.

DI-GOU: Imagine that. After I die, someone could be playing a violin with my fingerprint.

CHESTER: Funny, isn't it?

DI-GOU: You know, I used to play violin.

CHESTER: Really?

DI-GOU: Though I never had as fine an instrument as this.

CHESTER: Try it. Go ahead.

DI-GOU: No. Please. I get more pleasure looking at it than I would playing it. But I would get the most pleasure hearing you play.

CHESTER: No.

DI-GOU: Please?

CHESTER: All right. Later. How long did you play?

DI-GOU: Some years. During the Cultural Revolution, I put it down.

CHESTER: Must've been tough, huh? (CHESTER *directs* DI-GOU*'s attention to the back of his violin*) Look—the back's my favorite part.

DI-GOU: China is my home, my work. I had to stay there. (DI-GOU *looks at the back of the violin*) Oh—the way the light reflects—look. And I can see myself in it.

CHESTER: Yeah. Nice, huh?

DI-GOU: So you will take this violin and make music around the world.

CHESTER: Around the world? Oh, you probably got a misleading press clipping. See, my dad . . .

DI-GOU: Very funny.

CHESTER: (*Smiling*) Yeah. See, I'm just playing in the Boston Symphony. I'm leaving tomorrow.

DI-GOU: I am fortunate, then, to come today, or perhaps I would never meet you.

CHESTER: You know, I wasn't even planning to come here.

DI-GOU: That would be terrible. You know, in China, my wife and I had no children—for the good of the state. (DI-GOU *moves to where he left the Chinese toys earlier in the act. He picks them up and studies them*)

DI-GOU: All these years, I try to imagine—what does Hannah look like? What does her baby look like? Now, I finally visit and what do I find? A young man. A violinist. The baby has long since disappeared. And I learn I'll never know the answer to my question. (*Silence*)

CHESTER: Di-gou, why did you come here?

DI-GOU: My wife has died, I'm old. I've come for my sisters.

CHESTER: Well, I hope you're not disappointed to come here and see your sisters, your family, carry on like this.

DI-GOU: They are still my sisters.

CHESTER: I'm leaving here. Like you did.

DI-GOU: But, Chester, I've found that I cannot leave the family. Today—look!—I follow them across an ocean.

CHESTER: You know, they're gonna start bringing you to church.

DI-GOU: No. My sisters and their religion are two different things.

CHESTER: No, they're not. You've been away. You've forgotten. This family breathes for God. Ever since your aunt, Sec-goh-poh.

DI-GOU: See-goh-poh is not the first member of this family.

CHESTER: She's the first Christian.

DI-GOU: There are faces back further than you can see. Faces long before the white missionaries arrived in China. Here. *(He holds* CHESTER's *violin so that its back is facing* CHESTER, *and uses it like a mirror)* Look here. At your face. Study your face and you will see—the shape of your face is the shape of faces back many generations—across an ocean, in another soil. You must become one with your family before you can hope to live away from it.

CHESTER: Oh, sure, there're faces. But they don't matter here. See-goh-poh's face is the only one that has any meaning here.

DI-GOU: No. The stories written on your face are the ones you must believe.

CHESTER: Stories? I see stories, Di-gou. All around me. This house tells a story. The days of the week tell a story—Sunday is service, Wednesday and Friday are fellowship, Thursday is visitation. Even the furniture tells stories. Look around. See-goh-poh is sitting in every chair. There's nothing for me here.

DI-GOU: I am here.

CHESTER: You? All right. Here. *(CHESTER turns the back of the violin toward DI-GOU, again using it like a mirror)* You look. You wanna know what I see? I see the shape of your face changing. And with it, a mind, a will, as different as the face. If you stay with them, your old self will go, and in its place will come a new man, an old man, a man who'll pray.

DI-GOU: Chester, you are in America. If you deny those who share your blood, what do you have in this country?

AMA: *(From offstage)* All right? Ready?

CHESTER: Your face is changing, Di-gou. Before you know it, you'll be praying and speaking in tongues.

AMA: *(Still offstage)* One, two, three, four!

(The "Hallelujah Chorus" begins. The choir enters, consisting of WILBUR, JOANNE, ROBERT, HANNAH, and POPO. They are led by AMA, who stands at a movable podium which is being pushed into the room by ROBERT and WILBUR as they sing. The choir heads for the center of the room, where the podium comes to rest, with AMA still on it, and the "Hallelujah Chorus" ends. ROBERT begins singing the tenor aria "Every Valley Shall Be Exalted," from Handel's Messiah.*)*

ROBERT: "Every valley, every valley . . ."

HANNAH: Quiet, Robert!

ROBERT: But I want my solo!

JOANNE: *(To ROBERT)* Ssssh! We already decided this.

ROBERT: *(Continuing to sing)* ". . . shall be exalted . . ."

JOANNE: *(Yelling offstage)* Jenny!

AMA: *(To ROBERT)* Time for Family Devotions! Set up room! *(They begin to arrange the room like a congregation hall, with the pulpit up front)*

ROBERT: But it's a chance to hear my beautiful voice.

JENNY: *(From offstage)* Yeah! What?

POPO: *(To ROBERT)* Hear at home, hear in car. Now set up room.

JOANNE: *(Yelling offstage)* Jenny! Devotions!

JENNY: (From offstage) Aw, Mom.

JOANNE: *(Yelling offstage)* Devotions!

JENNY: *(Entering)* All right.

ROBERT: *(To* HANNAH*)* You know what this is? This is the breakdown of family authority.

HANNAH: *(To* ROBERT*)* You have all the authority, dear. Now shut up.

*(*JENNY *goes over to* CHESTER*)*

JENNY: Hey, you still here? I thought for sure you'd have split by now.

CHESTER: I will.

JENNY: You gotta take it easier. Do like me. I act all lotus blossom for them. I say, "Hi, uncle this and auntie that." It's easy.

ROBERT: Look—all this free time. *(Sings)* "Every valley . . ."

POPO: Shoot him!

(The room is set up)

AMA: We begin! Family Devotions!

*(*AMA *flips a switch. A neon cross is lit up)*

JENNY: *(To* CHESTER*)* Looks like a disco.

(Everyone is seated except DI-GOU. *The rest of the family waits for him. He walks over and sits down.* AMA *bows down to pray. Everyone bows except* CHESTER *and* DI-GOU, *but since all other eyes are closed, no one notices their noncompliance.* AMA *begins to pray)*

AMA: Dear Father, when we think of your great mercy to this family, we can only feel so grateful, privilege to be family chose for your work. You claim us to be yours, put your mark on our heart.

*(*CHESTER *gets up, picks up his violin, gets* DI-GOU*'s attention)*

AMA: Your blessing begin many year ago in China.

*(*CHESTER *begins playing; his music serves as underscoring to* AMA*'s prayer)*

AMA: When See-goh-poh, she hear your word—from missionary. Your spirit, it touch her heart, she accept you, she speak in tongue of fire.

(CHESTER *begins to move out of the room as he plays*)

AMA: You continue, bless See-goh-poh. She become agent of God, bring light to whole family, until we are convert, we become shining light for you all through Amoy.

(CHESTER *stops playing, looks at* DI-GOU, *waves good-bye, and exits.* DI-GOU *gets up, walks to where* CHESTER *was standing before he left, and waves good-bye*)

AMA: Let us praise your victory over Satan. Praise your power over demon. Praise miracle over our own sinful will. Praise your victory over even our very hearts. Amen.

(AMA *conducts the choir in the ending of the "Hallelujah Chorus." As they sing, she notices* DI-GOU*'s chair is empty. She turns and sees him waving. They look at each other as the "Hallelujah Chorus" continues*)

END OF ACT ONE

ACT TWO

A moment later. As the curtain rises, all are in the same positions they occupied at the end of Act One. AMA *and* DI-GOU *are looking at each other. The choir ends the "Hallelujah Chorus."* DI-GOU *walks back toward his chair and sits.* AMA *notices that* CHESTER's *seat is empty.*

AMA: Where is Chester?

HANNAH: I heard his violin.

AMA: This is Family Devotions.

ROBERT: The kid's got a mind of his own.

HANNAH: He probably went home to pack, Auntie. He's really in a hurry.

JENNY: Can I go look?

AMA: Why everyone want to go?

JENNY: But he forgot his suitcase. *(She points to the green suitcase, which* CHESTER *has left behind)*

POPO: *(To* JENNY*)* Di-gou . . . he will want to hear you give testimony.

(JENNY sits back down)

AMA: Now—Special Testimony. Let us tell of God's blessing! Who will have privilege? Special Testimony! Who will be first to praise?

(Silence)

AMA: He is in our presence! Open His arms to us!

(Silence)

AMA: He is not going to wait forever—you know this! He is very busy!

(ROBERT *stands up, starts to head for podium.* POPO *notices that* ROBERT *has risen, points to him.*)

POPO: No! Not him!

AMA: (*To* ROBERT) He is very bored with certain people who say same thing over and over again.

WILBUR: Why don't we sit down, Robert?

JENNY: C'mon, Uncle Robert.

HANNAH: Dear, forget it, all right?

ROBERT: But she needed someone to start. I just—

POPO: (*To* ROBERT) She did not include you.

WILBUR: Can't you see how bored they are with that, Robert?

ROBERT: Bored?

WILBUR: Everybody else has forgotten it.

ROBERT: Forgotten it? They can't.

JOANNE: We could if you'd stop talking about it.

ROBERT: But there's something new!

WILBUR: Of course. There always is.

ROBERT: There is!

JOANNE: (*To* WILBUR) Don't pay attention, dear. It just encourages him.

WILBUR: (*To* JOANNE) Honey, are you trying to advise *me* on how to be diplomatic?

JOANNE: I'm only saying, if you let Hannah—

WILBUR: You're a real stitch, you know that? You really are.

JOANNE: Hannah's good at keeping him quiet.

ROBERT: Quiet?

WILBUR: (*To* JOANNE) Look, who was voted "Mr. Congeniality" at the club last week—you or me?

ROBERT: Hannah, who are you telling to be quiet?

HANNAH: Quiet, Robert.

WILBUR: (*To* JOANNE) Afraid to answer? Huh? Who? Who was "Mr. Congeniality"? Tell me—were you "Mr. Congeniality"?

JENNY: *(To* WILBUR*)* I don't think she stood a chance, Dad.

WILBUR: *(To* JENNY*)* Who asked you, huh?

JENNY: "Mr. Congeniality," I think.

WILBUR: Don't be disrespectful.

AMA: We must begin Special Testimony! Who is first?

POPO: I talk.

JOANNE: Good.

POPO: Talk from here. *(She stands)* Long time since we all come here like this. I remember long ago, family leave China—the boat storm, storm, storm, storm, all around, Hannah cry. I think, "Aaah, why we have to leave China, go to Philippines?" But I remember Jonah, when he did not obey God, only then seas become—ah—dangerous. And even after, after Jonah eaten by whale, God provide for him. So if God has plan for us, we live; if not *(She looks at* DI-GOU*)* we die. *(She sits)* Okay. That's all. *(Everyone applauds)*

AMA: Very good! Who is next?

ROBERT: I said, I'd be happy to—

HANNAH: How about Jenny?

JENNY: Me?

JOANNE: Sure, dear, c'mon.

JENNY: Oh . . . well . . .

POPO: *(To* DI-GOU*)* You see—she is so young, but her faith is old.

JENNY: After I do this, can I go see what's happened to Chester?

POPO: *(To* JENNY*)* First, serve God.

ROBERT: Let her go.

POPO: Then, you may see about Chester.

JENNY: All right.
(She walks to the podium)

POPO: *(To* DI-GOU*)* I will tell you what each sentence meaning.

DI-GOU: I can understand quite well.

POPO: No. You are not Christian. You need someone—like announcer at baseball game—except announce for God.

JENNY: *(At podium, she begins testimony)* First, I want to say that I love you all very much. I really do.

POPO: *(To* DI-GOU*)* That meaning is, she love God.

JENNY: And I appreciate what you've done for me.

POPO: *(To* DI-GOU*)* She love us because we show her God.

JENNY: But I guess there are certain times when even love isn't enough.

POPO: *(To* DI-GOU*)* She does not have enough love for you. You are not Christian.

JENNY: Sometimes, even love has its dark side.

POPO: *(To* DI-GOU*)* That is you.

JENNY: And when you find that side, sometimes you have to leave in order to come back in a better way.

POPO: *(To* DI-GOU*)* She cannot stand to be around you.

JENNY: Please. Remember what I said, and think about it later.

POPO: *(To* DI-GOU*)* You hear? Think!

JENNY: Thank you.

(Everyone applauds)

AMA: Good, good.

JENNY: Can I go now?

ROBERT: *(To* HANNAH*)* What was she talking about?

AMA: *(To* JENNY*)* Soon, you can be best testifier—do testimony on TV.

JENNY: Can I go now?

JOANNE: All right, Jenny.

JENNY: Thanks.

(Exits)

ROBERT: *(To* POPO*)* Why don't you interpret for *me?* I didn't understand what she was talking about. Not a bit.

POPO: Good.

ROBERT: Good? Don't you want me to be a better Christian?

POPO: No. Not too good. Do not want to live in same part of Heaven as you.

ROBERT: Why not? It'll be great, Popo. We can tell stories, sing—

POPO: In Heaven, hope you live in basement.

ROBERT: Basement? C'mon, Popo, I'm a celebrity. They wouldn't give me the basement. They'll probably recognize my diplomacy ability, make me ambassador.

JOANNE: To Hell?

ROBERT: Well, if that's the place they send ambassadors.

POPO: Good. You be ambassador.

AMA: Special Testimony! Who is next?

ROBERT: *(Asking to be recognized)* Ama?

AMA: *(Ignoring him) Who is next?*

ROBERT: Not me. I think Wilbur should speak.

AMA: *(Disgusted)* Wilbur?

WILBUR: Me?

ROBERT: Yeah.

WILBUR: Well, I don't really . . .

ROBERT: Tell them, Wilbur. Tell them what kind of big stuffs happen to you. Tell them how important you are.

WILBUR: Well, I . . .

AMA: Would you . . . like to speak . . . Wilbur?

WILBUR: Well, I'd be honored, but if anyone else would rather . . .

ROBERT: We want to hear what you have to be proud of.

WILBUR: All right. (WILBUR *takes the podium;* AMA *scurries away)* Uh—well, it's certainly nice to see this family reunion. Uh—last week, I was voted Mr. Congeniality at the club.

ROBERT: What papers was it in?

WILBUR: Huh?

ROBERT: Was it in the L.A. *Times?* Front page? Otis Chandler's paper?

HANNAH: *(A rebuff)* Robert!

POPO: *(To* ROBERT*)* Devotions is not question-and-answer for anyone except God.

ROBERT: God sometimes speaks through people, doesn't He?

POPO: He has good taste. Would not speak through you.

ROBERT: *(Undaunted, to* WILBUR*)* Show me one newspaper clipping. Just one!

WILBUR: Well, besides the *Valley Green Sheet . . .*

ROBERT: The *Valley Green Sheet?* Who pays for that? Junk. People line their birdcages with it.

WILBUR: Well, I suppose from a media standpoint, it's not that big a deal.

AMA: *(To* JOANNE*)* What means "congeniality"?

JOANNE: It means, "friendly," sort of.

ROBERT: *(To* WILBUR*)* So why are you talking about it? Waste our time?

WILBUR: Look, Robert, it's obviously a token of their esteem.

ROBERT: Junk stuffs. Little thing. Who cares?

AMA: *(To herself)* "Mr. Friendly"?

ROBERT: It's embarrassing. What if clients say to me, "You're a bank president but your relative can only get into the *Valley Green Sheet*"? Makes me lose face. They think my relatives are bums.

AMA: *(To* JOANNE*)* He is "Mr. Friendly"?

WILBUR: Look, Robert, the business is doing real well. It's not like that's my greatest accomplishment.

AMA: *(To* JOANNE*)* How can he be "Mr. Friendly"? He always kill and laugh.

JOANNE: Mom!

ROBERT: *(To* WILBUR*)* Does your business get in the paper?

WILBUR: Computer software happens to be one of the nation's fastest-growing—

ROBERT: So what? Lucky guess. Big deal.

WILBUR: It was an educated choice, not luck!

(ROBERT gets up, starts to head for the podium)

ROBERT: Anyone can make money in America. What's hard is to become . . . a celebrity.

WILBUR: You're not a celebrity.

ROBERT: Yes, I am. That's the new thing. See, I just wanted to say that—*(He nudges* WILBUR *off the podium, takes his place)*—when I was kidnapped, I didn't know if I would live or die.

POPO: *(Turns and sees* ROBERT *at the podium)* Huh?

JOANNE: Robert, forget it!

POPO: How did he get up there?

WILBUR: *(To* JOANNE*)* I'm perfectly capable of handling this myself.

POPO: He sneak up there while we are bored!

WILBUR: *(To* POPO*)* I'm sorry you found my testimony boring.

ROBERT: *(To* WILBUR*)* It was. *(To the assemblage)* Now hear mine.

JOANNE: We've all heard it before.

HANNAH: *(To* ROBERT*)* They're tired, dear. Get down.

ROBERT: Why? They listened to Wilbur's stuff. Boring. Junk.

JOANNE: "I didn't know if I would live or die." "I didn't know if I would live or die."

ROBERT: Di-gou, he hasn't heard. Have you, Di-gou?

DI-GOU: Is this when you didn't know if you would live or die?

ROBERT: How did—? Who told him?

POPO: I cannot think of enough ways to shoot him! Rifle! Arrows!

HANNAH: *(To* ROBERT*)* Sit down!

ROBERT: But there's something new!

HANNAH: I think we better let him speak, or he'll never shut up.

ROBERT: She's right. I won't.

JOANNE: All right. Make it quick, Robert.

ROBERT: All right. As I was saying, I didn't know if I would live or die.

JOANNE: You lived.

ROBERT: But the resulting publicity has made me a celebrity. Every place I go, people come up to me—"Aren't you the one that got kidnapped?" When I tell them how much the ransom was, they can hardly believe it. They ask for my autograph. Now—here's the new thing. I met these clients last week, told them my story. Now, these guys are big shots and they say it would make a great movie. Yeah. No kidding. They made movies before. Not just regular movie, that's junk stuffs. We want to go where the big money is—we want to make a mini-series for TV. Like "Shogun." I told them, they should take the story, spice it up a little, you know? Add some sex scenes—we were thinking that I could have some hanky-panky with one of my kidnappers—woman, of course—just for audience sake—like Patty Hearst. I told them I should be played by Marlon Brando. And I have the greatest title: "Not a Chinaman's Chance." Isn't that a great title? "Not a Chinaman's Chance." Beautiful. I can see the beginning already: I'm walking out of my office. I stop to help a man fixing a flat tire.

HANNAH: All right, dear. That's enough.

ROBERT: Meanwhile, my secretary is having sex with my kidnapper.

HANNAH: Kidnap! Kidnap! That's all I ever hear about!

ROBERT: But, Hannah, I didn't know if I would live or die.

HANNAH: I wish you'd never even been kidnapped.

JOANNE: Well, what about Wilbur?

WILBUR: Leave me out of this.

JOANNE: Wilbur, you could be kidnapped.

WILBUR: I know, I know. It just hasn't happened yet, that's all.

HANNAH: Listen, Joanne. Count your blessings. It's not that

great a thing. If they live, they never stop talking about it.

ROBERT: But the publicity!—I sign newspapers all the time!

JOANNE: I'm just saying that Robert's not the only one worth kidnapping.

HANNAH: Joanne, no one's saying that.

AMA: Yes. We all desire Wilbur to be kidnapped also.

POPO: And Robert. Again. This time, longer.

JOANNE: I mean, Wilbur has a lot of assets.

ROBERT: Wilbur, maybe next time you can get kidnapped.

WILBUR: Never mind, honey.

JOANNE: You do.

WILBUR: I can defend myself.

ROBERT: But it takes more than assets to be kidnapped. You have to be cosmopolitan.

HANNAH: Hey, wait. What kind of example are we setting for Di-gou?

ROBERT: See? That's why I'm talking about it. To show Di-gou the greatness of America. I'm just an immigrant, Di-gou, an FOB—but in America, I get kidnapped.

HANNAH: I mean, a Christian example.

DI-GOU: Oh, do not worry about me. This is all very fascinating.

JOANNE: *(To* ROBERT*)* So, you think you're cosmopolitan, huh?

ROBERT: I am. Before they let me loose, those kidnappers— they respected me.

JOANNE: They probably let you go because they couldn't stand to have you in their car.

POPO: Probably you sing to them.

ROBERT: No. They said, "We've been kidnapping a long time, but—"

JOANNE: Because we can't stand to have you in our house!

(Pause)

ROBERT: *(To* JOANNE*)* Now what kind of example are you setting for Di-gou?

WILBUR: Joanne, just shut up, okay?

HANNAH: *(To* DI-GOU*)* It's not always like this.

JOANNE: *(To* WILBUR*)* You never let me talk! You even let him *(Refers to* ROBERT*)* talk, but you never let me talk!

AMA: *(To* JOANNE*)* He *(Refers to* WILBUR*)* cannot deprive you of right to speak. Look. No gun.

ROBERT: Joanne, I have to tell this because Di-gou is here.

DI-GOU: Me?

JOANNE: *(To* ROBERT*)* You tell it to waiters!

ROBERT: Joanne, I want him *(Refers to* DI-GOU*)* to understand America. The American Dream. From rags to kidnap victim.

JOANNE: *(To* ROBERT*)* Well, I don't like you making Di-gou think that Wilbur's a bum.

WILBUR: *(To* JOANNE*)* Dear, he doesn't think that.

JOANNE: *(To* DI-GOU*)* You see, don't you, Di-gou? This house. Wilbur bought this.

DI-GOU: It is a palace.

JOANNE: It's larger than Robert's.

HANNAH: Joanne, how can you sink to my husband's level?

ROBERT: My house would be larger, but we had to pay the ransom.

POPO: Waste of money.

JOANNE: Look, all of you always put down Wilbur. Well, look at what he's done.

WILBUR: *(To* JOANNE*)* Just shut up, all right?

JOANNE: *(To* WILBUR*)* Well, if you're not going to say it.

WILBUR: I don't need you to be my PR firm.

ROBERT: *(To anybody)* He doesn't have a PR firm. We do. Tops firm.

JOANNE: *(To* WILBUR*)* Let me say my mind!

WILBUR: There's nothing in your mind worth saying.

JOANNE: What?

WILBUR: Face it, honey, you're boring.

AMA: *(To* WILBUR*)* At least she does not torture!

WILBUR: Please! No more talking about torture, all right?

AMA: All right. I will be quiet. No need to torture me.

POPO: *(To* DI-GOU*)* This small family disagreement.

JOANNE: So I'm boring, huh?

WILBUR: *(To* JOANNE*)* Look, let's not do this here.

POPO: *(To* DI-GOU*)* But power of God will overcome this.

JOANNE: I'm boring—that's what you're saying?

HANNAH: Joanne! Not in front of Di-gou!

JOANNE: *(To* DI-GOU*)* All right. You're objective. Who do you think is more boring?

DI-GOU: Well, I can hardly—

WILBUR: Please, Joanne.

POPO: *(To* DI-GOU*)* Do you understand how power of God will overcome this?

JOANNE: He *(Refers to* WILBUR*)* spends all his time with machines, and he calls me boring!

AMA: Di-gou, see the trials of this world?

WILBUR: *(To* JOANNE*)* Honey, I'm sorry, all right?

JOANNE: Sure, you're sorry.

AMA: *(To* DI-GOU*)* Argument, fight, no-good husbands.

WILBUR: "No-good husbands"?

(ROBERT, *in disgust, exits into the house)*

AMA: *(To* DI-GOU*)* Turn your eyes from this.

(POPO *and* AMA *turn* DI-GOU*'s eyes from the fight)*

JOANNE: *(To* WILBUR*)* She's *(Refers to* AMA*)* right, you know.

WILBUR: All right, honey, let's discuss this later.

JOANNE: Later! Oh, right.

(WILBUR *runs off into the house;* JOANNE *yells after him)*

JOANNE: When we're with *your* family, that's when you want to talk about my denting the Ferrari.

HANNAH: Joanne! Don't be so boring!

JOANNE: *(To* HANNAH*)* With *our* family, it's "later."

AMA: *(To* DI-GOU*)* Look up to God!

(POPO *and* AMA *force* DI-GOU *to look up)*

DI-GOU: Please!

(DI-GOU *breaks away from the sisters' grip, but they knock him down)*

POPO: Now—is time to join family in Heaven.

AMA: Time for you to return to God.

HANNAH: *(To* JOANNE*)* Look—they're converting Di-gou.

POPO: Return. Join us for eternity.

AMA: Pray now.

(POPO *and* AMA *try to guide* DI-GOU *to the neon cross)*

DI-GOU: Where are we going?

AMA: He will wash you in blood of the lamb.

POPO: Like when you are a child. Now! You bow down!

HANNAH: Ask God for His forgiveness.

JOANNE: You won't regret it, Di-gou.

DI-GOU: Do you mind?

(He breaks away)

POPO: Why will you not accept Him?

AMA: There is no good reason.

DI-GOU: I want to take responsibility for my own life.

POPO: You cannot!

AMA: Satan is rule your life now.

DI-GOU: I am serving the people.

AMA: You are not.

POPO: You serve them, they all die, go to Hell. So what?

DI-GOU: How can you abandon China for this Western religion?

AMA: It is not.

POPO: God is God of all people.

DI-GOU: There is no God!

(Pause)

AMA: There is too much Communist demon in him. We must cast out demon.

POPO: Now, tie him on table.

DI-GOU: This is ridiculous. Stop this.

(The women grab DI-GOU, *tie him on the table)*

POPO: We have too much love to allow demon to live.

DI-GOU: What?

POPO: *(To* JOANNE *and* HANNAH *who are hesitating)* Now!

DI-GOU: You can't—!

POPO: Now! Or demon will escape!

AMA: We must kill demon.

POPO: Shoot him!

AMA: Kill for good.

POPO: Make demon into *jok!*

DI-GOU: This is barbaric! You live with the barbarians, you become one yourself!

POPO: Di-gou, if we do not punish your body, demon will never leave.

AMA: Then you will return to China.

POPO: And you will die.

AMA: Go to Hell.

POPO: And it will be too late.

DI-GOU: I never expected Chinese children to tie down their elders.

*(*DI-GOU *is now securely tied to the table)*

HANNAH: All right. We're ready.

POPO: Now—you give your testimony.

DI-GOU: I'll just lie here and listen, thank you.

AMA: You tell of God's mercies to you.

JOANNE: How He let you out of China.

AMA: Where you are torture.

JOANNE: Whipped.

POPO: After thirty year, He let you out. Praise Him!

DI-GOU: I will never do such a thing!

HANNAH: If you wait too long, He'll lose patience.

POPO: Now—tell of your trip with See-goh-poh.

AMA: The trip which begin your faith.

DI-GOU: I was only eight years old. I don't remember.

POPO: Tell how many were convert on her tour.

HANNAH: Tell them, Di-gou.

DI-GOU: I cannot.

JOANNE: Why? Just tell the truth.

POPO: Tell how you saw the miracle of a great evangelist, great servant of God.

HANNAH: Tell them before they lose their patience.

DI-GOU: I'm sorry. I will not speak.

POPO: Then we are sorry, Di-gou, but we must punish your body. Punish to drive out the demon and make you speak.

HANNAH: Don't make them do this, Di-gou.

AMA: If you will not speak See-goh-poh's stories in language you know, we will punish you until you speak in tongue of fire.

(AMA hits DI-GOU with an electrical cord, using it like a whip)

JOANNE: Please, Di-gou!

HANNAH: Tell them!

AMA: Our Lord was beat, nails drive through His body, for our sin. Your body must suffer until you speak the truth.

(AMA hits him)

HANNAH: Tell them, See-goh-poh was a great evangelist.

AMA: You were on her evangelism tour—we were not—you must remember her converts, her miracle.

(Hit)

JOANNE: Just tell them and they'll let you go!

AMA: Think of See-goh-poh! She is sit! *(Hit)* Sit beside God. He is praising her! Praise her for her work in China.

(CHESTER enters the tennis court; he looks into the sunroom and sees AMA hit DI-GOU)

AMA: She is watching you!

(Hit. CHESTER tries to get into the sunroom, but the glass door is locked. He bangs on it, but everyone inside stands shocked at AMA's ritual, and no one notices him. He exits off the tennis court, running)

AMA: Praying for you! Want you to tell her story!
(Hit)

AMA: We will keep you in float. Float for one second between life and death. Float until you lose will to hold to
either—hold to anything at all.

(AMA quickly slips the cord around DI-GOU's *neck, begins
pulling on it.* JOANNE *and* HANNAH *run to get* AMA *off of*
DI-GOU. CHESTER *enters from the house, with* JENNY *close
behind him. He pulls* AMA *off of* DI-GOU*)*

CHESTER: Ama! Stop it!

*(*DI-GOU *suddenly breaks out of his bonds and rises up on the
table. He grabs* CHESTER. *The barbecue bursts into flames.*
DI-GOU, *holding onto* CHESTER, *begins speaking in tongues)*

AMA: *(Looking up from the ground)* He is speaking in tongues!
He has returned!

(Everyone falls to their knees. As DI-GOU's *tongues continue,*
CHESTER *is suddenly filled with words, and begins interpreting*
DI-GOU's *babbling)*

CHESTER: Di-gou at eight goes with See-goh-poh on her
first evangelism tour. Di-gou and See-goh-poh traveling
through the summer heat to a small village in Fukien.
Sleeping in the straw next to See-goh-poh. Hearing a
sound. A human sound. A cry in my sleep. Looking up
and seeing a fire. A fire and See-goh-poh. See-goh-poh is
naked. Naked and screaming. Screaming with legs spread
so far apart. So far that a mouth opens up. A mouth
between her legs. A mouth that is throwing up blood,
spitting out blood. More and more blood. See-goh-poh's
hands making a baby out of the blood. See-goh-poh hits
the blood baby. Hits the baby and the baby cries. Watching the baby at See-goh-poh's breast. Hearing the sucking.

*(AMA *and* POPO *spring up)*

POPO: Such a thing never happened!

AMA: See-goh-poh never did this!

POPO: This is not tongues. This is not God. This is demon!

CHESTER: Sucking. Praying. Sucking. Squeezing. Crying.

AMA: He is possess by demon!

CHESTER: Biting. Blood. Milk.

POPO: Both have the demon!

CHESTER: Blood and milk. Blood and milk running down.

AMA: *(To the other women)* You pray.

CHESTER: Running down, further and further down.

POPO: We must cast out the demon!

> *(DI-GOU's tongues slowly become English, first overlapping, then overtaking* CHESTER's *translation.* CHESTER *becomes silent and exhausted, drops to the ground)*

CHESTER *and* DI-GOU: Down. Down and into the fire. The fire down there. The fire down there.

> *(DI-GOU breaks the last of his bonds, gets off the table)*

DI-GOU: *(To the sisters)* Your stories are dead now that you know the truth.

AMA: We have faith. We know our true family stories.

DI-GOU: You do not know your past.

AMA: Are you willing to match your stories against ours?

> *(DI-GOU indicates his willingness to face* AMA, *and the two begin a ritualistic battle.* POPO *supports* AMA *by speaking in tongues.* AMA *and* DI-GOU *square off in seated positions, facing one another)*

AMA: We will begin. How many rooms in our house in Amoy?

DI-GOU: Eighteen. How many bedrooms?

AMA: Ten. What year was it built?

DI-GOU: 1893. What year was the nineteenth room added?

AMA: 1923.

DI-GOU: On whose instructions?

AMA: See-goh-poh.

DI-GOU: What year did See-goh-poh die?

AMA: 1945. What disease?

DI-GOU: Malaria. How many teeth was she missing?

AMA: Three.

DI-GOU: What villages were on See-goh-poh's evangelism tour?

(Silence)

DI-GOU: Do you know?

AMA: She preached to all villages in Fukien.

DI-GOU: Name one.

(Silence)

DI-GOU: Do you know? Your stories don't know. It never happened.

AMA: It did! What year was she baptized? *(Silence)* What year was she baptized?

DI-GOU: She was never baptized.

AMA: You see? You don't remember.

DI-GOU: Never baptized.

AMA: It was 1921. Your stories do not remember.

DI-GOU: Who was converted on her evangelism tour?

AMA: Perhaps five hundred or more.

DI-GOU: Who? Name one.

(Silence)

AMA: It is not important.

DI-GOU: You see? It never happened.

AMA: It did.

DI-GOU: You do not remember. You do not know the past. See-goh-poh never preached.

AMA: How can you say this?

DI-GOU: She traveled.

AMA: To preach.

DI-GOU: To travel.

AMA: She visited many—

DI-GOU: I was there! She was thrown out—thrown out on her evangelism tour when she tried to preach.

(Silence)

AMA: It does not matter.

DI-GOU: You forced her to invent the stories.

AMA: We demand nothing!

DI-GOU: You expected! Expected her to convert all Amoy!

AMA: She did!

DI-GOU: Expected many miracles.

AMA: She did! She was a great—

DI-GOU: Expected her not to have a baby.

AMA: She had no husband. She had no baby. This is demon talk. Demon talk and lie.

DI-GOU: She turned away from God.

AMA: We will never believe this!

DI-GOU: On her tours she could both please you and see China.

(POPO's tongues become weaker; she starts to falter)

AMA: See-goh-poh was a great—

DI-GOU: Only on her tours could she see both China and her baby.

AMA: She was a great . . . a great evangelist . . . many . . .

DI-GOU: Where is she buried?

AMA: . . . many miracle . . .

DI-GOU: She is not buried within the walls of the church in Amoy.

AMA: . . . many miracle a great evangelist . . .

(POPO collapses)

DI-GOU: In her last moment, See-goh-poh wanted to be buried in Chinese soil, not Christian soil. You don't know. You were in the Philippines.

(Pause)

DI-GOU: I come to bring you back to China. Come, sisters. To the soil you've forsaken with ways born of memories, of stories that never happened. Come, sisters. The stories written on your face are the ones you must believe.

(AMA rises from her chair)

AMA: We will never believe this!

(She collapses back into her chair, closes her eyes)

(Silence)

DI-GOU: Sisters?

(Silence)

DI-GOU: Sisters!

(JENNY, CHESTER, JOANNE, HANNAH, *and* DI-GOU *stare at the two inert forms*)

CHESTER: Jenny! Jenny!

*(*JENNY *goes to* CHESTER*'s side)*

JOANNE: Hannah? Hannah—come here.

*(*HANNAH *does not move)*

HANNAH: I see.

JOANNE: No! Come here!

HANNAH: I know, Joanne. I see.

DI-GOU: Once again. Once again my pleas are useless. But now—this is the last time. I have given all I own.

*(*POPO *and* AMA *have died.* DI-GOU *picks up his suitcase and the Chinese toys, heads for the door)*

JOANNE: *(To* DI-GOU*)* Are you leaving?

DI-GOU: Now that my sisters have gone, I learn. No one leaves America. And I desire only to drive an American car—very fast—down an American freeway.

*(*DI-GOU *exits)*

JOANNE: *(Yelling after him)* This is our home, not yours! Why didn't you stay in China! This is not your family!

*(*JENNY *starts to break away from* CHESTER, *but he hangs onto her.* JOANNE *turns, sees the figures of* AMA *and* POPO*)*

JOANNE: Wilbur! Wilbur, come here!

JENNY: *(To* CHESTER*)* Let go of me! Get away! *(She breaks away from* CHESTER*)* I don't understand this, but whatever it is, it's ugly and it's awful and it causes people to die. It causes people to die and I don't want to have anything to do with it.

*(*JENNY *runs out onto the tennis court and away. On her way, she passes* ROBERT, *who has entered onto the court.* ROBERT *walks into the sunroom. Silence)*

ROBERT: What's wrong with her? She acts like someone just died. *(Silence. He pulls up a chair next to* CHESTER*)* Let's chit-chat, okay?

CHESTER: Sure, Dad.

ROBERT: So, how's Dorrie? *(Silence)* How much they paying you in Boston? *(Silence)* Got any new newspaper clippings? *(Silence)*

(CHESTER gets up, picks up his suitcase, walks onto the tennis court, and shuts the glass doors)

(AMA and POPO lie in the center of the room. JOANNE and HANNAH stare at them. ROBERT sits, staring off into space)

(CHESTER turns around, looks through the glass door onto the scene)

(The LIGHTS BEGIN TO DIM until there is a single spotlight on CHESTER's face, standing where DI-GOU stood at the beginning of the play)

(The shape of CHESTER's face begins to change)

CURTAIN

THE HOUSE
OF
SLEEPING
BEAUTIES

From the Short Story
by Yasunari Kawabata

To Natolie

Playwright's Note

This play is a fantasy. In historical fact, Kawabata's composition of his novelette *House of the Sleeping Beauties* and his unexplained suicide occurred many years apart.

Many people helped me develop this play, and I'd like to thank especially Grafton Mouen, Jean Brody, John Harnagel, Marcy Mattox, Natolie Miyawaki, Nancy Takahashi, Mitch Motooka, and Helen Merrill.

The House of Sleeping Beauties was produced by Joseph Papp with *The Sound of a Voice* under the omnibus title "Sound and Beauty" at the New York Shakespeare Festival Public Theater, where it opened in LuEsther Hall on November 6, 1983, with the following cast:

WOMAN.................................... Ching Valdes
KAWABATA................................ Victor Wong

An additional dancer was added to the cast, performed by Elizabeth Fong Sung.

Directed by John Lone and Lenore Kletter; set by Andrew Jackness; lighting by John Gisondi; costumes by Lydia Tanji; music by Lucia Hwong.

CHARACTERS

YASUNARI KAWABATA, seventy-two, a leading Japanese novelist.
WOMAN, Japanese, late seventies.

PLACE

Tokyo.

TIME

The year 1972.

SYNOPSIS OF SCENES

Scene 1. The sitting room of the House of Sleeping Beauties. Night.
Scene 2. The sitting room, following evening.
Scene 3. The sitting room, several months later, evening.
Scene 4. The sitting room, one week later, evening.

Scene 1

A sitting room. Not richly decorated. Desk, pillows, low table, equipment for tea, cabinet, screen, mirror, stove. It is night. WOMAN sits at desk, writing. KAWABATA paces.

WOMAN: Now, you mustn't do anything distasteful.

KAWABATA: Distasteful?

WOMAN: You mustn't stick your fingers in the girl's mouth or anything like that.

KAWABATA: Oh, no. I wouldn't think of it.

WOMAN: Good. All my guests are gentlemen.

KAWABATA: Would you please put that down?

WOMAN: *(Indicating the pen)* This?

KAWABATA: Yes. I'm not here to be interviewed.

WOMAN: Perhaps. *I* am, however, accountable to my girls—

KAWABATA: Fine.

WOMAN: —and must therefore ask a few questions of those who wish to become my guests.

KAWABATA: You assume too easily, madame.

WOMAN: Oh?

KAWABATA: You assume that my presence here identifies me as just one type of man.

WOMAN: On the contrary, sir.

KAWABATA: Why did you assume I was going in there, then?

WOMAN: I never assumed any such thing. Did you assume I was going to allow you in there?
(Pause)

152

KAWABATA: "Allow me"?

WOMAN: Actually, I identify two types of men, sir—gentlemen and those who do not behave. My guests are all gentlemen. They do not disgrace the house. Obviously, very few men meet these requirements.

KAWABATA: What are you talking about?

WOMAN: I must protect my girls—and the house.

KAWABATA: Well, I mean, I'm certainly not going to assault a girl, if that's what you mean. Is that what you think? That I look like a man who goes to brothels?

WOMAN: Neither looks nor brothels has much to do with it, sir. My experience has taught me that in most cases if you scratch a man you'll find a molester.

KAWABATA: Well, if you take that kind of attitude . . .

WOMAN: A look in most men's bottom drawers confirms this.

KAWABATA: . . . how is any man to prove he's a . . . a gentleman, as you say?

WOMAN: I take a risk on all my guests. But I have my methods; I judge as best I can.

KAWABATA: That's ridiculous. That men must be . . . tested to become your customers. But all your customers are practically ghosts anyway—of course they don't object. Their throats are too dry to protest.

WOMAN: Guests.

KAWABATA: I'm sorry?

WOMAN: They're not customers, they're guests.

KAWABATA: Well, I, for one, do not intend to become a guest, understand?

WOMAN: You are very proud.

KAWABATA: Proud?

WOMAN: But that doesn't necessarily mean you are not a gentleman. Sometimes the proudest men are the best behaved. So, you don't want to be my guest. What *do* you want?

KAWABATA: I only want to talk.

WOMAN: About what?

KAWABATA: Your house.

WOMAN: Window shopping?

KAWABATA: No.

WOMAN: I'm sorry.

KAWABATA: I want to know why the old men come here.

WOMAN: But all your answers are in there.

KAWABATA: No, they're not. I could never feel what they feel, what brings them back—a parade of corpses—night after night. But you—perhaps they share their secrets.

WOMAN: I have no secrets.

KAWABATA: Old Eguchi—

WOMAN: And I'm no gossip.

KAWABATA: He talked to me last week.

WOMAN: Yes, he called and said you were coming.

KAWABATA: Said he comes here almost every night. I wanted him to tell me more, but he said I could only know more by talking to you.

WOMAN: He said you wished to gain entrance.

KAWABATA: No—he's making the same mistake as you. I won't be able to feel what he feels because my mind's different.

WOMAN: Oh?

KAWABATA: Eguchi's so old.

WOMAN: And you're young?

KAWABATA: Well, no. Not in years.

WOMAN: Oh.

KAWABATA: But my mind is young. Eguchi's is gone. He sits on his *futon* each afternoon swatting bees with tissue paper. Listen, I know you're a woman of business—may I offer you some fee for what you know?

WOMAN: Money?

KAWABATA: Don't worry. I'm not with the police or anything.

WOMAN: Don't be ridiculous. What do you take me for?

KAWABATA: What do I—?

WOMAN: You might as well pay me to tell you how one falls in love.

KAWABATA: What do you take yourself for, madame—acting like a sorceress, a *sensei*. You're just an old woman running this house. I have questions, and I'm willing to pay for the answers.

WOMAN: I have questions also. Fair, sir? *(Pause)* How old are you?

KAWABATA: I won't answer just anything, you know.

WOMAN: Don't worry. Neither will I.

KAWABATA: Seventy-two.

WOMAN: Married?

KAWABATA: My wife passed away . . . several years ago.

WOMAN: I'm sorry. Children?

KAWABATA: Yes. Two. Daughters. Why are you asking this?

WOMAN: Don't worry. I'm no gossip. Retired?

KAWABATA: Uh—no . . . I mean, yes.

WOMAN: Yes or no?

KAWABATA: Uh—no.

WOMAN: No? No. Profession?

KAWABATA: Uh—teacher.

WOMAN: Teacher.

KAWABATA: University level, of course.

WOMAN: There. That wasn't so bad, was it?

KAWABATA: That's all?

WOMAN: Now, what would *you* like to know?

KAWABATA: From that, you decide?

WOMAN: I *would* like you to join me in a game, though.

KAWABATA: A game?

WOMAN: Yes. And as we play, we can talk about the rooms. Do you mind?

KAWABATA: Well, if it's harmless.

WOMAN: Quite. Would you like some tea?

KAWABATA: Oh, yes. Please. Thank you. This game—what's it called?

WOMAN: I don't know. It's old. Geishas used to play it with their customers, to relax them. *(She brings the tea, pours it)*

KAWABATA: Relax? Perhaps it will relax me. *(He laughs softly)* Now, why do you want me to play this?

(WOMAN pulls a box out of the desk and opens it. Inside are twenty-five smooth tiles, five times as long as they are wide. While she speaks, she stacks them in five layers of five tiles each, such that the tiles of each layer are perpendicular to those of the layer below it)

WOMAN: So we can get to know each other. As I said, I must protect my girls from men who do not behave.

KAWABATA: You talk as if men should be put on leashes.

WOMAN: No, leashes aren't necessary at all. *(The tower is finished)* There. We'll take turns removing tiles from the tower until it collapses. Understand?

KAWABATA: Is this a game you ask all your customers to play?

WOMAN: Guests. You can't touch the top layer, though, and you can only use one hand.

KAWABATA: But what's the object? Who wins, who loses?

WOMAN: There are no winners or losers. There is only the tower—intact or collapsed. Just one hand—like this. *(She removes a piece)*

KAWABATA: My turn? What am I trying to do?

WOMAN: Judge the tiles. Wriggle that one, for instance— yes, that one you're touching—between your fingers. Is the weight of the stack on it? If so, don't force it. Leave it and look for another one that's looser. If you try to force the tiles to be what they're not, the whole thing will come crashing down.

KAWABATA: A test of skills? There—*(He removes a piece)* —Your turn.

WOMAN: See? Simple.

KAWABATA: What kind of a test—? You're just an old woman. What kind of a contest is this?

WOMAN: Let's talk about you, sir. We want to make you happy.

(They continue to take turns through the following section)

KAWABATA: Happy? No, you don't understand. You can't—

WOMAN: Our guests sleep much better here. It's the warmth, they say.

KAWABATA: I don't have any trouble sleeping.

WOMAN: Don't you?

KAWABATA: Sometimes . . . sometimes I choose not to go to bed. But when I do, I sleep.

WOMAN: Our guests are never afraid to go to sleep.

KAWABATA: It's not that I'm afraid.

WOMAN: The darkness does not threaten them.

(Pause)

KAWABATA: Old Eguchi—he says that the girls . . . that they are naked.

WOMAN: Yes.

KAWABATA: He says they are very beautiful, but I hardly . . .

WOMAN: For you, I would pick an especially pretty one.

KAWABATA: For me—? Don't start—

WOMAN: How old was your wife when you first met her?

KAWABATA: My wife? Oh, I don't know. She must have been—oh, maybe nineteen.

WOMAN: Nineteen. That is a beautiful age. I would pick one who is nineteen.

KAWABATA: Don't be ridiculous. She'd see me and—

WOMAN: But you forget, sir—our girls won't see anything.

KAWABATA: I suppose you have some way of guaranteeing this. I suppose it's never happened that some girl has opened her eyes—

WOMAN: No. Never.

(KAWABATA is having a particularly difficult time with a tile)

KAWABATA: Look at this. *(He holds out his hand, laughs)*

Shaking. Would you mind putting some more wood in the furnace?

WOMAN: Of course. *(WOMAN rises to do so as she talks)* I know what girl I would pick for you. She is half Japanese, half Caucasian. She has the most delicate hair—brown in one light, black in another. As she sleeps, she wriggles her left foot, like a cat, against the mattress, as if to draw out even the last bits of warmth.

(She returns to the table, sits. As she does, KAWABATA *causes the tower to fall)*

KAWABATA: Ai! You shook it.

WOMAN: No.

(During the next section, WOMAN *gets up, goes to the cabinet, removes a small jar filled with clear liquid and a tiny cup. She pours the liquid into the cup)*

KAWABATA: Maybe an accident, but still—

WOMAN: I assure you.

KAWABATA: —when you sat down.

WOMAN: I was perfectly still.

KAWABATA: No, you shook the table.

WOMAN: I didn't touch it.

KAWABATA: Just a bit.

WOMAN: Really.

KAWABATA: But at the crucial moment.

WOMAN: Please, sir.

KAWABATA: Just as it was about to give.

WOMAN: Thank you for playing.

KAWABATA: It wasn't fair.

WOMAN: Please—

KAWABATA: It was my first time.

WOMAN: —take this cup.

KAWABATA: What?

WOMAN: Here.

(He takes it)

KAWABATA: What is this?

WOMAN: To help you sleep.

KAWABATA: Sleep?

WOMAN: To assure you a restful evening—in there. *(Pause)* If you wish to, you may now go in. You're my guest. If you still have questions after tonight, I'll try to answer some—

KAWABATA: I can just—

WOMAN: —on your next visit.

KAWABATA: —go in?

WOMAN: Welcome. Your name?

KAWABATA: My name?

WOMAN: We keep names of all our guests.

KAWABATA: But I don't see why . . .

WOMAN: Our guests are our friends. Sometimes we like to let our friends know if we have something special. Don't worry, it is confidential.

KAWABATA: "Kawabata."
(He drinks from the cup)

WOMAN: May I help you undress, Mr. Kawabata?

KAWABATA: Oh, yes. Thank you. *(They go behind the screen)* I can just . . . go in?

WOMAN: Yes. On the right, second door. *(Pause)* She's a very pretty girl.

KAWABATA: Second door.

WOMAN: On the right. She's asleep, waiting for you.
(Pause)

KAWABATA: I'm really only curious.

WOMAN: I know. That's why you should go in.

KAWABATA: What if . . . something happens?

WOMAN: Something?

KAWABATA: What if she wakes up?

WOMAN: Even if you were to try your utmost— You could cut off her arms and she wouldn't wake up till morning. Don't worry. *(They come out from behind the screen. He wears a light robe)* Sleep well, Mr. Kawabata. A boy will wake you and bring you tea in the morning.

KAWABATA: Uh—thank you.
   (She opens the door)
WOMAN: Listen.
KAWABATA: Listen?
WOMAN: To the waves. And the wind. *(Silence)* Good night, Mr. Kawabata.
   (He walks in. She closes the door. She moves to the table, begins cleaning up the tiles, as LIGHTS FADE TO BLACK*)*

Scene 2

It is the following evening. Before the LIGHTS COME UP, *we see a flame.* LIGHTS UP. WOMAN *sits at the desk.* KAWABATA *is burning his record from yesterday; he tosses it into the stove.*

KAWABATA: I'm not a teacher, madame. I'm a writer.
WOMAN: Oh. A writer?
KAWABATA: Have you read my novels, short stories?
WOMAN: Have you ever been published in this?
   (She holds up a magazine)
KAWABATA: *Shifuno Tomo*? Trash.
WOMAN: Then I haven't read you.
KAWABATA: I don't write about beauty tips *or* American movie stars.
WOMAN: So you're going to write a report on us.
KAWABATA: I'm not a reporter. I write stories, novels. For some time now, I've been thinking about old men. How it must—
WOMAN: If you wish to write your report, Mr. Kawabata, you must realize the consequences of your actions. You understand, don't you, that we can't let the outside know we're here. That would mean the end of the house.

KAWABATA: And that should worry me?

WOMAN: Does it? Didn't you sleep well?

KAWABATA: Hardly. I was afraid to touch the covers and disturb her. I studied the walls until I fell asleep, watched the colors change in the dark.

WOMAN: I see.

KAWABATA: But what I've learned about the state to which men come—to think they return—night after night—for that.

WOMAN: Then why have *you* returned?

KAWABATA: Me?

WOMAN: Why didn't you just write your report and destroy the house?

KAWABATA: Story. I wanted . . . to burn that.

WOMAN: Is that all?

KAWABATA: Yes. That's all. *(He chuckles)* I certainly have no desire to repeat last night's experience. It's been so many years since I've had to share a bed. No room to stretch.

WOMAN: Well, then, go.

KAWABATA: What?

WOMAN: If you've done what you've come for, then you must want to leave.

KAWABATA: Yes. I will. But first, I thought I might talk . . . to you.

WOMAN: What about? You've burned your record, you're no longer a guest, you plan to write your report without concern for the house, my girls, or myself.

KAWABATA: Yourself?

WOMAN: Our relationship is hardly suited to polite conversation.

KAWABATA: You will be all right.

WOMAN: "All right"? How can you be so insensitive? You talk like a man who lives in other men's beds.

KAWABATA: You are very defiant, madame. Defiance is admirable in a woman. Defiance in a man is nothing more than a trained response, since we always expect to get our way. But a woman's defiance is her own.

WOMAN: Mr. Kawabata, you must not write this report.

KAWABATA: What if I do?

WOMAN: Then my life is over.

KAWABATA: Don't be melodramatic.

WOMAN: Please. Don't talk of things you know nothing about. I can tell you. Only one other time—twenty years ago—have I ever misjudged a guest. He came back the next evening, as you have tonight, and informed me he was . . . with the authorities. Then he left. I didn't know what to do. First, I tried to imagine all the awful things that could happen, hoping that by picturing them, I would prevent them from taking place, since real life never happens like we envision it will. Finally, after an hour of this, I decided to sleep. As I lay in bed, I began to wonder, what else could I do? Where else could I go? I saw myself being carried up to Mount Obasute. My girls were carrying me up. "You're old now, Mama!" they cried. "We'll join your bones when we ourselves become old!" They left me in a cave and danced a *bon-odori* down the mountain, singing "Tokyo Ondo" as they went. *(She sings a little of it)* I thought, "Look at them dancing. That's why I'm here and they're leaving me. Anyone who can dance down the mountain is free to go." And the next thing I knew, I was dancing a *bon-odori* right up there, on my bed—the springs making the sounds young people make in beds. And I danced down the hall to a telephone and began looking for a new house for my girls. *(Pause)* That was twenty years ago. Look at me today. I can't even raise a foot for three seconds, let alone dance. I'm old, and I have no savings, no money, no skills. This time, Mr. Kawabata, I would have to stay on Mount Obasute.

KAWABATA: Look, madame, even if I wrote this story, it's possible that your house wouldn't be affected.

WOMAN: Why? Don't people read them?

KAWABATA: Of course. But people will likely think it's all from my head. You haven't read my stories. Like what you said to me—"Listen to the waves," you said.

WOMAN: Yes, they often help men sleep.

KAWABATA: In one of my novels, the boy always makes love to the woman while listening to the waves. The critics would probably laugh—"Old Kawabata and waves. Can't he think of anything new?"

WOMAN: And if the authorities—some of whom already suspect our existence—if they read your story, that won't make them certain? *(Pause)* What is that story to you?

KAWABATA: I want to write this story. I can do it, I know. I haven't written a story in . . . in . . .

WOMAN: That's just one story to you. This is my life.

KAWABATA: Better if you were rid of it.

WOMAN: Then you must change the facts—

KAWABATA: You made a mistake, madame.

WOMAN: to confuse the authorities.

KAWABATA: You chose not to cooperate with me yesterday.

WOMAN: But even that—

KAWABATA: You thought I was like the rest of them.

WOMAN: No, you mustn't write this report!

KAWABATA: You misjudged me. Now you see I'm different.

WOMAN: Yes, you are a reporter.

KAWABATA: You should have just told me about the house.

WOMAN: Mr. Kawabata—

KAWABATA: But you assumed—

WOMAN: —think of the girls.

KAWABATA: The girls?

WOMAN: The money they receive here.

KAWABATA: You shame them.

WOMAN: They are from poor families.

KAWABATA: They would be better off—

WOMAN: They come of their own will.

KAWABATA: —doing—working at . . . any other job.

WOMAN: And the old men.

KAWABATA: Don't tell me that.

WOMAN: We care about them. Look at this.

KAWABATA: At what?

WOMAN: At what you'll destroy.

KAWABATA: You humiliate them. Their despair—it's so great.

WOMAN: What do you know?

KAWABATA: Your girls—are they all still virgins?

WOMAN: Was yours?

KAWABATA: Yes. Do you see the depth of the old men's despair?

WOMAN: How do you know?

KAWABATA: That they can't even find the manhood to—

WOMAN: Mr. Kawabata, how do you know she was still a virgin?

(Pause)

KAWABATA: Don't worry. I didn't . . . molest her. I walked into the room. I didn't believe she was going to be naked. I knew you'd told me, but I thought, no, you couldn't go that far, it would be unfair to give men exactly what they want. But she was lying on her back, the blanket leaving bare two white shoulders and her neck. I couldn't see clearly yet, so I ran my fingers from one shoulder, across her neck, to the other shoulder. Nothing blocked my finger's path—nothing, no straps, only taut, smooth skin. I still couldn't believe it, so I placed my index finger at the base of her throat and moved down, under the blanket, farther and farther down—one unbroken line—all the way. When I knew, I pulled my hand away. She moaned and turned away from me. I looked at my finger, placed it at the top of her spine and followed the hard bumps all the way down. I looked at my finger again, tasted it. Then I placed it against the back of her knee, under her nostrils, behind her ear, in the hair under her arm. And every place my finger touched, it pressed. And everywhere it pressed, her skin resisted with the same soft strength, and I thought, "This . . . is youth." I lay down and buried my nose against her scalp, my nose rubbing up and down as her foot rubbed against the sheets. When I woke up, it was just past dawn. The room was bright. That's when I tried to assault her—yes, it's true, I *tried*. But I'm an honorable man, so don't worry for her. If I had known she was a virgin, I would never have even thought of it to begin with.

(Pause)

WOMAN: Well, this is too bad. You know the rules of the house, don't you?

KAWABATA: Yes.

WOMAN: But still . . .

KAWABATA: But I didn't.

WOMAN: Very technical.

KAWABATA: I don't know why. It was too bright in the room. I became sad, then angry. I wanted to hit her or something. But instead, I tried that instead.

WOMAN: Can I get you some tea?

KAWABATA: Huh? Yes, please. Thank you.

WOMAN: Why do you do that kind of thing anyway?

KAWABATA: I told you, I don't know. And don't make it sound like I do it often.

WOMAN: No, I mean about sleeping with your head in her hair.

KAWABATA: Oh, that.

WOMAN: Don't you worry about suffocating?

KAWABATA: I have my reasons.

WOMAN: Well, go on. There's very little you can't tell me now.

(Pause)

KAWABATA: Her hair—the girl last night. It had a special smell. Like a lady friend of mine.

WOMAN: Your wife?

KAWABATA: No, I'm afraid not. Maybe thirty years ago. She was married to—oh, some kind of Hong Kong business-man, maybe even a movie producer—I can't remember. I do remember she lived alone with her servants—he was always away—in a huge castle in Kowloon. It really was—a castle in Kowloon. I didn't know they had castles either. Where did we meet? Kyoto? I can't—you see, I'd even forgotten her until I smelled that girl's hair. My lady friend, I'd smell her hair and she'd cry, "Don't do that. It's filthy!" But I'd smell her hair for hours. I wonder what she's doing now, She was the only woman who ever winked at me.

WOMAN: Mr. Kawabata . . .

KAWABATA: I was shocked. This was many years ago, you know.

WOMAN: I apologize. For my hysteria.

KAWABATA: Have you . . . seen my point?

WOMAN: Yes.

KAWABATA: About the story? My writing?

WOMAN: Yes. Would you like to be our guest again tonight?

KAWABATA: What? Even after—?

WOMAN: I misjudged you. You are honest. That's a rare quality. I was irrational. This time, no charge. Only please stay.

KAWABATA: I came here to burn my record.

WOMAN: We can make you a new one. The girl I've picked out for you tonight is more experienced than the one before.

KAWABATA: It's not the same one?

WOMAN: No. Isn't it better to have a different one?

KAWABATA: You understand that I won't . . . do anything like . . . last night.

WOMAN: Of course, Mr. Kawabata. I see you're a gentleman after all. Your sleeping medicine?

KAWABATA: My— Oh, thank you. I don't quite understand.

WOMAN: Don't understand. Just enjoy tonight's sleep. May I help you undress?

KAWABATA: Thank you. I suppose . . . I can't refuse your generosity.

WOMAN: Thank you.
(They go behind the screen. Again she helps him undress and put on a kimono)

KAWABATA: Uh—where was your house located before?

WOMAN: Before? We've always been here.

KAWABATA: No, but that story you told—the one about your guest the policeman.

WOMAN: Oh, that.

KAWABATA: Where did you move from?

WOMAN: We didn't. *(Pause)* Things just worked out.
(They come out. She opens the door, gives him a key) Third door on your left. This one's even prettier—and more experienced.

KAWABATA: What do you mean, "more experienced"? After all, she's sound asleep.

WOMAN. Good night, Mr. Kawabata.
(He goes in. She closes the door. She returns to the desk, pulls out her record book, and begins to write. LIGHTS TO BLACK)

Scene 3

It is several months later. KAWABATA *is sitting alone. Silence.*
WOMAN *enters from door to rooms.*

WOMAN: Yes, I can arrange something tonight. *(Pause)* But you should know better. You've been a guest for five months now. Why didn't you call first, instead of just bursting in?

KAWABATA: *(Sharply)* I'm sorry!

WOMAN: It will be a few minutes before things are ready.
(Pause)

KAWABATA: Can you give me some of that sleeping medicine?

WOMAN: Now? Well, if you like.

KAWABATA: No, not that. The kind you give the girls.

WOMAN: The girls?

KAWABATA: Yes. I want to sleep as deeply as they do.

WOMAN: Sir, that kind of medicine isn't healthy for old men.

KAWABATA: I can take it. I'm your guest, aren't I? You always say so. You always say you want to serve your guests, don't you?

WOMAN: What's wrong with this?
(She holds up the usual cup)

KAWABATA: I wake up. I wake up at two, three in the morning. Sometimes, it takes me an hour to fall back to sleep. I just lie there.

WOMAN: Your body shouldn't be building up resistance.

KAWABATA: That's not it.

WOMAN: If you're tired of my girls, I can arrange something special.

KAWABATA: Will it help me sleep? *(Pause)* See? Whatever you do with the girls—it doesn't matter if I have to lie there like a stone.

WOMAN: Is there a girl here you'd like to see again?

KAWABATA: No. It's not the girls, it's me. When I began coming here, I'd lie awake at nights, too, but I'd love it, because I'd remember . . . things I'd forgotten for years—women, romances. I stopped writing—even exercises—it all seemed so pointless. But these last few weeks, I smell their skin, run my fingers between their toes—there's nothing there but skin and toes. I wake up in the middle of the night, and all I can remember was what it was like to remember, and I'm a prisoner in that bed.

WOMAN: I'm sorry. I can't—

KAWABATA: No. Listen. It's getting worse. Last night, when I woke up, all I could think of was the death of my friend.

WOMAN: I'm sorry.

KAWABATA: I hadn't thought of Mishima's suicide in a year. But last night—it began again—what must it have been like? *(Pause) Hara-kiri.* How does a man you know commit *hara-kiri*? A loved one, a friend. Strangers, of course. They kill themselves daily. But someone you know—how do they find that will? *(Pause)* The will. To feel your hands forcing steel through your stomach and if the hands stopped the pain would stop, but the hands keep going. They must become another being, your hands. Yes. Your hands become another being and the steel becomes you.

WOMAN: You shouldn't give your friend more respect than he deserves.

KAWABATA: He was a man, though. He had his lover stand behind him and chop off his head when the cutting was done.

WOMAN: I'm not going to give you dangerous drugs. I'm sorry. *(Pause)* Don't worry so much about your friend, Mr. Kawabata. People commit suicide for themselves. That's one thing I know. I had a sister, Mr. Kawabata. My parents sent her away to Tokyo, hoping that she would be trained in the tea, the dance, the *koto,* to attract a man of wealth. I wept with envy at the fine material Mother bought for her kimonos—gold thread, brocade. The day she left, I was angry—she was crying at her good fortune. Years went by; we were both engaged. She came back from Tokyo for her wedding and we could barely recognize her—she had neither the hands nor the speech of anyone we knew. I got very angry at her haughtiness. My chore was to pick the maggots from the rice, and I purposely left a few in, hoping she would get them . . .

Their wedding was the most beautiful I'd ever seen. Just before she was to leave, my sister cornered me outside, tears streaming down her face, and begged my forgiveness . . . They tried to keep the story a secret from us, but, well . . . such a romantic story; the stuff legends are made of. It seems my sister had a lover in the village, that they had pledged fidelity long before she left for Tokyo. The next morning, my father went to draw water from the well. In the dim light before dawn, two faces came rushing up to the water's surface. Two faces—my sister and my fiancé . . . So don't worry about your friend, Mr. Kawabata. People kill themselves to save themselves, not others. *(Pause)* Now, I'm going to prepare something special. There will be two girls. There will be twice the warmth.

(She exits. He goes to the cabinet, takes out the vials and a cup. He pours and drinks three glasses of the sleeping potion. He returns the items. She reenters)

KAWABATA: Madame?

WOMAN: Yes.

KAWABATA: If I were to commit *hara-kiri,* would you chop off my head?

WOMAN: Mr. Kawabata—

KAWABATA: No! Answer me. If I gave you a sword—I'd pay you, you know—I wouldn't expect you to do it for nothing.

WOMAN: This type of question doesn't help either of us.

KAWABATA: Listen—would you chop off my head when I whispered, "Now. Please. Now." Or would you walk away laughing, counting your change?

WOMAN: Will you stop that? Will you stop that selfishness?

KAWABATA: No! The question is—answer it!—would you chop—

WOMAN: No! No! That's *your* question, yours only. You never think of anyone else's suffering—you're so self-centered, all you men, every last one of you. Have some woman chop off your head, leave her alone, do you think of her? She takes her few dollars, she buys some vegetables, she eats them and slowly withers away—no glory, no honor, just a slow fading into the background—that's all you expect. No, Mr. Kawabata, if *I* wanted to commit *hara-kiri*, would you chop off *my* head?

KAWABATA: Women don't commit *hara-kiri*.

WOMAN: What if I did? What if I were the first?

KAWABATA: This is pointless.

WOMAN: I know—you think I would do it the woman's way, just slipping the tiny knife in here. *(Points to base of neck)* But what if I wanted to do it like a man? Completely. Powerfully.

KAWABATA: That's a foolish question.

WOMAN: I would do it better than you.

KAWABATA: Don't be absurd.

WOMAN: I would be braver.

KAWABATA: What a ridiculous notion!

WOMAN: If you didn't chop off my head, I'd be glad.

KAWABATA: This is a waste of time.

WOMAN: Because then, I'd be braver than you or your friend.

KAWABATA: Don't blaspheme Mishima.

WOMAN: I'd die like the generals.

KAWABATA: You're just an old woman.

WOMAN: I'd be the old woman who died like the generals.

KAWABATA: Show some respect.

(Pause)

WOMAN: So quiet now, aren't you, Mr. Kawabata. Why don't you spout glorious phrases about chopping off my head? *(Pause)* Or why don't you write your report and destroy us all? *(Pause)* Your room is ready. Should I help you undress?

KAWABATA: No.

(He starts to leave, still dressed)

WOMAN: Don't forget your key. *(He returns, takes the key)* Fourth door on your right.

(He exits. She closes the door. Pause. She goes to her desk, takes out a makeup kit. She stands next to the mirror, powders her face completely white, does her eyes, her mouth. She then goes to the door to the rooms, pulls up a chair, and sits facing it)

KAWABATA: [Offstage] Madame! Madame!

(He enters, wearing only his pants. He is in a panic, but the large amount of sleeping potion he's taken has started to take effect. He stares at her. She says nothing. He is speechless. Long pause)

Your . . . one of your girls. She's . . . not breathing. No pulse.

WOMAN: Her body is being removed even as you speak. Now go back to bed. There is still the other girl.

KAWABATA: Other girl?

WOMAN: Yes, there were two, remember?

KAWABATA: I can't . . . your face. Why is it that way? I can't go back in there. She's dead. Do something. Go in.

WOMAN: Very little I can do. She took too much of her sleeping medicine, I think.

KAWABATA: This is inhuman.

WOMAN: It's difficult, but these things happen.

KAWABATA: This is . . . not human.

WOMAN: Now, go back. It won't do to be walking the streets at this hour.

KAWABATA: Why do people come here? Why don't they leave? I won't . . . I'm leaving.

WOMAN: You can't leave.

KAWABATA: I'm leaving. Where's my shirt, my coat?

WOMAN: Where will you go?

KAWABATA: Out. Home.

WOMAN: In your condition? Look at you—what happened, anyway?

KAWABATA: No, I don't care. I'll sleep in the streets.

WOMAN: You'll die in the cold, that's what you'll do.

KAWABATA: Yes. I'll die in the cold. I'll die in the cold before I become like Old Eguchi. Look at him—pathetic— here every damn night.

WOMAN: Like Old Eguchi? How are you *not* like Old Eguchi?

KAWABATA: I can still sleep somewhere else.

WOMAN: Today, perhaps. Tomorrow, no.

KAWABATA: Where's my shirt?

WOMAN: Here. *(She leads him to the mirror)* Look at yourself. Even as we speak, the lines are getting deeper, the hair is getting thinner, your lips are getting drier. Even as we speak, the shape of your face is changing, and with it, a mind, a will, as different as the face. You can leave now, Mr. Kawabata, but as much as you deny it, your face will continue to change, as if your will didn't even exist. See my face? Look at it. Close. I try and powder it like a young girl. But look—all that's here is an obscene mockery of youth. Don't be like this, Mr. Kawabata. Go back to sleep and let's not hear any more of your grandstanding. *(KAWABATA is firmly in the grip of the drug now)*

KAWABATA: I'm . . . so tired. I drank too much of the potion.

WOMAN: That? I'm sorry. My fault. I shouldn't have left it there. Well, you should be all right. That's not as strong as the stuff you wanted.

KAWABATA: I would leave, I would, you know.

WOMAN: But you're too tired?

KAWABATA: I'm not coming back.

WOMAN: Of course not. Here. I'll help you to your room. *(She starts to sing the "Tokyo Ondo" softly as they exit together.* LIGHTS FADE SLOWLY, *and we can still hear the song)*

Scene 4

A week later. It is evening. KAWABATA *is alone in the room. He is wrapping something in a small box. He completes the wrapping, puts the box into the breast pocket of the suit he is wearing.* WOMAN *enters from the door to the rooms. She carries a manuscript.*

WOMAN: You've sent this to your publisher?

KAWABATA: Yes. It will be in print in time.
  (Pause)

WOMAN: You go very easy on yourself.

KAWABATA: In what sense?

WOMAN: You don't even name the main character after yourself. You call him Old Eguchi.

KAWABATA: Maybe I'm writing about him, not me.

WOMAN: And here . . . this story. That never happened. No man ever died here.

KAWABATA: Are you sure?

WOMAN: Who told you that?

KAWABATA: No one. I just thought . . . maybe.

WOMAN: And look at this. All this talk about the girls with their electric blankets. We don't even have electric blankets.

KAWABATA: Madame, I write stories, not newspaper copy. I don't—

WOMAN: This woman—she's very . . . uh . . . she seems so hard.

KAWABATA: The story's not about her.

WOMAN: She has no feelings, no heart. She's so . . . above it all, like she never cries, like her heart has gone through life without stumbling. She's like a ghost that walks through men's houses without creaking the floorboards.

KAWABATA: It's rather depersonalized, objective . . .

WOMAN: "Objective"? How can you say that? Look at the

end—here—when the girl dies—like last week—and she says, "There's still the other girl." Doesn't that make her just one kind of woman?

KAWABATA: What I mean is that—

WOMAN: Doesn't it? Yes, I said that. But I shared things with you, stories. I let you see me ridiculous, hideous, a fool in my powder. Where is that? Is this all you remember? Just an old, cruel woman who serves you tea and takes your money?

KAWABATA: You have to understand . . . the joy was that I could finally write again at all.

WOMAN: Yes. That is surprising.

KAWABATA: I wasn't going to stop it.

WOMAN: I was surprised wc hadn't seen you all week.

KAWABATA: Do you understand?

WOMAN: Do you still think that the house will survive this story? Even after revealing the girl's death?

KAWABATA: I don't know. Who can say?

WOMAN: You didn't change anything, make it harder for them to find us.

KAWABATA: I'm sorry. I wanted to, but I couldn't. I'm sorry.

WOMAN: No. Sorry has nothing to do with it. We each do our work.

KAWABATA: When I told you last week—drugged—that I wasn't coming back again, did you believe me?

WOMAN: Of course not. But there was a part of me . . . *(Pause)* Up to a point, you'd acted like all my guests. The game with the tiles, being unable to assault my girl when you found her a virgin, you fit right into the gentleman's pattern. But your memories—leaving you so soon. There was a part of me that wondered. I wanted to call you. Once I even finished dialing your number. But I hung up before it rang. I sat here and thought up tortures for you. I thought you'd gone away . . . committed *hara-kiri,* and that you were waiting for me to come and chop off your head. I decided to stay right here.

KAWABATA: Did you think I wasn't coming back?

WOMAN: After a time, I began to wonder. *(Pause. She goes to the mirror, looks at it)* Well, there're many things I could do now. I could move to another city. Try to start again, from the ground. Or I could sit here, the same as always. Who knows? Perhaps no one will believe your story.

KAWABATA: That's quite possible. I've told you that.

WOMAN: Which would you recommend?

KAWABATA: Me? I don't know what kind of risks you take, or what's involved in starting over.

WOMAN: No. You don't.

KAWABATA: I think, though, that at our age, starting again is only worthwhile if one enjoys the process.

WOMAN: "At our age"?

KAWABATA: It's—uh—difficult to make long-range plans, you know.

WOMAN: Since when are we the same age?

KAWABATA: We are, aren't we?

WOMAN: Yes, we are.

KAWABATA: Give or take five years—

WOMAN: And you, then—

KAWABATA: —which hardly matters at this point.

WOMAN: —what will you do? Will you come back here?

KAWABATA: No.

WOMAN: Oh.

KAWABATA: No. My life becomes very simple now. *(He takes out a packet of bills, offers them to her)* Here. Here. Take it. Enough for you to . . . I don't know, buy a new house, anywhere you want. Or retire. Yes, retire and never worry about a thing again.

WOMAN: This is . . . so much . . . amazing. I can't take this. Why?

KAWABATA: I want you to serve me.

WOMAN: This is . . . an outrageous amount, Mr. Kawabata. I cannot accept it.

KAWABATA: Please. You'll need the money. An even trade.

WOMAN: Do you want a girl? A room?

KAWABATA: No.

WOMAN: I can fix you something special.

KAWABATA: Fix me some tea.

WOMAN: Oh, I forgot. I'm sorry.

KAWABATA: No. Don't apologize.

WOMAN: I'm sorry. So rude of me. It's such a cold night.

KAWABATA: You make very wonderful tea.

WOMAN: No, it's not.

KAWABATA: Yes.

WOMAN: It's nothing.

(Pause)

KAWABATA: I've grown in this house.

WOMAN: You feel young here?

KAWABATA: I did. As I've slept here, I've grown older. I've seen my sweethearts, my wife, my mistresses, my daughters, until there's only one thing left. *(She comes with the tea)* Will you powder your face again?

WOMAN: Mr. Kawabata, don't—

KAWABATA: Please.

WOMAN: You're mocking me—an old woman.

KAWABATA: No, I've brought you something. *(He reaches into a bag he is carrying, pulls out a kimono)*

WOMAN: Oh!

KAWABATA: Yes. Take it.

WOMAN: It's . . . No, this isn't for me.

KAWABATA: Yes. See? Gold thread. Brocade.

WOMAN: I can't accept this. Please. Give it to someone who deserves it.

KAWABATA: It's for you.

WOMAN: One of your young admirers. You are a famous writer. You must have many.

KAWABATA: Please. Put it on. It's just like the one you told me about.

WOMAN: It's gorgeous, too beautiful—

KAWABATA: Put it on and powder your face.

WOMAN: You're so foolish, Mr. Kawabata. I'll disgrace these clothes. Once they drape down my old bones, especially with my face in that powder, they'll change into something else completely, believe me.

KAWABATA: Don't be shy. You'll do me a great honor to wear my gift.

(Pause)

WOMAN: If you insist.

KAWABATA: Yes. Please. *(She starts to leave)* No. Please. Do it in here. I want to watch.

WOMAN: Women don't like men to watch them making up.

(Pause. She sits, begins making up)

KAWABATA: I finished that story several days ago, you know. It came out of me like a wild animal, my hands were cramping at the pen. I wanted to show it to you while it was still warm, but I kept turning back. It's the same way I've felt before when I've written the end of a story, yet known that the story had more to do before I could rest. So I trusted my instincts—I watched television for two full days, since usually, what hasn't yet been revealed will rise to the surface in its own time. Yesterday, I woke up and knew what had to be added, and words weren't the question at all, so I sent the manuscript as it was to my publisher and went out shopping.

WOMAN: For the kimono? It's so beautiful.

KAWABATA: I tried to imagine the one you described.

WOMAN: This is every bit as beautiful.

KAWABATA: It's not the same?

WOMAN: It's difficult for me to remember. I was so young. But my sister's couldn't have been any finer.

(She takes the kimono, goes behind the screen, begins changing

into it. He takes the small box out of his breast pocket, removes his jacket, takes off his tie, unbuttons his collar, takes off his shoes. Finally, she speaks)

WOMAN: After the war, when we realized Father wasn't coming back, and the family was dispersed, I moved here to Tokyo. And I thought, "Now I'll dress in brocade also. I'll wear gold threads, too." But when I remembered my sister, I lost any desire to have anything like that. It's just as well, that being after the war and all. And I've never had the money, even to this day—ai! You'd think at my age, I'd have earned the right to stop worrying about money.

KAWABATA: But I've given you your security.

WOMAN: Yes, yes. I still can't— But why? *(She steps out from behind the screen)* See? Don't I look hideous?

KAWABATA: You're exactly what I want.

WOMAN: Is this what you want? An old hag pretending to be young again?

KAWABATA: Please. Sit down.

WOMAN: The tea—it's probably cold.

KAWABATA: No, it's fine. Open that box.

WOMAN: This one?

KAWABATA: Yes.

WOMAN: It's beautifully wrapped.

(She starts to open it)

KAWABATA: It took me several hours to buy the kimono, and the rest of the day to buy that.

(She removes a vial of clear liquid)

KAWABATA: Please. Add it to the tea. *(Pause)* Go on. You said it was all right for us to bring our own medicine, didn't you? *(Pause)* The top lifts off. *(Pause)* Don't worry. I'm not going to ask you to drink it or anything. It's for me. Now, go on.

WOMAN: Respect me, Mr. Kawabata.

KAWABATA: I do.

WOMAN: Tell me—this isn't a sleeping potion.

KAWABATA: No.

WOMAN: Do you want a room?

KAWABATA: No.

WOMAN: I want to give you one. Free.

KAWABATA: I've already paid.

WOMAN: For what?

KAWABATA: Paid not to have a room.

WOMAN: For me?

KAWABATA: Please, empty the vial.

WOMAN: No.

(Pause)

KAWABATA: Isn't this your job? Isn't this what you get paid to do? For your life's security, madame, you should be willing to endure a little more than usual. *(Pause)* What's the matter? I thought of all people in the world, you would understand this. *(Silence. She empties the vial into the teapot)* Good. I'm sorry. I didn't mean to do that, say those things. But I assume . . . we have an understanding. Do we?

WOMAN: Look at me. See this? *(Points to her face)* This? *(Pointing to her dress)* That should answer your question. What should I do now?

KAWABATA: Tell me again, why I should come to your house.

WOMAN: *(As before)* Our guests sleep very well here. It's the warmth, they say.

KAWABATA: Warmth?

WOMAN: Our guests are not afraid to sleep at night. The darkness does not threaten them.

KAWABATA: Oh, it's so cold tonight. Look at my hand. Could you pour me some tea, please?

(Pause)

WOMAN: Yes. Certainly *(She does; her eyes are fixed on him. She watches him drink as she speaks)* The girl I've picked out for you is . . . she's . . . half Japanese, half Caucasian, very beautiful, like a child, like a pearly-white snowflake child, whose foot never—always—moves, traces circles around the snow—uh—sheet, fleeing—uh—feeling the warmth, the heart—uh—the heat, finding it, the warmth, the heart—uh—the heat, taking it, the warmth, the heat, always . . .

(He puts down the cup. It is empty. Pause. She refills his cup. It sits on the table, untouched. Silence)

KAWABATA: Now, we are as we should be.

WOMAN: Yes, I suppose so.

KAWABATA: And you look so beautiful.

WOMAN: Don't be cruel.

KAWABATA: But you do.

WOMAN: I won't listen.

KAWABATA: If we were thirty, maybe even twenty years younger, who knows?

WOMAN: Mr. Kawabata, for so long now, you've been trying to show me that you're different from my other guests.

KAWABATA: I'm sorry.

WOMAN: No, no, you've done it. You've gotten your wish. How does it make you feel?

KAWABATA: I wasted so much time.

WOMAN: You've proven to me that you're a thousand times more terrible and wonderful than any of my other guests.

KAWABATA: How sad. I don't even care about that anymore. If I'm different, it's only because I believed you when you showed me that I was the same as the rest of them. *(Pause)* It's funny. I've known you all this time, and I don't even know your name.

WOMAN: "Michiko."

KAWABATA: Michiko. Wonderful. You have the hands of a young woman, did you know that, Michiko?

WOMAN: No. My hands are ugly.

KAWABATA: Let me see them, Michiko.

WOMAN: They are the hands of a crow.

KAWABATA: Please. Let me see them. *(She does)* Amazing. And you—from the country. *(He touches them)* They are long. And firm. And warm with blood. *(He kisses them)* I'm starting to become tired. May I rest in your lap? *(She nods)* Thank you, Michiko. *(Silently, she begins to stroke his hair)* You've been very kind for allowing me to . . . take these liberties with you. I'm sorry I said those things about you. But I was afraid that you weren't as strong as I expected, that you couldn't give me what I needed. I shouldn't have doubted. *(Pause)* Please. Take the money. Be happy. Enjoy these last years. Buy what you've always wanted. *(Pause)* I do want you to take care of yourself. *(Silence)* You can't believe what a comfort it is for me to be falling asleep, yet able to open my eyes, look up, and see you.

(His eyes are closed. She looks around the house, continues to stroke his hair. She begins to sing the "Tokyo Ondo" as a lullaby)

(She picks up the remaining cup of tea, drinks it)

(She resumes singing, strokes his hair, as LIGHTS FADE TO BLACK*)*

CURTAIN

THE SOUND
OF A VOICE

The Sound of a Voice was produced by Joseph Papp with *The House of Sleeping Beauties* under the omnibus title "Sound and Beauty" at the New York Shakespeare Festival Public Theater, where it opened on November 6, 1983, with the following cast:

WOMAN........................... Natsuko Ohama
MAN .... John Lone
MOVEMENT .... Ching Valdez
                                        Elizabeth Fong Sung

Directed by John Lone and Lenore Kletter; set by Andrew Jackness; lighting by John Gisondi; costumes by Lydia Tanji; music by Lucia Hwong.

CHARACTERS

MAN, fifties, Japanese.
WOMAN (Hanako), forties or fifties, Japanese.

PLACE

Woman's house, in a remote corner of a forest.

SYNOPSIS OF SCENES

Scene 1. Evening.
Scene 2. Dawn.
Scene 3. Day.
Scene 4. Night.
Scene 5. Day.
Scene 6. Night.
Scene 7. Morning.
Scene 8. Day.
Scene 9. Night

DEFINITION

Shakuhatchi: Japanese end-blown bamboo flute

Scene 1

It is evening. WOMAN *warms tea for man.* MAN *rubs himself, trying to get warm.*

MAN: You are very kind to take me in.

WOMAN: This is a remote corner of the world. Guests are rare.

MAN: The tea—you pour it well.

WOMAN: No.

MAN: The sound it makes—in the cup—very soothing.

WOMAN: That is the tea's skill, not mine. *(She hands the cup to him)*

WOMAN: May I get you something else? Rice, perhaps?

MAN: No.

WOMAN: Some vegetables?

MAN: No, thank you.

WOMAN: Fish? *(Pause)* It is at least two days walk to the nearest village. I saw no horse. You must be very hungry. You would do a great honor to dine with me. Guests are rare.

MAN: Thank you.

*(*WOMAN *gets up, leaves.* MAN *gets up, walks to kitchen door, listens. The room is sparsely furnished, except for one shelf on which stands a vase of brightly colored flowers. The flowers stand out in sharp contrast to the starkness of the room. He crosses to the vase of flowers. He touches them. Quickly, he*

187

takes one of the flowers from the vase, hides it in his clothes.
WOMAN *reenters. She carries a tray with food)*

WOMAN: Please. Eat. It will give me great pleasure.

MAN: This—this is magnificent.

WOMAN: Eat.

MAN: Thank you.

(He motions for WOMAN *to join him)*

WOMAN: No, thank you.

MAN: This is wonderful. The best I've tasted.

WOMAN: You are reckless in your flattery, sir. But anything you say, I will enjoy hearing. It's not even the words. It's the sound of a voice, the way it moves through the air.

MAN: How long has it been since you last had a visitor?
(Pause)

WOMAN: I don't know.

MAN: Oh?

WOMAN: I lose track. Perhaps five months ago, perhaps ten years, perhaps yesterday. I don't consider time when there is no voice in the air. It's pointless. Time begins with the entrance of a visitor, and ends with his exit.

MAN: And in between? You don't keep track of the days? You can't help but notice—

WOMAN: Of course I notice.

MAN: Oh.

WOMAN: I notice, but I don't keep track. *(Pause)* May I bring out more?

MAN: More? No. No. This was wonderful.

WOMAN: I have more.

MAN: Really—the best I've had.

WOMAN: You must be tired. Did you sleep in the forest last night?

MAN: Yes.

WOMAN: Or did you not sleep at all?

MAN: I slept.

WOMAN: Where?

MAN: By a waterfall. The sound of the water put me to sleep. It rumbled like the sounds of a city. You see, I can't sleep in too much silence. It scares me. It makes me feel that I have no control over what is about to happen.

WOMAN: I feel the same way.

MAN: But you live here—alone?

WOMAN: Yes.

MAN: It's so quiet here. How can you sleep?

WOMAN: Tonight, I'll sleep. I'll lie down in the next room, and hear your breathing through the wall, and fall asleep shamelessly. There will be no silence.

MAN: You're very kind to let me stay here.

WOMAN: This is yours.

(She unrolls a mat)

MAN: Did you make it yourself?

WOMAN: Yes. There is a place to wash outside.

MAN: Thank you.

WOMAN: Goodnight.

MAN: Goodnight.

(He starts to leave)

WOMAN: May I know your name?

MAN: No. I mean, I would rather not say. If I gave you a name, it would only be made up. Why should I deceive you? You are too kind for that.

WOMAN: Then what should I call you? Perhaps—"Man Who Fears Silence"?

MAN: How about, "Man Who Fears Women"?

WOMAN: That name is much too common.

MAN: And you?

WOMAN: Hanako.

MAN: That's your name?

WOMAN: It's what you may call me.

MAN: Good night, Hanako. You are very kind.

WOMAN: You are very smart. Good night.

(MAN exits. She picks up the dishes and teapot, returns them

offstage to kitchen. She goes to the vase. She picks up the flowers, studies them. She carries them out of the room with her. Man reenters. He glimpses the spot where the vase used to sit. He listens at the various screens, then suddenly hears a sound. He prepares to draw his sword, then hears a shakuhatchi. *He sits on the mat, looks at the flower, puts it away. Then he sits on guard with his sword ready at his side)*

Scene 2

Dawn. MAN *is packing.* WOMAN *enters with food.*

WOMAN: Good morning.

MAN: Good morning, Hanako.

WOMAN: You weren't planning to leave?

MAN: I have quite a distance to travel today.

WOMAN: Please.

   (She offers him food)

MAN: Thank you.

WOMAN: May I ask where you're traveling to?

MAN: It's far.

WOMAN: I know this region well.

MAN: Oh? Do you leave the house often?

WOMAN: I used to. I used to travel a great deal. I know the region from those days.

MAN: You probably wouldn't know the place I'm headed.

WOMAN: Why not?

MAN: It's new. A new village. It didn't exist in "those days."

   (Pause)

WOMAN: I thought you said you wouldn't deceive me.

MAN: I didn't. You don't believe me, do you?

WOMAN: No.

MAN: Then I didn't deceive you, did I? I'm traveling. That much is true.

WOMAN: Are you in such a hurry?

MAN: Traveling is a matter of timing. Catching the light. (WOMAN *exits.* MAN *finishes eating, puts down his bowl.* WOMAN *reenters with the vase of flowers*)

MAN: Where did you find those? They don't grow native around these parts, do they?

WOMAN: No, they've all been brought in by visitors. Such as yourself. They were left here. In my custody.

MAN: But—they look so fresh, so alive.

WOMAN: I take care of them. They remind me of the people and places outside this house.

MAN: May I touch them?

WOMAN: Certainly.

MAN: These have just blossomed.

WOMAN: No, they were in bloom yesterday. If you'd noticed them before, you would know that.

MAN: You must have received these very recently. I would guess—within five days.

WOMAN: I don't know. But I wouldn't trust your estimate. It's all in the amount of care you show to them. I create a world which is outside the realm of what you know.

MAN: What do you do?

WOMAN: I can't explain. Words are too inefficient. It takes hundreds of words to describe a single act of caring. With hundreds of acts, words become irrelevant. *(Pause)* But perhaps you can stay.

MAN: How long?

WOMAN: As long as you'd like.

MAN: Why?

WOMAN: To see how I care for them.

MAN: I *am* tired.
WOMAN: Rest.
MAN: The light?
WOMAN: It will return.

Scene 3

Day. MAN *is carrying chopped wood. He is stripped to the waist.*
WOMAN *enters.*

WOMAN: You're very kind to do that for me.

MAN: I enjoy it, you know. Chopping wood. It's clean. No
questions. You take your ax, you stand up the log, you
aim—pow!—you either hit it or you don't. Success or
failure.

WOMAN: You seem to have been very successful today.

MAN: Why shouldn't I be? It's a beautiful day. I can see to
those hills. The trees are cool. The sun is gentle. Ideal. If
a man can't be successful on a day like this, he might as
well kick the dust up into his own face. (MAN *notices*
WOMAN *staring at him.* MAN *pats his belly, looks at her)*
Protection from falls.

WOMAN: What? (MAN *touches his belly, showing some fat)* Oh.
Don't be silly.

(MAN begins slapping the fat on his belly to a rhythm)

MAN: Listen—I can make music—see? That wasn't always
possible. But now—that I've developed this—whenever I
need entertainment . . .

(He continues slapping)

WOMAN: You shouldn't make fun of your body.

MAN: Why not? I saw you. You were staring.

WOMAN: I wasn't making fun. I was just—stop that!

(He stops)

MAN: Then why were you staring?

WOMAN: I was . . .

MAN: Laughing?

WOMAN: No.

MAN: Well?

WOMAN: I was—your body. It's . . . strong.

(Pause)

MAN: People say that. But they don't know. I've heard that age brings wisdom. That's a laugh. The years don't accumulate here. They accumulate here. *(He pats his stomach)* But today is a day to be happy, right? The woods. The sun. Blue. It's a happy day. I'm going to chop wood.

WOMAN: There's nothing left to chop. Look.

MAN: Oh. I guess . . . that's it.

WOMAN: Sit. Here.

MAN: But . . .

WOMAN: There's nothing left. Learn to love it.

MAN: Don't be ridiculous.

WOMAN: Touch it.

MAN: It's flabby.

WOMAN: It's strong.

MAN: It's weak.

WOMAN: And smooth.

MAN: Do you mind if I put on my shirt?

WOMAN: Of course not. Shall I get it for you?

MAN: No. No. Just sit there. *(Picks up his shirt. He pauses, studies his body)* You think it's cute, huh?

WOMAN: I think you should learn to love it.

(Man pats his belly)

MAN: *(To belly)* You're okay, sir. You hang onto my body like a great horseman.

WOMAN: Not like that.

MAN: *(Still to belly)* You're also faithful. You'll never leave me for another man.

WOMAN: No.

MAN: What do you want me to say?

   (WOMAN leans over to MAN. *She touches his belly with her hand)*

Scene 4

Night. MAN *is alone. Flowers are gone from stand. Mat is unrolled.* MAN *lies on it, sleeping. Suddenly, he starts, awakened by the sound of the* shakuhatchi. *He sits up and grabs his sword, then relaxes as he recognizes the instrument. He crosses to a screen and listens, then returns to the mat and sits. He takes out the stolen flower. He stares into it.*

Scene 5

Day. WOMAN *is cleaning while* MAN *exercises. She is on her hands and knees, scrubbing the floor.*

MAN: I heard your playing last night.

WOMAN: My playing?

MAN: *Shakuhatchi.*

WOMAN: Oh.

MAN: You played very softly. I had to strain to hear it. Next time don't be afraid. Play out. Fully. Clear. It must've been very beautiful, if only I could've heard it clearly. Why don't you play for me sometime?

WOMAN: I'm very shy about it.

MAN: Why?

WOMAN: I play for my own satisfaction. That's all. It's something I developed on my own. I don't know if it's at all acceptable by outside standards.

MAN: Play for me. I'll tell you.

WOMAN: No, I'm sure you're too knowledgeable in the arts.

MAN: Who? Me?

WOMAN: You being from the city and all.

MAN: I'm ignorant, believe me.

WOMAN: I'd play, and you'd probably bite your cheek.

MAN: Ask me a question about music. Any question. I'll answer incorrectly. I guarantee it.

WOMAN: *(Looking at the floor)* Look at this.

MAN: What?

WOMAN: A stain.

MAN: Where?

WOMAN: Here? See? I can't get it out.

MAN: Oh. I hadn't noticed it before.

WOMAN: I notice it every time I clean.

MAN: Here. Let me try.

WOMAN: Thank you.

MAN: Ugh. It's tough.

WOMAN: I know.

MAN: How did it get here?

WOMAN: It's been there as long as I've lived here.

MAN: I hardly stand a chance. *(Pause)* But I'll try. One—two—three—four! One—two—three—four! See, you set up . . . gotta set up . . . a rhythm—two—three—four. Used to practice with a rhythm. One—two—three—four.

Yes, remember. Like battle . . . like fighting, one—two—three—four. One—two—three—four. *(The stain starts to fade away)* Look . . . there it goes . . . got the sides . . . the edges . . . fading away . . . fading quick . . . toward the center to the heart . . . two—three—four. One—two—three—four—dead!

WOMAN: Dead.

MAN: I got it! I got it! A little rhythm! All it took! Four! Four!

WOMAN: Thank you.

MAN: I didn't think I could do it . . . but there—it's gone—I did it!

WOMAN: Yes. You did.

MAN: And you—you were great.

WOMAN: No—I just watched.

MAN: We were a team! You and me!

WOMAN: I only provided encouragement.

MAN: You were great! You were!

   (MAN grabs WOMAN. Pause)

WOMAN: It's gone. Thank you. Would you like to hear me play *Shakuhatchi*?

MAN: Yes I would.

WOMAN: I don't usually play for visitors. It's so . . . I'm not sure. I developed it—all by myself—in times when I was alone. I heard nothing . . . The air began to be oppressive—stale. So I learned to play *Shakuhatchi*. I learned to make sounds on it. I tried to make these sounds resemble the human voice. The *Shakuhatchi* became my weapon. It kept me from choking on many a silent evening.

MAN: I'm here. You can hear my voice.

WOMAN: Speak again.

MAN: I will.

Scene 6

Night. MAN *is sleeping. Suddenly, a start. He lifts his head up. He listens. The shakuhatchi melody rises up once more. This time, however, it becomes louder and more clear than before. He gets up. He cannot tell from what direction the music is coming. It seems to come from all directions at once, as omnipresent as the air. Slowly, he moves toward the wall with the sliding panel through which the woman enters and exits. He puts his ear against it, thinking the music may be coming from there. Slowly, he slides the door open just a crack, ever so carefully. He peeks through the crack. As he peeks through, the upstage wall of the set becomes transparent, and through the scrim, we are able to see what he sees.* WOMAN *is upstage of the scrim. She is carrying the vase of flowers in front of her as she moves slowly through the cubicles upstage of the scrim. She is also transformed. She is beautiful. She wears a brightly colored kimono.* MAN *observes this scene for a long time. He then slides the door shut. The scrim returns to opaque. The music continues. He returns to his mat. He picks up the stolen flower. It is brown and wilted, dead. He looks at it, throws it down. The music slowly fades out.*

Scene 7

Morning. MAN *is practicing sword maneuvers. He practices with the feel of a man whose spirit is willing but flesh is inept. He tries to execute deft movements but is dissatisfied with his efforts.*

Suddenly, he feels something buzzing around his neck—a mosquito. He slaps his neck, but misses it. He sees it flying near him. He swipes at it with his sword. He keeps missing. Finally, he thinks he's hit it. He runs over, kneels down to recover the fallen insect. He picks up the two halves of the mosquito on two different fingers. WOMAN *enters the room. She looks as she normally does. She is carrying a vase of flowers, which she places on its shelf.*

MAN: Look.

WOMAN: I'm sorry?

MAN: Look.

WOMAN: What?

   (He brings over the two halves of the mosquito to show her)

MAN: See?

WOMAN: Oh.

MAN: I hit it—chop!

WOMAN: These are new forms of target practice?

MAN: Huh? Well—yes—in a way.

WOMAN: You seem to do well at it.

MAN: Thank you. For last night. I heard your *shakuhatchi*. It was very loud, strong—good tone.

WOMAN: Did you enjoy it? I wanted you to enjoy it. If you wish, I'll play it for you every night.

MAN: Every night!

WOMAN: If you wish.

MAN: No—I don't—I don't want you to treat me like a baby.

WOMAN: What? I'm not.

MAN: Oh, yes. Like a baby who you must feed in the middle of the night or he cries. Waaah! Waaah!

WOMAN: Stop that!

MAN: You need your sleep.

WOMAN: I don't mind getting up for you. *(Pause)* I would enjoy playing for you. Every night. While you sleep. It will make me feel . . . like I'm shaping your dreams. I go through long stretches when there is no one in my dreams. It's terrible. During those times, I avoid my bed as much as possible. I paint. I weave. I play *shakuhatchi*. I sit on mats and rub powder into my face. Anything to keep from facing a bed with no dreams. It is like sleeping on ice.

MAN: What do you dream of now?

WOMAN: Last night—I dreamt of you. I don't remember what happened. But you were very funny. Not in a mocking way. I wasn't laughing at you. But you made me laugh. And you were very warm. I remember that. *(Pause)* What do you remember about last night?

MAN: Just your playing. That's all. I got up, listened to it, and went back to sleep.

(Gets up, resumes practicing with his sword)

WOMAN: Another mosquito bothering you?

MAN: Just practicing. Ah! Weak! Too weak! I tell you, it wasn't always like this. I'm telling you, there were days when I could chop the fruit from a tree without ever taking my eyes off the ground. *(Continuing to practice with his sword)* You ever use one of these?

WOMAN: I've had to pick one up, yes.

MAN: Oh?

WOMAN: You forget . . . I live alone . . . out here . . . there is . . . not much to sustain me but what I manage to learn myself. It wasn't really a matter of choice.

MAN: I used to be very good, you know. Perhaps I can give you some pointers.

WOMAN: I'd really rather not.

MAN: C'mon—a woman like you—you're absolutely right. You need to know how to defend yourself.

WOMAN: As you wish.

MAN: Do you have something to practice with?

WOMAN: Yes. Excuse me. *(She exits. She reenters with two wooden sticks)* Will these do?

MAN: Fine. *(He takes one)* Nice. Now, show me what you can do.

WOMAN: I'm sorry?

MAN: Run up and hit me.

WOMAN: Please.

MAN: Go on—I'll block it.

WOMAN: I feel so . . . undignified.

MAN: Go on! *(She taps him playfully)* Not like that! C'mon!

WOMAN: I'll try to be gentle.

MAN: What?

WOMAN: I don't want to hurt you.

MAN: You won't. Hit me!

(WOMAN charges at MAN, quickly, deftly. She scores a hit)

WOMAN: Did I hurt you?

MAN: No—let's try that again.

(They square off again. WOMAN rushes forward. He blocks an apparent strike. She rushes in for another. She scores)

WOMAN: Did I hurt you? I'm sorry.

MAN: No.

WOMAN: I hurt you.

MAN: Don't be ridiculous!

WOMAN: Do you wish to hit me?

MAN: No.

WOMAN: Do you want me to try again?

MAN: No. Just practice there—by yourself—let me see you run through some maneuvers.

WOMAN: Must I?

MAN: Yes! Go! *(WOMAN goes to an open area)* My greatest strength always was as a teacher.

(WOMAN executes a series of movements. Her whole manner is transformed. MAN watches with increasing amazement. Her movements end. She regains her submissive manner)

WOMAN: I'm so embarrassed. My skills—they're so—inappropriate. I look like a man.

MAN: Where did you learn that?

WOMAN: There is much time to practice here.

MAN: But you—the techniques . . .

WOMAN: I don't know what's fashionable in the outside world. *(Pause)* Are you unhappy?

MAN: No.

WOMAN: Really?

MAN: I'm just . . . surprised.

WOMAN: You think it's unbecoming for a woman.

MAN: No, no. Not at all.

WOMAN: You want to leave.

MAN: No!

WOMAN: All visitors do. I know. I've met many. They say they'll stay. And they do. For a while. Until they see too much. Or they learn something new. There are boundaries outside of which visitors do not want to see me step. Only who knows what those boundaries are? Not I. They change with every visitor. You have to be careful not to cross them, but you never know where they are. And one day, inevitably, you step outside the lines. The visitor knows. You don't. You didn't know that you'd done anything different. You thought it was just another part of you. The visitor sneaks away. The next day, you learn that you had stepped outside his heart. I'm afraid you've seen too much.

MAN: There are stories.

WOMAN: What?

MAN: People talk.

WOMAN: Where? We're two days from the nearest village.

MAN: Word travels.

WOMAN: What are you talking about?

MAN: There are stories about you. I heard them. They say that your visitors never leave this house.

WOMAN: That's what you heard?

MAN: They say you imprison them.

WOMAN: Then you were a fool to come here.

MAN: Listen.

WOMAN: Me? Listen? You. Look! Where are these prisoners? Have you seen any?

MAN: They told me you were very beautiful.

WOMAN: Then they are blind as well as ignorant.

MAN: You are.

WOMAN: What?

MAN: Beautiful.

WOMAN: Stop that! My skin feels like seaweed.

MAN: I didn't realize it at first. I must confess. I didn't. But over these few days—your face has changed for me. The shape of it. The feel of it. The color. All changed. I look at you now and I am no longer sure you are the same woman who had poured tea for me just a week ago. And because of that I remember—how little I know about a face that changes in the night. *(Pause)* Have you heard those stories?

WOMAN: I don't listen to old wives tales.

MAN: But have you heard them?

WOMAN: Yes. I've heard them. From other visitors—young—hotblooded—or old—who came here because they were told great glory was to be had by killing the witch in the woods.

MAN: I was told that no man could spend time in this house without falling in love.

WOMAN: Oh? So why did you come? Did you wager gold that you could come out untouched? The outside world is so flattering to me. And you—are you like the rest? Passion passing through your heart so powerfully that you can't hold onto it?

MAN: No! I'm afraid.

WOMAN: Of what?

MAN: Sometimes—when I look into the flowers, I think I hear a voice—from inside—a voice beneath the petals. A human voice.

WOMAN: What does it say? "Let me out"?

MAN: No. Listen. It hums. It hums with the peacefulness of one who is completely imprisoned.

WOMAN: I understand that if you listen closely enough, you can hear the ocean.

MAN: No. Wait. Look at it. See the layers? Each petal—hiding the next. Try and see where they end . . . You can't. Follow them down, further down, around and as you come down—faster and faster—the breeze picks up. The breeze becomes a wail. And in that rush of air—you can hear a voice.

(WOMAN grabs flower from MAN)

WOMAN: So, you believe I water and prune my lovers? How can you be so foolish? *(She throws the flower to the ground)* Do you come only to leave again? To take a chunk of my heart, then leave with your booty on your belt, like a prize? You say that I imprison hearts in these flowers? Well, bits of my heart are trapped with travelers across this land. I can't even keep track. So kill me. If you came here to destroy a witch, kill me now. I can't stand to have it happen again.

(MAN begins to pull out sword—cannot use it)

MAN: I won't leave you.

WOMAN: I believe you.

Scene 8

Day. Woman is modeling her kimono.

WOMAN: Do you like it?

MAN: Yes, it's beautiful.

WOMAN: I wanted to wear something special today.

MAN: It's beautiful. (MAN *takes out his sword*) Excuse me. I must practice.

WOMAN: Shall I get you something?

MAN: No.

WOMAN: Some tea, maybe?

MAN: No, thank you. (*He resumes swordplay*)

WOMAN: Perhaps later today—perhaps we can go out—just around here. We can look for flowers.

MAN: All right.

WOMAN: We don't have to.

MAN: No. Let's.

WOMAN: I just thought if . . .

MAN: Fine. Where do you want to go?

WOMAN: There are very few recreational activities around here, I know.

MAN: All right. We'll go this afternoon.

(*Pause*)

WOMAN: Can I get you something?

MAN: What?

WOMAN: You might be . . .

MAN: I'm not hungry or thirsty or cold or hot.

WOMAN: Then what are you?

MAN: Practicing.

(MAN *resumes practicing; woman exits.* MAN *sits down. He examines his sword, thinks. He stands up. He places the sword on the ground with the tip pointed directly upward. He keeps it from falling by placing the tip under his chin. He experiments with different degrees of pressure.* WOMAN *reenters. She sees him in this precarious position*)

WOMAN: Don't do that!

MAN: What?

WOMAN: You can hurt yourself!

MAN: I was practicing!

WOMAN: You were playing!

MAN: I was practicing!

WOMAN: It's dangerous.

MAN: What do you take me for—a child?

WOMAN: Sometimes wise men do childish things.

MAN: I knew what I was doing!

WOMAN: It scares me.

MAN: Don't be ridiculous.

WOMAN: Don't! Don't do that!

MAN: Get back!

WOMAN: But . . . .

MAN: Ssssh!

WOMAN: I wish . . .

MAN: Listen to me! The slightest shock, you know—the slightest shock—surprise—it might make me jerk or—something—and then . . . So you must be perfectly still and quiet.

WOMAN: But I . . .

MAN: Ssssh! *(Silence, then . . .)* I learned this exercise from a friend—I can't even remember his name—good swordsman—many years ago. He called it his meditation position. He said, like this, he could feel the line between this world and the others because he rested on it. If he saw something in another world that he liked better, all he would have to do is let his head drop, and he'd be there. Simple. No fuss. One day, they found him with the tip of his sword run clean out the back of his neck. He was smiling. I guess he saw something he liked. Or else he'd fallen asleep.

WOMAN: Stop that.

MAN: Stop what?

WOMAN: Tormenting me.

MAN: I'm not.

WOMAN: Take it away!

MAN: You don't have to watch, you know.

WOMAN: Do you want to die that way—an accident?

MAN: I was doing this before you came in.

WOMAN: If you do, all you need to do is tell me.

MAN: What?

WOMAN: I can walk right over. Lean on the back of your head.

MAN: Don't try to threaten . . .

WOMAN: Or jerk your sword up.

MAN: . . . or scare me. You can't threaten . . .

WOMAN: I'm not. But if that's what you want.

MAN: You wouldn't do it.

WOMAN: Oh?

MAN: Then I'd be gone. You wouldn't let me leave that easily.

WOMAN: Yes, I would.

MAN: You'd be alone.

WOMAN: No. I'd follow you. Forever. *(Pause)* Now, let's stop this nonsense.

MAN: No! I can do what I want! Don't come any closer!

WOMAN: Then release your sword.

MAN: Come any closer and I'll drop my head.

*(*WOMAN *slowly approaches* MAN. *She grabs the sword. She pulls it out from under his chin)*

WOMAN: There will be no more of this.

(She exits with the sword. He starts to follow her, then stops. He touches under his chin. On his finger, he finds a drop of blood)

Scene 9

Night. MAN *is leaving the house. He is just about out when he hears a* shakuhatchi *playing.* WOMAN *appears in the doorway to the outside.*

WOMAN: It's time for you to go?

MAN: Yes. I'm sorry.

WOMAN: You're just going to sneak out? A thief in the night? A frightened child?

MAN: I care about you.

WOMAN: You express it strangely.

MAN: I leave in shame because it is proper. *(Pause)* I came seeking glory.

WOMAN: To kill me? You can say it. You'll be surprised at how little I blanch. As if you'd said, "I came for a bowl of rice," or "I came seeking love," or "I came to kill you."

MAN: Weakness. All weakness. Too weak to kill you. Too weak to kill myself. Too weak to do anything but sneak away in shame.

(WOMAN brings out MAN's sword)

WOMAN: Were you even planning to leave without this? *(He takes sword)* Why not stay here?

MAN: I can't live with someone who's defeated me.

WOMAN: I never thought of defeating you. I only wanted to take care of you. To make you happy. Because that made me happy and I was no longer alone.

MAN: You defeated me.

WOMAN: Why do you think that way?

MAN: I came here with a purpose. The world was clear. You changed the shape of your face, the shape of my heart— rearranged everything—created a world where I could do nothing.

WOMAN: I only tried to care for you.

MAN: I guess that was all it took.

(Pause)

WOMAN: You still think I'm a witch. Just because old women gossip. You are so cruel. Once you arrived, there were only two possibilities: I would die or you would leave. *(Pause)* If you believe I'm a witch, then kill me. Rid the province of one more evil.

MAN: I can't—

WOMAN: Why not? If you believe that about me, then it's the right thing to do.

MAN: You know I can't.

WOMAN: Then stay.

MAN: Don't try to force me!

WOMAN: I won't force you to do anything. *(Pause)* All I wanted was an escape—for both of us. The sound of a human voice—the simplest thing to find, and the hardest to hold on to. This house—my loneliness is etched into the walls. Kill me, but don't leave. Even in death, my spirit would rest here and be comforted by your presence.

MAN: Force me to stay.

WOMAN: I won't. *(MAN starts to leave)* Beware.

MAN: Of what?

WOMAN: The ground on which you walk is weak. It could give way at any moment. The crevice beneath is dark.

MAN: Are you talking about death? I'm ready to die.

WOMAN: Fear for what is worse than death.

MAN: What?

WOMAN: Falling. Falling through the darkness. Waiting to hit the ground. Picking up speed. Waiting for the ground. Falling faster. Falling alone. Waiting. Falling. Waiting. Falling.

(WOMAN goes out through the door to her room. MAN reenters from the outside. He looks for her in the main room. He goes to the mat, sees the shakuhatchi. *He puts down his sword, takes*

off his bundle and coat. He goes inside. He comes out. He goes to the mat, picks up the shakuhatchi, *clutches it to him. He moves everything else off the mat, sits, and puts the* shakuhatchi *to his mouth. He begins to blow into it. He tries to make sounds. He continues trying through the end of the play.)*

(The upstage scrim lights up. Upstage, we see the woman. She is hanging from a rope suspended from the roof. She has hung herself. Around her swirl the thousands of petals from the flowers. They fill the upstage scrim area like a blizzard of color.)

*(*MAN *continues to attempt to play.* LIGHTS FADE TO BLACK*)*

CURTAIN

RICH RELATIONS

To Lenore

Rich Relations was produced by The Second Stage, Carole Rothman and Robyn Goodman, artistic directors, where it opened on April 21, 1986, with the following cast:

HINSON .... Joe Silver
KEITH.............................. Keith Szarabajka
JILL .... Phoebe Cates
BARBARA .... Susan Kellermann
MARILYN.......................... Johann Carlo

Directed by Harry Kondoleon; sets by Kevin Rupnik; lighting by Pat Collins; costumes by Candice Donnelly; Robin Rumpf was production stage manager.

CHARACTERS

HINSON, male, early fifties.
KEITH, his son, late twenties.
JILL, Keith's girlfriend, sixteen.
BARBARA, Hinson's younger sister, late forties.
MARILYN, Barbara's daughter, early twenties.

TIME

Present.

PLACE

The second living room of a large home in the hills above
Los Angeles.

SYNOPSIS OF SCENES

Act One, Scene 1. Evening.
Act One, Scene 2. Morning of the following day.
Act Two. Dusk and evening of that same day.

ACT ONE

Scene 1

The second living room of a large home in the hills above Los Angeles. The upstage wall is covered with floor-to-ceiling picture windows through which we see a spectacular view of the L.A. basin at night. A set of glass doors upstage open onto a balcony with a railing, which hangs out over the city. There are two other doors: One leads outside to the driveway, the other onto a hallway which connects to the rest of the house. A huge television faces upstage. The room is littered with numerous high-tech appliances— VCRs, stereos, telephones, etc.

On an easy chair sits KEITH, *twenty-nine, leaning back, eyes closed. He is dressed in an East Coast preppy style. Next to him is an overstuffed suitcase.* HINSON, *a man in his early fifties, sits on the couch wearing a monogrammed red velvet bathrobe and slippers. He holds a remote control unit in his hands and leans toward the TV, changing stations.*

HINSON: *(To TV)* Hello? Hello? Can you hear me? *(Pause)* Wait. *(He punches a button on the remote control. From the TV speakers, we hear a telephone dial tone)* OK. Watch this. Keith, are you watching?

(KEITH's eyes remain closed)

KEITH: Yeah. I'm watching.

HINSON: No, you're not. You got your eyes closed. How can you be watching?

KEITH: With my ears.

215

HINSON: What? What's that?

KEITH: I'm watching with my ears.

HINSON: What's that supposed to mean?

KEITH: Look—I'm tired, my eyes hurt.

HINSON: I'm showing you something important!

KEITH: The air on planes—it's dry.

HINSON: I'm sorry about that.

KEITH: So I'll just listen. That's a dial tone. Why do I have
to look?

HINSON: Find out! C'mon—open your eyes!

(KEITH opens his eyes)

HINSON: See?

KEITH: What's that?

HINSON: Now, watch. When I dial the number, you can see
it on the TV.

KEITH: Why would anyone want to do this?

HINSON: Watch. 283-40—see?

KEITH: I see.

HINSON: Beautiful, isn't it, Keith?

KEITH: Why can't you use a phone like everyone else?

HINSON: Look!

KEITH: Why do you have to talk into your TV?

(Over the television speaker, we hear the ringing of a telephone)

HINSON: See? Isn't that beautiful?

KEITH: I mean, why don't you just use a phone?

HINSON: This *is* a phone! That's the beauty!

*(Over the television speaker, we hear the "click" of a phone
being answered, then a very weak and tinny-sounding male
voice)*

HINSON: *(To TV)* Hello? Hello?

VOICE: Hello?

HINSON: Fred?

FRED: Hello? Is anyone there? Who is—?

HINSON: Fred, it's me. Hinson. I—

FRED: What? Speak up.

HINSON: It's Hinson!

FRED: Hinson?

HINSON: Yeah. Isn't this beau—

FRED: What?

HINSON: *(Screaming)* Isn't this beautiful!

FRED: Hinson, you sound like you're at the bottom of a sewer!

HINSON: No, I'm talking through my TV!
   (Pause)

FRED: Look, we got a really bad connection.

HINSON: I said, I'm talking through my TV!

KEITH: Dad, will you just pick up the phone?

FRED: Your TV?

HINSON: Yes, yes! My TV!
   (Pause)

FRED: How come?

HINSON: It's a modern convenience.

KEITH: This is ridiculous!
   (KEITH picks up the phone. As he speaks into it, his voice blares over the TV speaker, with feedback)

KEITH: Uncle Fred?

HINSON: *(To KEITH)* Hey! Careful! What do you want to do?

KEITH: Turn it off!

HINSON. *(Turning off TV)* You break the speaker that way.

KEITH: This is Keith.

HINSON: A modern device, and you abuse it.

KEITH: Yeah. I'm back in L.A. No real reason—just felt like a visit. *(Beat)* Probably a week—maybe longer—we'll see.
   (HINSON turns the TV back on)

HINSON: Fred—I just got the TV.

FRED: Hinson? Bring it back.

HINSON: This is state-of-the-art stuff.

FRED: See you Sunday, Keith?

KEITH: At church? Yeah. Probably.

FRED: OK. Bye, Keith. Hinson, get rid of that thing.
(*Dial tone*)

HINSON: What does he know? Small thinker, Fred. Very
jealous. (HINSON *turns off the TV*)
Hey, I also got one in my car—it's a new thing.

KEITH: A TV?

HINSON: No. A phone.

KEITH: That's not so new. I've been seeing them in movies
for years.

HINSON: Movies? This is real life. You want to see my spy
pens?

KEITH: No, thanks. I don't want to be overwhelmed.

HINSON: You know, your Uncle Fred—he may be a small
thinker, but he really likes you.

KEITH: Think so?

HINSON: He wants you to marry Marilyn.

KEITH: What?

HINSON: No—I'm telling you!

KEITH: That's ridiculous!

HINSON: It is one of the few times he has thought big!

KEITH: Dad—

HINSON: He's crazy. I know.

KEITH: —Marilyn is my cousin.

HINSON: I know. I told you, he's crazy.

KEITH: Why would he—?

HINSON: Oh—you don't know. After the kind of guys that
she goes out with, you would be like manna from heaven.

KEITH: What kind of guys—?

HINSON: And, then, you know, he—Fred—he also thinks
about being related to me.

KEITH: What?

HINSON: That would be a big thing for him.

KEITH: He's already related to you!

HINSON: What?

KEITH: He's already your brother-in-law!

HINSON: You see? Why do you think he married Barbara?

KEITH: Wait.

HINSON: You think for her looks? Of course not! Pleasant personality? Ha!

KEITH: Just hold on, OK?

HINSON: He saw there was an opportunity to get hooked up with some real money—

KEITH: Dad! Ssssh! *(Pause)*

OK. He's related to you right now. What difference would it make if I married Marilyn?

HINSON: Double relations!

KEITH: God, that's the stupidest—

HINSON: No, listen. Right now, he's only got my sister. OK, if they need money, sometimes I say yes, sometimes I say, let them work it out themselves. Sometimes I say, "Barbara, I know you're my sister, but shut up and go home." I say that. But with you—well, he knows I'll have to give you money if you ask.

KEITH: I never ask!

HINSON: If you married Marilyn, *then* you'd ask!

KEITH: You think everyone wants to marry me.

HINSON: They do.

KEITH: So they can be related to you.

HINSON: Not just that.

KEITH: But mostly.

HINSON: Don't sell yourself short, son. You're a good catch. Most men today—bums, derelicts, two steps above the gutter. No, really. I walk out there. Downtown. I go to lunch, I see them. They don't have good jobs, insurance, pensions—nothing. And even if they do, they don't have the good heart like you. They go out, sleep with everybody, fool around. Bad upbringing. Not like you. They didn't have your privileges. You have manners, dating is no big deal, you don't have funny thoughts about other men. That's rare today. You're a real catch, son.

(Pause)

KEITH: Well, I'd better unpack.

HINSON: Of course, they want to be related to me, too.

KEITH: We'll discuss this some other time.

HINSON: I mean, being related to a real estate baron.

KEITH: A—what?

HINSON: Son, I have to tell you this—

KEITH: Dad, I want to unpack.

HINSON: Just wait. Wait a second, OK? Last week, this client—I'm supposed to meet her. She's the daughter of a big shipping tycoon. This guy is worth—I don't know—thirty, forty million. I'm supposed to meet his daughter for lunch. She drives up—this big limousine—black—haaaa—one of those big antennas on back. She steps out—oh!—it's this young, pretty girl. Everyone in my office looks at her. I get into the limousine—into the back seat, right next to her. She's so beautiful. It makes my heart go—top speed. The car is driving—seventy, eighty down the freeway. And my heart is shaking—top speed. When it's all over, she looks at me and says, "Hinson, you're a baron."

KEITH: That's good. I'm glad you're dating.

HINSON: You know what I said to her?

KEITH: Dad, you don't have to tell me.

HINSON: You know? Just like this—I said, "What's a baron?"

KEITH: You don't know?

HINSON: She told me. She said, "A baron is like a king."

KEITH: Well, not exactly.

HINSON: So, I'm a real estate baron.

KEITH: It's lower than a king.

(Pause)

HINSON: So what?

KEITH: Nothing. I was just explaining—

HINSON: It's close enough. Once you get up there, who cares? King, baron—it's all good.

KEITH: That's true.

HINSON: So I'm having a sign made for my office: "Hinson Orr, Baron."

KEITH: What?

HINSON: You like that? I'm going to hang it over the light sculpture.

KEITH: But, see, "baron" has bad connotations.

HINSON: King? King has bad connotations?

KEITH: A baron's not a king!

HINSON: Why do you keep bringing that up?

KEITH: Baron implies you're shady.

HINSON: She called me shady?

KEITH: Not exactly.

HINSON: After what I did for her? In the back seat of her car? She calls me shady?

KEITH: It's not bad to be shady in business.

HINSON: You're right. It's not. Sometimes, you got to bend the rules a little. Not like in your world.

KEITH: But I wouldn't put it on my wall. You don't want to tip off your clients, do you?

HINSON: Why not? I want them to know I'm honest. If I'm shady, I tell them—right away.

(Pause)

KEITH: Just forget it. I gotta unpack.

HINSON: That's good. That you unpack first thing. Shows you're organized.

KEITH: I guess.

HINSON: Not like me. I never know when to unpack. I leave clothes in the suitcase. They get wrinkled, smelly.

KEITH: Why don't you take them out?

HINSON: I just can't. I had a bad upbringing.

KEITH: What does that have to do with it?

HINSON: Lots. We were brought up—like peons. Look at Barbara. You think that's a girl with social grace, class? Ha! She's lucky to get any husband at all, even an auto mechanic like Fred.

KEITH: OK, Dad.

HINSON: She's funny up here, Barbara.

KEITH: I'm going in, now.

HINSON: Me, too. It's late. For me—that's nine o'clock. Not like you, huh?

KEITH: Good night.

HINSON: Swinger.

KEITH: Dad!

HINSON: Why not come into my bedroom, we can chit-chat.

KEITH: We just did.

HINSON: More! You just got home!

KEITH: Dad, if I talk to you in bed, you always fall asleep.

HINSON: So? That's conversation. I'm your father—you should be happy to put me to sleep.

KEITH: Maybe tomorrow.

HINSON: OK. Well, good night.

KEITH: 'Night.

HINSON: Good to have my son home.

KEITH: Nice to be here.

(HINSON *exits*)

(KEITH *walks around the room, then exits out onto the driveway. He returns, propping up a young girl,* JILL, *very beautiful, sixteen years old. She wears jeans and a silk blouse, and, drowsy with sleep, she clutches a blanket*)

KEITH: Want a drink or anything?

(JILL *shakes her head wearily, curls up on the couch with her head in* KEITH's *lap, and goes back to sleep*) Jill? (*She doesn't budge*) We should go into the bedroom.

(*He picks up the remote control, turns on the TV, watches music videos*)

(FADE TO BLACK)

Scene 2

Day. JILL *is still asleep in* KEITH's *lap, the TV is still on.*
HINSON, *in a suit, stands in front of both of them.*

HINSON: Who's that?
KEITH: Sssh. Not so loud. She's an insomniac.
  (Pause)
HINSON: How did she get in the house? Did you forget to
  turn the burglar alarm on?
KEITH: She's a student. Could you turn off the TV?
  (He does)
HINSON: I thought you were going to sleep last night.
KEITH: I did.
HINSON: Here? With the TV on? That's not sleep.
KEITH: I fell asleep.
HINSON: You didn't lie down. If you don't lie down, it's
  rest.
KEITH: OK. So I rested.
HINSON: But you should've slept. Where'd she come from?
KEITH: Sssh! I told you—she's an insomniac.
HINSON: Then why's she asleep?
KEITH: She hadn't slept—
HINSON: Nothing wakes her up.
KEITH: —in days.
HINSON: How can she be insomniac?
KEITH: She was exhausted.
HINSON: Who is she?
KEITH: I told you—a student.
HINSON: Oh, oh. Right.
KEITH: Now go to work and—
HINSON: Where'd she come from?
KEITH: She was in the car.

HINSON: Whose car? My car?

KEITH: My car. The one I rented.

HINSON: She was there last night? While we were chit-chatting?

KEITH: Yeah.

HINSON: In the cold?

KEITH: Dad, it's seventy outside.

HINSON: I don't care. She could've come in here. Why didn't you—?

KEITH: I just didn't feel like introducing her right away, that's all.

HINSON: And this is better? I stare at her when she's asleep? Why didn't you ask her in? She'll think I'm cheap.

KEITH: What does cheap have to do with it?

HINSON: You make a guest stay outside in the car, that's cheap. You should invite them in, make coffee, show off the wallpaper!

(JILL *turns over, opens her eyes*)

JILL: What time is it? *(She sees* HINSON*)* Hi.

HINSON: Hi, there. It's six-thirty.

JILL: Six-thirty? That's so early . . .

HINSON: Not for me. I get up—

KEITH: Dad, this is Jill. Jill, my dad.

JILL: Hi, Mr. Orr.

HINSON: Jill? Nice to meet you.

JILL: I've heard a lot about you.

HINSON: Yeah? He talks about me?

JILL: Oh, all the time.

HINSON: I've never heard anything about you.

KEITH: *(To* JILL*)* Dad and I don't discuss personal details on the phone.

HINSON: What do you mean? I always ask, "What's new?"

JILL: This is quite a place you've got here.

HINSON: You like it?

JILL: It's great. Look at the view!

HINSON: Here. You don't have the full effect. *(He raises one of the blinds)* This home, you know—it wasn't just built by anyone.

KEITH: Dad?

HINSON: It was built by an architect. A man with inside knowledge.

KEITH: Shouldn't you be getting to work?

HINSON: What business is that for you to worry about?

KEITH: I just thought—

HINSON: The baron decides when to come and go.

JILL: *(Looking out window)* That's all L.A., huh? Wow— It really *is* a big wasteland.

HINSON: This is your first time here?

JILL: *(Nods)* I like the burrito stands at the airport. And then we passed these traffic lights that were made to look like hitching posts.

HINSON: Right. In Pacific Palisades.

JILL: Sharp. Definitely. Mr. Orr, I hope you didn't mind my staying here last night.

HINSON: Mind? Look at this place—it's huge! Stay as long as you like! *(Points to* KEITH*)* Him—he makes you wait in the car.

JILL: Oh—that was okay.

HINSON: Keith, did you see how they redid your room?

KEITH: No, I haven't been in there.

HINSON: Why not? Go now! Beautiful!

KEITH: Dad, I'll see it—

HINSON: Go! Go! It'll just take a second!

JILL: C'mon, Keith.

*(*KEITH *exits;* HINSON *turns to* JILL*)*

HINSON: Tell me something—uh-uh—

JILL: Jill.

HINSON: Can I call you Jill?

JILL: It's my name.

(Pause)

HINSON: Ha, ha. I like you, Jill.

JILL: I like you, too, Mr. Orr.

HINSON: Isn't that wonderful? Two seconds ago, we were strangers. Now, we're friends!

JILL: It helps that I'm dating your son.

HINSON: No doubt about it. But I tell you, I don't like all the girls he dates.

JILL: Well, who would? Keith's taste in girls is kinda—well, I mean, yuck-o!

HINSON: That's what I say. Did you ever meet Agnes?

JILL: Oh, he told me about her.

HINSON: Unbelievable! I said, "Son, this is the bottom of the barrel." But you—you're different. Classy.

JILL: That's really sweet.

HINSON: Tell me. Does he—does he talk a lot about me?

JILL: Oh, yeah. Can I see your spy pens?

HINSON: He tell you about all that?

JILL: And your TV watch. And your robot arm.

HINSON: Does he tell you about my business?

JILL: Sometimes.

HINSON: That's the best part! How I started from nothing but tuberculosis? Does he tell you about my great love for God? *(Pause)* Here—let me show you. This is our last shareholder's report. Beautiful, huh? See? The eagle. The theme is, "God bless America." Here—see?—the lyrics to the song. And here's my bio.

JILL: That's a really nice picture.

HINSON: Yeah? You like it? See?—"With God's help, he rose from the dead in 1948 to attend the University of Southern California."

JILL: You must've really wanted to go to college.

HINSON: I had TB. Doctors said, "No hope," but I prayed to God, "Save my life and I will be a shining light for thee." I thought I was dead, but then I saw this light— aaaah!—so bright. And this hand reached out to me. When I took it, it was not a ghost, but one of my sisters.

Then, I knew—God had answered my prayers. *(Pause)* Look at my hands—just look at them.

JILL: What?

HINSON: They say I'm supposed to be dead. But I'm not. I had too much personal initiative.

(KEITH enters)

HINSON: Do you like your new room?

KEITH: What new room? It looks exactly the same.

HINSON: The curtains! Didn't you see the curtains?

KEITH: What curtains?

HINSON: They must've been up.

KEITH: I guess, 'cuz I didn't—

HINSON: So, let them down!

KEITH: Dad, I'll do it later.

JILL: We're doing fine here, Keith.

HINSON: Hear that? *(KEITH exits)* So, what do you do?

JILL: I'm in high school.

HINSON: Right, right—he told me. Keith's school, huh? You must be a smartie.

JILL: No. I don't like school.

HINSON: Hey—that's like me! I had terrible grades. The worst.

JILL: My grades are OK, I just hate school.

HINSON: It was my upbringing.

JILL: Oh.

HINSON: But look where I am today.

JILL: I'm on Keith's debate team. *(Pause)* It was winter when we met. One night, we were cutting research in my room. No big deal. I mean, he bought beer for the boys and blew kisses at the girls—I couldn't take the guy seriously. But there we were in my room. It was cold that night. The wind was crazy. All these strange sounds out there—doors slamming shut, tiles ripped off roofs, and a lot of things I couldn't remember ever hearing before. I looked out the window. It was white, completely white—I couldn't see past the snow, beyond, to what was making all that noise. Keith said, "I'm from California. I'm still not used to snow." I wanted to laugh. Like "Is that your idea of a line?" But instead, I looked outside. The wind blew right through the room. And I pulled him to me in a flash. Then everything that wasn't nailed down flew out the window. I was pulling him back from the storm. All I could hear was the rush of wind, my teeth chattering, and my heart laughing away. *(Pause)*

HINSON: Yeah. It makes your heart go—so fast. Like you think you might die. The same thing happened to me. Last week. In a limousine. I thought I was going to die. And I did. But I came back. And she called me a baron.

(KEITH enters)

KEITH: They're not curtains, they're blinds.

HINSON: You like them?

KEITH: Well, yeah, but—

HINSON: Beautiful, huh?

KEITH: I mean, they're not so unusual.

HINSON: Why's everything have to be unusual? They're classic.

JILL: I asked your father about his spy pens.

HINSON: I like her, Keith.

KEITH: Oh. Great.

HINSON: Yeah. She's . . . *(To JILL)* I just go on my gut feelings.

JILL: Me, too. I like that, too.

HINSON: I see someone, I know in a second. I love them or I hate them.

KEITH: He never changes his mind.

HINSON: Like this one girl he used to date—Margie.

KEITH: Dad, there's no need to dredge up the past.

HINSON: Face like this. Sad.

JILL: Yeah.

HINSON: I could tell—she'd be the one to commit suicide one day.

JILL: And she did?

HINSON: Well, no. Not yet. But someday— You really want to see the spy pens?

JILL: Sure. It'd be fun.

KEITH: No wonder he likes you.

HINSON: What's wrong with that? She's interested in technology. Progress. American spirit.

(HINSON *exits*)

KEITH: You two seem to be getting along.

JILL: Your dad's cute.

KEITH: That's bizarre. I never think of my dad as being attractive to women. But everyone tells me so.

JILL: He's—you know—open. Confident. That's hard to find in guys.

KEITH: Guys your age.

JILL: Guys your age, too.

(HINSON *reenters with a large cardboard crate*)

HINSON: Here they are.

KEITH: You bought a whole boxload?

HINSON: I figured, you never know when they'll come in handy. I was on a business trip to Hong Kong. One dollar ninety-eight each. A steal. That's how much you pay here for pens that can't do anything but write.

(JILL *takes one out of the box*)

KEITH: They don't look like much.

HINSON: That's the beauty of it. What good is a spy pen that looks like a spy pen, huh?

JILL: He's right.

KEITH: And these things work?

HINSON: Sure they work! I use them to spy on my employees. (*To* JILL) That's what business is like.

JILL: Oh, I know.

HINSON: Shady.

KEITH: So, you catch anyone yet?

HINSON: Well, no—not yet. I don't—I don't really get it. That's why I was hoping Keith—he's good at these electronic—

JILL: Him?

KEITH: Dad, I'm totally inept at these kinds of things!

JILL: He is.

HINSON: Maybe. But he has a good heart.

KEITH: What's that got to do with—?

HINSON: You never know. Sometimes, a good heart, it can—it just—look, I need another opinion. Watch this. *(HINSON turns on the radio)* You turn to FM 106.7. Is that right?

KEITH: I think so.

HINSON: OK. Now you unscrew the top just a little—like this. *(They each pick up a pen, unscrew the cap)* Now, if you talk into the pen, we should hear it on the radio. *(To pen)* Hello? Hello?

KEITH: Hello? Hello? Jill, can you hear us? *(JILL crouches next to the stereo speakers)* Hello?

HINSON: *(To pen)* "Fourscore and seven years ago . . ."

JILL: I can't tell what I'm hearing. Keith, why don't you go into the next room?

HINSON: That's a good idea.

KEITH: All right.

HINSON: Because my employees—they're in other rooms when I spy on them.

KEITH: Yes—this simulates actual working conditions. *(KEITH exits)*

HINSON: *(To JILL)* He likes to joke with us.

JILL: *(To KEITH, Offstage)* OK. Start talking! *(Nothing on the radio but static)* I don't—

HINSON: Turn it up. Turn up the volume.

JILL: *(To KEITH)* Keep talking!

HINSON: Louder. Louder.

JILL: Maybe we're on the wrong channel.

(She flips the dial; stations come on and off at full blast)

HINSON: Wait. *(To* KEITH*)* Keith, we can't hear you!

KEITH: *(Offstage)* Sorry! I'm talking into the pen!

HINSON: There! I heard him!

JILL: But—

HINSON: *(To* KEITH*)* Keep talking!

JILL: But he's not on the speakers.

HINSON: *(To* KEITH*)* Louder! We're losing you! Louder!

KEITH: *(Offstage, screaming)* Testing!! Testing!!

HINSON: Wonderful. Beautiful.

JILL: Mr. Orr—see, it's not coming from the speakers.

HINSON: Huh?

KEITH: *(Offstage)* One! Two! Three! Four!!

JILL: It's not—

(She turns off the radio)

KEITH: *(Offstage)* Testing! Hello!!

HINSON: Oh.

JILL: Sorry.

KEITH: *(Offstage)* One! Two!!

HINSON: Dumb.

KEITH: *(Offstage)* Three! Four!!

JILL: Keith! Forget it!

HINSON: Dumb. That Hong King guy—he gyped me. It worked in the store.

(KEITH enters, clutching his throat)

KEITH: When they tell secrets, make sure they're screaming real loud.

HINSON: Dumb. Dumb guy.

KEITH: Who's dumb?

(Pause)

HINSON: Aaah, that's business, I guess. Sometimes, you eat. Sometimes, you get eaten.

JILL: You can still use them to write.

(She uncaps one, tries writing)

HINSON: I'll give them to my clients as gifts. It worked in the store. That guy—I gotta hand it to him.

KEITH: They don't write.

JILL: Gimme another one.

HINSON: I spent a whole year listening to static for nothing.

KEITH: Dad, they don't even write.

(Pause)

HINSON: What a guy. If I ever open a Hong Kong office, he'll be my top man. Well, I better get going to the office. Gotta set a good example for my employees. *(To* JILL*)* You going to be here a few days?

JILL: If it's OK with you.

HINSON: OK? I love to have people around! Otherwise, this showcase feels empty. *(*HINSON *exits, then returns, picks up crate)* Guess I'll give them away anyway. No one expects free pens to write.

(He exits with the crate)

JILL: So, which room is going to be mine?

KEITH: Well, I thought you could stay with me.

JILL: Under the same roof as your father? Keith, don't you have any shame?

KEITH: I mean, if you want, there's a few guest rooms.

JILL: Good. You think your dad will give me some money to redecorate?

KEITH: What?

JILL: Oh, just a whim. Forget I even brought it up.

KEITH: How long do you intend to stay here?

JILL: How long do you intend to stay here? A while, I bet, since you're kinda short on options.

KEITH: Wait, wait, wait. I thought you were just coming for the weekend. *(*JILL *turns the TV on, watches music videos)* When I told you yesterday I was leaving, you said you'd come along for the weekend.

JILL: Yeah, I did.

KEITH: Good. I'm glad we agree on that.

JILL: When you're right, you're right.

KEITH: 'Cuz with everything that's happened—

JILL: But, then—

KEITH: I thought I was going crazy for a second.

JILL: —why did I leave my folks a note saying I was running away forever?

KEITH: What? You left what? You were going to tell them you were staying at Amy's for the weekend!

JILL: You know, Keith, there's only one conclusion we can reach here.

KEITH: That's what you told me!

JILL: I guess I lied.

KEITH: What? How could you—?

JILL: You're right. That's was awful. Here— I'm leaving.

KEITH: Wait! What? Where are you going?

JILL: Back to my stupid parents.

KEITH: You're going to leave me alone with my Dad?

JILL: Isn't that what you want?

KEITH: No! I—I want . . .

JILL: Then I can stay?

KEITH: Why do you do this? If you want to stay, why don't you just ask? Why do you have to run around me in circles?

JILL: You would've said no.

KEITH: Of course I would've said no! You're a minor! If they catch me—especially after that letter I wrote—they'll lock me up.

JILL: See? You're already backing down.

KEITH: Who wouldn't? I just wrote a letter to the headmaster that'll ruin my career for life, expose me to criminal charges, and ensure that everyone in Connecticut thinks I'm a pervert! And now, they catch me in L.A. with my runaway student? I'm not completely stupid!

(Pause)

JILL: I don't think you're a pervert.

KEITH: That's why they have laws. Look, I'll call up your mom, tell her . . . tell her . . . something . . .

JILL: You're going to explain this to my mom? That I'm 3,000 miles from home? With you?

KEITH: I can be very persuasive. I'm a debate coach, aren't I?

JILL: Keith, my mother could take on a wrestling coach.

KEITH: *(Into phone)* Hello? *(He yells into receiver)* Hello! *(To* JILL*)* Someone picked up the phone, but all I hear is your TV.

JILL: I don't think mom watches videos.

KEITH: *(To* JILL*)* Turn it off! *(To phone)* Hold on, please.

JILL: Which button is "Off"?

(She tries one, the volume of the TV increases)

KEITH: No! Wrong! Give it to me! *(He turns off the TV, then returns to the receiver)* They hung up.

JILL: And who can blame them?

KEITH: *(Dialing again)* Why does my dad have to buy these things?

JILL: He's lonely. A TV you can talk to is like having a son in the house.

KEITH: OK—it's ringing.

(Suddenly, the TV comes on at full volume)

(To phone, yelling) Hello? Hello?

(He hangs up the phone—the TV goes off. Silence)

JILL: *(Pointing to the TV)* Maybe if you ask nicely, it'll let you make your call.

KEITH: I refuse to negotiate with a television! There must be other phones in the house that work!

JILL: They're probably all hooked up to different appliances.

KEITH: What's wrong with these stupid things? How does my dad ever call anyone?

JILL: Guess he goes to the office.

KEITH: This is ridiculous! There're a million phones in this house. They're everyplace—in TV's, in radios, pens, cars, walls, lamps—one of them has got to work!—

(He exits)

(JILL *goes to her bag, pulls out a bag of cheese-puffs, begins eating them. Then she picks up the phone, dials. The TV does not interfere*)

JILL: Randy, hi! I can probably only talk for a sec. Keith, the loony, is running all around trying to find a phone that works. *(Pause)* What am I using? A phone that works. *(Pause)* How should I know? It's temperamental—it likes me, OK? Listen, Randy, I'm not coming back to Greenwich. I like it here. Who wants to hang out with a bunch of boys? *(Pause)* Don't take it personally. If you start acting your age, I'll never speak to you ever again! *(Pause)* That's better. Now, do any of the girls know that Keith's left? What about Bonnie, or Ginger, or Karen, or Tina? Well, let me know. I can't wait to hear what they say when they find out we've run off together. *(Pause)* Randy? No, don't—don't read it—I hate poetry, you know that. *(Pause)* Especially when it's about me! No, no—just mail it. Hold it— Randy, I think he's coming back.

(She hangs up the phone. KEITH *enters)*

KEITH: This is all your fault!

JILL: What, sweetheart?

KEITH: Every phone in this house plays rock music!

JILL: Told you your dad was cool.

KEITH: Why did I leave that letter? No one had to know.

JILL: You wanted to tell the truth.

KEITH: What good is that?

JILL: It got you out of that awful place.

KEITH: And right into jail.

JILL: No one's gonna press charges. Come here.

KEITH: What?!

JILL: Don't bark. I'm trying to be nice.

KEITH: Sorry.

JILL: You're not making it easy.

KEITH: This is all your fault.

JILL: Yes, it is. Everything is my fault. When the rain falls, it's my fault. When water in the sink backs up, it's my fault. When rivers run off-course, mountains collapse, damns burst, it's all my fault. So don't you worry about a thing. Just lie here. And know who's at fault. And smile in your sleep, and dream of rain, and love me, love me, love me.

KEITH: What am I going to do with you?

JILL: I just told you, silly.

KEITH: You talked me into making the biggest mistake of my life.

JILL: Did I say a thing? You did it yourself. Your conscience was your guide.

KEITH: I don't have a conscience.

JILL: You're getting one. Out of thin air.

KEITH: And you think we could be comfortable living here?

JILL: Sure. We'd never have to call anyone. We'd isolate ourselves from the rest of the world.

KEITH: With my father.

JILL: Right. We have our own groceries, our own beds, our own view.

KEITH: They're not ours, they're his.

JILL: He's a what's-mine-is-yours kinda guy. Especially where it comes to you, sweetheart.

KEITH: You think so?

JILL: I can tell. I'm intuitive—like him. *(Pause)* Did your father really rise from the dead?

KEITH: God, he tells anyone that old story. "I rose from the dead . . . I rose from the dead." Why doesn't he just go make up bumper stickers?

JILL: So— What? He was sick, then he got better?

KEITH: No. See, well, Dad—he used to be a gangster.

JILL: Yeah?

KEITH: Not really a gangster, but he trafficked in drugs, laundered other people's money, dealt in graft and extortion— Yeah, he was a gangster. And Grandma—she was a faith healer. Now, she wanted Dad to become a pastor, like his father.

JILL: But, instead, he became a gangster.

KEITH: Right. Sort of missed the mark, there. So, Grandma and all the aunts prayed for him.

JILL: That he'd become a Christian.

KEITH: No—that he'd get hit by a truck.

JILL: Oh.

KEITH: It's this old movie that some Christian broadcasting company made about this guy who breaks his mother's heart by leaving the church and becoming a nightclub singer. Until one day, he's hit by a truck, and, in the hospital, he tells God that he'll serve the Lord if he's given back his voice. Then God performs a miracle, and he becomes this big Christian singer.

JILL: You miss some great entertainment being brought up atheist.

KEITH: Anyway, they're praying for a truck, and Dad—he doesn't get run over, but he gets something better: he gets TB.

JILL: Oh.

KEITH: Doctors tell him: no chance to live. Grandma and the aunts are ecstatic. They say, "Dedicate your life to pastoring, and we'll pray for a miracle." So, he does.

JILL: And it worked, huh?

KEITH: He was declared dead an hour, then he just came back. Even today, if he goes to a palm reader, they'll tell him his lifeline is too short—he shouldn't be alive.

JILL: So, how come he's not a pastor?

KEITH: Wait. He was. But he hated it. Then, he meets my mom. She convinces him to go into real estate.

JILL: And he makes a small fortune.

KEITH: No—then Mom is hit by a truck.

JILL: Oh.

KEITH: Dies instantly. I was five. I looked for her—all

around the house. In the clothes hamper, behind the shower curtain, underneath the bed, behind the bedroom dresser. Until all the drawers in the house were open, all the cans flung out of all the pantries, all the closets empty, all the windows open. And I sat in the center of it. The wind blew right through the house. I looked at the ground, then I put my ear against the floor. I listened and listened until I heard a thud, a banging. My heart jumped, I looked up, and it was my dad—home from work. I asked where she was. And he got on his knees and put his ear to the ground, and he listened, then we listened—together.
(Doorbell)

JILL: Who's that?

KEITH: It might be the cops! Lie down! Don't make a sound!
(Someone bangs on the door)

WOMAN'S VOICE: *(Offstage)* Keith? Keith? You home?

KEITH: Oh, shit.

JILL: What?

KEITH: It's my Auntie Barbara.

BARBARA: *(Offstage)* It is Barbara.
(JILL starts to get up)

JILL: Well, shouldn't you—?

KEITH: Get down! This is worse than the cops!

BARBARA: *(Offstage)* I want to discuss many important life topics.
(Someone fiddles with the door)

KEITH: Fuck. I forgot.

JILL: What?

KEITH: She can pick locks.
(The door opens. BARBARA shuffles in. A woman in her late forties, she wears mostly synthetic fabrics, and brandishes a hairpin as she spots KEITH and JILL lying on the floor)

KEITH: Oh—is it morning already?

BARBARA: Keith. Why did you not answer the door?

KEITH: I was asleep.

BARBARA: You sleep here? In the rec room? A girl and a boy? Without marriage?

KEITH: Actually, we were just resting.

BARBARA: Don't you know the danger of such immoral behavior? You will grow up to become like my husband!

KEITH: It's not sleep unless you're in bed.

BARBARA: *(To JILL)* And you will become like my husband's mistress. Bonnie.

KEITH: Auntie, this is Jill. Jill—my Auntie Barbara.

JILL: Bonnie? You know her name?

BARBARA: Of course. I am a faithful wife.

KEITH: They have a—

BARBARA: Interested in all his affairs.

KEITH: —a living arrangement.

BARBARA: So, sit down. Please. *(She sits down and brandishes the hairpin)* Still very skillful, huh?

KEITH: Yeah. Good work.

BARBARA: *(To JILL)* As children, we were poor—but resourceful. *(She spots JILL's bag of munchies)* Oh! Cheez-puffs! I love cheez-puffs!

(She grabs the bag, begins devouring them)

JILL: Please. Help yourself.

BARBARA: So fresh! Where did you buy these?

KEITH: *(To JILL)* Where?

JILL: L.A. airport. The American Airlines snack stand.

BARBARA: Excellent. You have a pen?

KEITH: Yeah.

BARBARA: *(Scratching notes)* "American . . ." I will send Fred there with his pickup. If he refuses, then Bonnie—she goes back to Ohio!

KEITH: That seems reasonable.

BARBARA: He may get the adultery, but I get the cheez-puffs! Well, Keith, my husband tells me you are presently in Los Angeles, correct?

KEITH: Well . . . yeah.

(JILL *pulls out another bag of cheez-puffs from her bag.*
BARBARA *takes it matter-of-factly*)

BARBARA: *(To* JILL*)* Thank you. *(To* KEITH*)* You know, we
pray for you all the time.

KEITH: Thanks, but I—

BARBARA: Especially at potluck dinners. We pray you will
return to God.

KEITH: I'm grateful that you're concerned, but—

BARBARA: Who do you think you are fooling?

KEITH: Huh?

BARBARA: You think I am stupid? Always, at church, after
the potluck, I sit with my prayer group—twenty, thirty
women. We discuss all the problems of everyone we
know: our sons, our husbands, nephews and neighbors,
unfixed animals. Everyone is so anxious to talk. All the
disgusting infidelity and poking in the Xerox room, and
suspicious skin rashes, and sweats and grunts and things
with tongues— Oh! the world is one giant filth-pot! I
know! Even my own home! My own bed! Now, do you
want to be discussed in a group like that? Not if you have
any self-respect. But I discuss you there. Because after
we are all done, and it is ten, eleven at night, after we have
finished all the Kentucky Fried Chicken—after that, we
pray. *(Pause)* We pray that God will improve the whole lot
of you. And we pray for ourselves, too. We pray that
next time, we will not enjoy the prayer meeting so much.
This is a balanced scheme for prayer. *(Pause)* Would you
like to marry Marilyn?

KEITH: What?

BARBARA: Oh, nothing.

KEITH: Auntie Barbara, I happen to be going around with
Jill.

JILL: I'm the one with the cheez-puffs, remember?

BARBARA: But, Marilyn—she is a woman.

KEITH: Auntie Barbara!

BARBARA: *(To* JILL*)* This is not to insult you. It is good to be a girl. Learn to ride horses.

KEITH: Look, if you want to discuss Christianity, that's one thing. But leave Jill out of this.

BARBARA: I do not come here only to discuss Christianity! I come for good general conversation! Like your father— look at the mistake he made.

KEITH: Quitting the ministry?

BARBARA: First, marrying your mother.

KEITH: What's that supposed to mean?

BARBARA: We—at church—we offered to counsel them! We even offered to provide dinner! But he turned his nose up! At me—his own sister!

KEITH: That was thirty years ago.

BARBARA: Look where it has led—his wife is dead and he is unemployed as a pastor.

KEITH: He's a millionaire!

BARBARA: Someday, all this will be gone.

KEITH: I think Dad seems happy.

BARBARA: You think so? Then why does he need to live in a house like this? Why does he buy these ridiculous objects, such as three different car phones?

JILL: I don't see why people can't throw their money out the window if they've earned it.

(Pause)

BARBARA: *(To* JILL*)* I will be understanding with you, because you were generous with the cheez-puffs. You think Hinson throws his money out the window? Then why has so little of it landed near Fred and me?

JILL: Why should it?

BARBARA: *(To* KEITH*)* This is where Marilyn comes in.

KEITH: I can't believe it. My father said you were thinking all this, and I told him he was crazy! I can't believe how blatant you're being in pursuit of his money!

BARBARA: Not blatant. Honest. This is a Biblical virtue.

JILL: If his money is so evil, why do you even want it?

BARBARA: No. It is the *love* of money which is the root of all evil.

JILL: And you don't love it by wanting it so much?

BARBARA: I do not want it so much. If I wanted it so much, I would work for it! Please do not mind this talk of Marilyn. You are young. There will be many men besides him in your future. How old are you?

JILL: Sixteen.

BARBARA: Sixteen? Then, you will have many, many more men.

KEITH: Don't talk to her like that!

JILL: And how many have you had?

BARBARA: What is she—at sixteen—to ask such questions?

KEITH: *(To* BARBARA*)* You started it.

JILL: Since you seem to be such an expert.

BARBARA: Is she one of your argument people?

KEITH: Debaters, Auntie Barbara.

JILL: Just answer the question.

BARBARA: What a ridiculous thing, this debate.

JILL: We concede the point.

KEITH: We do not!

BARBARA: Teaching people how to argue. Who needs to be taught?

KEITH: It's not just arguing, it's learning how to think logically.

BARBARA: You see? If you think logically, you will never win your arguments.

JILL: Stop changing the subject!

BARBARA: Now, let us reconsider Marilyn. She does not attend church, it is true. But she has great potential for virtue.

JILL: *(To* BARBARA*)* How many men have you slept with?

BARBARA: *(To* JILL*)* One. *(To* KEITH*)* You are the same kind of case.

JILL: Oh.

BARBARA: Perhaps, together—the two of you will return to the values of your youth.

KEITH: I'm not going to marry my cousin!

BARBARA: Why not? Marilyn—all the boys find her attractive.

KEITH: Several dozen, I've heard.

BARBARA: Hundreds.

JILL: Women!

KEITH: What?

JILL: *(To* BARBARA*)* I've got it— How many women have you slept with?
(Dead silence)

KEITH: Auntie Barbara?

BARBARA: One. Again, only one. And I do it only from duty to my husband. The Bible demands that wives be submissive. I cannot argue with the holy word.
(Pause)

JILL: Look, I just didn't like what you were implying about me, OK?

KEITH: *(To* BARBARA*)* What are you saying?

BARBARA: Do not be such an idiot! You have been to our house.

KEITH: Not in years.

BARBARA: You see a small room with only one queen-sized bed. You see myself, you see Fred, you see the harlot Bonnie—it is only a matter of simple arithmetic.

KEITH: I thought . . . one of you slept in Marilyn's room or something . . .

BARBARA: Marilyn? Ha! Her door is bolted with three different locks. What does she think is so precious inside? The crown jewels? King Tut? Once, I walked in, and she was naked. She screamed like I was a man. She wrapped herself up like there was so much to see. Then she beat me with her fists until I ran back to the bed where Bonnie lies. I wasn't trying to see her naked. But, once I was there, she should not have covered herself so quickly. *(BARBARA looks out the window)* There is great potential for virtue in Marilyn. In you. In all of us. *(She opens the doors leading to the balcony, walks out onto it)* Look at this. Why would your father buy a house on a mountain? One rain, the whole thing goes away. *(Pause)* Marilyn is waiting in the car.

KEITH: No, Auntie Barbara. Take her home.

BARBARA: It is so far down.

KEITH: You should get going, too.

BARBARA: And the rocks beneath are sharp.

(She climbs over the balcony, sits on the railing, feet dangling over the edge)

JILL: Keith? Look!

KEITH: Auntie Barbara!

BARBARA: Stand back! Or I will jump!

KEITH: You will not!

BARBARA: I have attempted suicide before!

KEITH: So? You've never succeeded!

JILL: *(To KEITH)* That's a terrible thing to say!

BARBARA: I failed before because I used chemicals! This time, I will use gravity! Will you marry my daughter?

KEITH: I'm just going to sit here like nothing's happening.

JILL: Keith, are you sure she's bluffing?

BARBARA: It is the last hope, for both of you!

JILL: It's windy out there!

BARBARA: Not to mention for me!

KEITH: I'm going to watch TV.

(He turns it on. At that instant, the phone starts to ring)

BARBARA: Marry my daughter and return to God!

(JILL picks up the phone, but it continues to ring)

JILL: Hello? What's going on here?

KEITH: It's only ringing because the TV's on. Just ignore it.

BARBARA: Keith—this is not a sturdy railing!

JILL: Ignore it?

KEITH: Ignore everything! Just watch TV!

JILL: But—

KEITH: Sit down! Watch the man eat the Mars bar!

BARBARA: I can see my body—broken on those rocks . . .
(The phone continues to ring. There is a banging on the door)

JILL: Keith? What's that?

KEITH: Just sit!

BARBARA: . . . blood streaming, my face a twisted thing!
(Banging continues)

MAN'S VOICE: *(Offstage)* Hollywood police! Is anyone at home?

JILL: Keith?!

KEITH: Who cares?

MAN'S VOICE: *(Offstage)* Hello? Hello! This is the police!

BARBARA· Keith? Keith?

WOMAN's VOICE: *(Offstage)* Ma? Ma!

MAN'S VOICE: *(Offstage)* Hello? Hello?
(KEITH just stares blankly at the television. JILL's eyes dart around the room. Banging and phone rings continue)

(FADE TO BLACK)

END OF ACT ONE

ACT TWO

Dusk. The front door has been broken in. MARILYN *sits on the couch, watching music videos. She is shapely and somewhat attractive, but trying too hard—she wears too much makeup, and her clothes are very tight.* BARBARA *is still perched on the railing, legs dangling in space. They are alone.*

BARBARA: I'm doing this for you, you know. *(No response)* It's as easy to marry rich as to marry poor. *(No response)* Otherwise, you end up like me. Sitting on a railing threatening suicide so a man will marry your daughter. You think I would have to do this if we were rich? Ha!
   *(*JILL *enters with a blanket, hands it to* BARBARA *as she walks gently onto the balcony)*
JILL: Careful. Steady.
BARBARA: Thank you. You are very generous.
JILL: Need anything else, Auntie Barbara?
BARBARA: No, no. You are too kind. *(Pause;* JILL *slowly lowers herself onto her hands and knees, and puts her ear to the ground)* What are you doing?
JILL: Ssssh.
BARBARA: Please yell if you hear anything crack.
JILL: Ssssh. I'm listening.
BARBARA: To what?
JILL: My father. And my mother. Keith—this was something he told me about. *(Pause)* They're talking about the

246

note they found on my bed. What to do with her? Don't give her an inch. We've given her too much of everything already. The car! American Express! Trips to Europe! The pony! We should've let her struggle. Know the value of a dollar. Like my father, dear. Like your mother, dear. Ooooh, she's obviously so spoiled. She makes up problems in her sleep. A pain. A child. A bore. Well, we'll show her. Call your brother. Get the cops after her. Tell her not to bother coming home. That'll be a big surprise, huh? She'll zip back in no time. Psychology 1A. And we'll teach her the value of everything she's got! Pick up that phone! Briing, briiing. (JILL *starts pounding the balcony floor furiously*) Then, bang! bang! bang!

BARBARA: Careful! You want to vibrate me to death?

JILL: *(To ground)* Hello? Hello?

BARBARA: I would like to choose the time of my own suicide, please.

(JILL stops)

JILL: That's what I get for having parents who are shrinks. Can you believe a parent would do that? Have the cops track down their only child—tell her not to bother coming home?

BARBARA: I cannot even believe the police deliver messages.

JILL: My Uncle William is regional commissioner for New England. Like my father says, it's all who you know. Don't they have any shame?

BARBARA: Psychology people never do. They make you tell all your disgusting sexual thoughts; then they want cash for listening.

JILL: They suck, don't they?

BARBARA: Yes, the—how do you say it?—the big one.

JILL: Yup.

BARBARA: Tell me—just what is this "big one"?

JILL: Auntie Barbara . . .

BARBARA: Oh. This is what they suck? I remember discussing that topic at prayer meeting.

JILL: You talk about oral sex in church?

BARBARA: Yes. This is how born-again Christians differ from the Catholics—we are not afraid to face the issues of our day. *(Pause)* It is not so terrible sitting here, you know?

JILL: No?

BARBARA: At first—yes, it is frightening. But after several hours have passed and you have not yet fallen to your death, it seems to feel natural.

JILL: I don't know.

BARBARA: Look at this view—it is beautiful.

JILL: You can see it from inside, too.

BARBARA: It is not the same. When you are behind glass, it is pretty—like a picture—but it is not real. It is harmless. But here—you do not only see the view, you feel it. All of Los Angeles is close enough to touch!

(She reached out her hand)

JILL: Auntie Barbara, be careful!

BARBARA: *(Leaning out dangerously far)* This is God's creation!

JILL: No! If you fall, Keith will never marry Marilyn!

BARBARA: *(Regaining balance)* And if I do not—they will be married then? You—will you help me in convincing Keith?

JILL: Me? I'm his girlfriend!

BARBARA: Yes—he will listen to you! Otherwise, what will become of her?

JILL: She'll find someone on her own.

BARBARA: Ha! I have left her to her own devices for too long. She brings home everything from the alleys larger than a cat.

JILL: Give her time.

BARBARA: She does not understand the importance of marrying well. In my experience, no one does until after they have married poorly.

JILL: Auntie Barbara, I can't help you with this. Gimme a break—I just lost both my parents.

BARBARA: Oh, yes—this is true.

JILL: I'm not in any shape to be generous with my loved ones.

BARBARA: I can understand.

JILL: I never expected them to do this. It's awful. What do I do now?

BARBARA: Suffer misery with me.

JILL: OK. (JILL *climbs over the railing, sits next to* BARBARA *on the balcony*) Don't mind me. I just need time to think.

BARBARA: About how much do you weigh?

(KEITH *enters with coffee mugs on a tray*)

KEITH: Who wants coffee? Jill—! What are you—?

JILL: Keith, walk slowly onto the balcony. No quick moves, no heavy steps, and try to breathe in some regular pattern. I would appreciate all that a lot.

KEITH: Jill, get off there!

BARBARA: And me? You would like me to get off?

KEITH: Jill!

BARBARA: It is in your power. There is my daughter.

JILL: You're right.

KEITH: Who? What?

JILL: (*To* BARBARA) This isn't so bad.

KEITH: Don't be ridiculous!

(*Over the course of* JILL'S *speech,* KEITH *puts down the tray and tries to sneak slowly onto the balcony, intending to grab her*)

JILL: It's like on a roller coaster. The second before you take the plunge. Like your car stops just before the fall—stops and hangs there. You're in a state of complete excitement. Heart beats faster, senses sharper, your body starts to change. Into a different animal altogether.

BARBARA: Hey! Jill!

(JILL *turns to see* KEITH *sneaking up on her*)

JILL: Keith! No!

BARBARA: If you grab her, I will jump!

KEITH: What?

JILL: *(To* BARBARA*)* You would do that? For me?

BARBARA: Why not? I would do it for her. *(Nodding toward room behind her)* And she is worthless except for the fact of being my daughter.

KEITH: Jill. Listen—this is a trick by your parents.

JILL: *(To* BARBARA*)* Well, then, I would jump for you.

KEITH: No suicide pacts, please! Your parents are just calling your bluff! This is exactly the reaction they want!

JILL: Oh, they exactly want me to risk my life?

KEITH: No! They want you to panic!

JILL: And, then, risk my life. It's so difficult being a modern parent.

KEITH: Jill, come down!

JILL: Leave me alone! I'm doing this for my own bene-fit!

BARBARA: I am not doing this for my own benefit.

KEITH: Shut up, Auntie Barbara!

BARBARA: I have been here so many more hours than her—why do I get so little sympathy?

KEITH: *(To* BARBARA*)* This is your fault. You instigated this crisis.

JILL: Don't talk to her like that! At least she loves her daughter!

BARBARA: Yes. It is "agape-love." Not based on merit. Fortunately for my daughter.

(Pause)

KEITH: This all started because of that letter.

JILL: You're right. It's all your fault.

KEITH: My fault?

JILL: You and your stupid conscience.

KEITH: My . . . But you . . . you made me . . .

JILL: *Made* you? Gimme a break. I didn't write a letter. I didn't even suggest a letter.

KEITH: You said everytime you looked at the way I was living, it made you sick.

JILL: It did. So? Who cares what I think?

KEITH: I do!

JILL: Well, that was your first mistake.

KEITH: So I thought . . . I thought I oughta come clean.

JILL: Right. You thought. It was your conscience. It was your choice.

KEITH: I was fine before I met you. I was happy. Everything went my way. I was respected, I made enough to live, I had friends. We'd laugh, drink, kid around. I'd look out the window and say to myself, I really got it made.

JILL: And you were fucking fourteen-year-olds.

KEITH: Then you came along. And you were smarter than the rest. And prettier. And funnier. And you had some kind of power. I saw it at work. You'd walk by a pound, and all the dogs would run up to you. Babies that you held refused to go back to their mothers. And, in the moment that I met you, I was no longer special. Oh, no. You were the special one. And my life began to change. One by one, the planks I stood on were kicked away. By a turn of your cheek, the curve of your neck. I felt it all giving way. I hated it. So I hated you. But all I could do was call your name as I fell—rising up—falling to places higher than I ever imagined.

(Pause)

JILL: I don't like this. You're a grown man! Don't go pinning the weight of your decisions to my shoulders!

BARBARA: *(To* KEITH*)* How many girl students did you know? Five? Ten? Lose count?

KEITH: This is none of your business, Auntie Barbara.

BARBARA: And this letter you wrote—it was to confess your crimes? *(Pause)* There are so many secrets in each of our hearts. In the beginning, we were not meant to die. But, as sin spread, death came into the race. With more people come more atrocity, until the planet stank with sins hidden and left to rot. The sum of this decay spreads a cloud over the earth, blocking out the sun, leaving us in darkness.

KEITH: I don't believe in that stuff. I believe in myself, and I believe in mistakes I've made, and, Jill, I believe my life was different before I met you.

(KEITH *exits; silence*)

BARBARA: Some cheez-puffs would improve the mood, eh?

JILL: I don't know what's happening to me. I feel so heavy. And so tired.

BARBARA: Please—leave the balcony, now. I will take this shift.

JILL: Not yet. I can't. I feel like the weight of the world is pinned to my shoulders, keeping me here. There's some pain, then everything goes blurry. And planets are passing through the night, leaving me alone on this spot, seeing everything, feeling nothing, wondering how I got here and when I'll be going. Eyes on the skies, daydreaming of sleep.

(HINSON *enters through the broken-down front door*)

HINSON: Keith? What happened to the door? Did the decorators do this? Keith? *(He sees* MARILYN*)* Oh, hello.

MARILYN: Hi.

HINSON: How did you get in here?

MARILYN: Door's open.

HINSON: Oh, right. Ha, ha. Is your mother here?

MARILYN: Yeah.

HINSON: Where's Keith?

BARBARA: I am out here, Hinson!

HINSON: Oh, good. Enjoying the view? Beautiful, isn't it? When I first saw this view at night, I thought, "This is the kind of home that Clark Gable would have. Clark—" You know, that's a little dangerous.

BARBARA: We know, Hinson.

HINSON: Usually we sit on these chairs. See? Leather.

BARBARA: Hinson, I came to talk about Marilyn.

HINSON: Marilyn, why don't you join us? Sit here.

MARILYN: Nope.

HINSON: *(To* JILL *and* BARBARA*)* Why don't you two sit in these chairs?

JILL: We like it here.

HINSON: Why won't anyone sit in these things? What do you think I buy them for? They aren't just showpieces!

BARBARA: Hinson, I want Keith to marry Marilyn.

HINSON: Uh-huh. What does Marilyn have to say about it?

BARBARA: She agrees.

HINSON: Marilyn—

BARBARA: But she is shy.

HINSON: —do you want to marry my son?

MARILYN: I'm sure.

BARBARA: You see? She does not deny it.

HINSON: Well, there're a lot of people who want to marry Keith, you know.

JILL: Name one.

MARILYN: Keith is short.

HINSON: Well, Mark Murray—

BARBARA: *(To* MARILYN*)* No, *you* are tall!

HINSON: —he's a millionaire sewer contractor. He said his daughter should marry Keith. Then, I buy the condos, he builds the sewers. And Roger Olsen—he said he'd give Keith a dowry of a million dollars. But his daughters are ugly.

JILL: So marry him off.

BARBARA: *(To* JILL*)* If you are releasing your boyfriend, then support my case!

JILL: OK. Have him marry Marilyn.

HINSON: C'mon! They're first cousins!

BARBARA: Yes—the families already know one another.

HINSON: Stupid talk. Their kids will all be born blind.

254 David Henry Hwang

BARBARA: Hinson, if you do not agree to this, I will jump.

HINSON: What—you think that's supposed to be a threat?

BARBARA: I will.

HINSON: So jump. At least we won't have to pump your stomach like last time.

BARBARA: You are a horrid brother! Horrid!

HINSON: Always talking junk, Barbara. Jump.

BARBARA: What makes you think I will not?

HINSON: I don't think anything. Prove it to me.

BARBARA: I will.

HINSON: Let's see. Make me suffer.

BARBARA: You? You suffer?

HINSON: Make me feel guilty. Jump!

BARBARA: If I jump, I will suffer, not you. It will be my body on the rocks, not yours!

HINSON: I work a hard day at the office, then come home to this—it's all wrong!

BARBARA: Oh! You are so self-centered—all your life! I fall, you think only of your own suffering!

HINSON: A man's home is his castle, ever hear that before?

BARBARA: Of course you are rich— Father gave you the inheritance.

HINSON: What inheritance? Four hundred dollars and a stamp collection?

BARBARA: And then you mailed the stamps! Well, I will not give you the satisfaction!

(She climbs back onto the balcony)

HINSON: I knew you wouldn't. Dumb girl.

BARBARA: Not if my death will serve as an excuse for self-pity.

HINSON: You'll never kill yourself—no matter how hard you try.

BARBARA: Where is my daughter? C'mon, Marilyn—we are going home.

MARILYN: I want to watch cable. We don't have cable.

BARBARA: We have been insulted in countless ways.

MARILYN: I said I didn't wanna come, but then you drag me down here—

BARBARA: So, now, you may go!

MARILYN: At least let me stay and watch what I want!

HINSON: She's staying, Barbara. Why don't you get back on your balcony?

BARBARA: Why don't you lend me three thousand dollars?

HINSON: What?

BARBARA: I want to send her to charm school—in Switzerland.

HINSON: That costs three thousand dollars?

BARBARA: Who knows? This idea just entered my head. But three thousand seems like a good amount.

HINSON: Barbara, three thousand dollars—my cash flow isn't always that good.

BARBARA: How much did each car phone cost?

HINSON: Those are for business!

BARBARA: And this is more important than the future security of your niece? You want her to become like me? Forced to beg money from relatives who do not care if I kill myself or die naturally?

HINSON: What happened to this door? Keith? Keith!

BARBARA: They gave you their inheritance because they expected you to become a pastor! And, now, you are cheap with it!

HINSON: I did become a pastor.

BARBARA: You quit. That is disgraceful. There is a great history of men being pastors—a family heritage—and you broke it. This is why you suffer.

HINSON: Suffer? I'm the one you're asking for money to go to Switzerland!

BARBARA: You see? Is this not complete aggravation?

HINSON: I have a great love for God. I told—uh-uh—Jill.

Jill, didn't I tell you that? *(No response)* Well, I did. I tell everyone. At work, I deal with these hot-shot guys. You think some little pastor with only a tiny pension plan is going to impress them? You don't know! These guys—they deal with the Rockefellers—they've been to the White House a dozen times—they're worth twenty, thirty million—sometimes more! These are the guys that I witness to, because I'm in their league. They see on my wall—pictures of me shaking hands with Gerry Ford, with Jim Carter, with Ron Reagan—all my good friends! So they know I'm a top guy—a real estate superstar. I give them my card, they go, "Whaa—are you the one who built up that best-performing corporation? Are you the baron?" They kiss my ring! Then, we're golfing, and I say, "You know, I'm a Christian." Whaaaa—this is so impressive to them. They say, "No. Really? But you're a baron." They respect me more. But, what's important is—they come to respect God. I love God with a deep-felt yearning, for he has been so good to me. *(He begins singing the hymn, "Were You There When They Crucified My Lord?")* "Were you there when they crucified my Lord"—this is what I sing in the showers—while the others compare organ lengths—I sing, "Were you there when they crucified my Lord?"

BARBARA: It is not the same as being a pastor and suffering poverty! *(*HINSON *starts to sing the hymn, plugging his ears to* BARBARA'*s speech)* Do you hear me? The Bible says it is harder for a camel to go through the eye of a needle than a rich man to enter the Kingdom of God! Are you listening? Have you ever seen a camel? Here—wait—I have a needle!

(She digs in her purse, as HINSON *sings more loudly, overlapping dialogue)*

HINSON: "Sometimes I wonder/Wonder, wonder/Were you there when they crucified my Lord?/Were you there when

they laid Him in the ground? (etc.)/Were you there when
He rose up from the grave? (etc.)/"

MARILYN: Hey! Keep it down!

(MARILYN turns up the TV volume.

BARBARA *finds a needle)*

BARBARA: Here, see? A camel—it is bigger than me!

MARILYN: Uncle Hinson!

BARBARA: Now—watch!

MARILYN: I can't hear the TV!

(Everyone's volume goes up. BARBARA *bumps her head against the eye of the needle)*

BARBARA: See? I am trying to get through the eye of a needle. Pretty difficult, huh?

MARILYN: I said, shut up!

(Everything continues to rise in volume)

BARBARA: You think this is difficult?

MARILYN: It won't get any louder!

(She punches the remote control button)

BARBARA: Just wait until you reach judgment day!

MARILYN: C'mon! That's enough!

BARBARA: This will be you.

MARILYN: Ma! Uncle Hinson!

BARBARA: "I'll be up in just a second!"

MARILYN: Shit!

BARBARA: "As soon as I squeeze through!"

MARILYN: Fucking no-good TV!

(She throws the remote control to the ground. The TV explodes. Stage BLACKS OUT *except for erratic flashes of light from the TV screen)*

(Stage lights slowly flicker back on, we see everyone thrown slightly by the force of the blast)

*(*JILL *is gone)*

HINSON: What was that? Where's the warranty?

BARBARA: Look! Where is Jill?

(BARBARA *rushes to the balcony, with Hinson in quick pursuit.* *They look over the edge.* MARILYN *stares blankly at the broken* *TV)*

HINSON: You sure she was sitting here?

BARBARA: I cannot see her.

HINSON: This is all your fault! Keith? Keith!

BARBARA: She was sitting here—I am sure.

HINSON: I told you—didn't I tell you?—to sit on the leather showpieces? Dumb! Dumb!

BARBARA: There! Is that her? That speck!

HINSON: No—that's a speck. Stupid!

BARBARA: Here— I will drop this compact.

HINSON: What are you doing?

BARBARA: Where it lands, she must be.

HINSON: You want to kill her?

BARBARA: Kill her? She must already be dead!

HINSON: It picks up speed when it falls. By the time it hits the ground, it could kill her!

BARBARA: If she is dead, it can only dent her!

HINSON: Stupid! Keith? Where's Keith!

BARBARA: Is there a path down the hill?

HINSON: Yes, but we haven't had time to install the designer lights!

BARBARA: Come—there is no time to waste!

(BARBARA *and* HINSON *exit out onto the driveway)*

(MARILYN *just stares at the TV)*

MARILYN: Oh, shit.

(KEITH *enters from the hall)*

KEITH: I hate it when he calls my name like that. Makes me feel like a dog. *(He looks at the balcony)* Where's Jill? That's the thing with her. One minute, she's ready to kill herself, the next she's rummaging in the 'fridge. *(He sits down next to* MARILYN, *flips on the TV. It goes on with no*

problem) Listen, Marilyn—you know, all that stuff about
not wanting to marry you—you don't take it personally
or anything, do you?
(Pause)

MARILYN: Keith? I was all set.

KEITH: What?

MARILYN: To run away from home.

KEITH: Oh.

MARILYN: You woulda liked him, too. Maybe you already
do.

KEITH: This is some guy I know?

MARILYN: Well, you've seen him. On TV. In videos. He
plays with that band. You know, "The Commotions"?

KEITH: Yeah?

MARILYN: You've seen 'em, right?

KEITH: The singer? That guy?

MARILYN: No, that's Hudd. I'm talkin' 'bout the bass
player.

KEITH: Oh, yeah.

MARILYN: The shiny blue tie? In the videos?

KEITH: Sure. That guy?

MARILYN: That's Rick.

KEITH: How'd you meet him?

MARILYN: Friend of a friend of a friend's.

KEITH: Well, is he nice?

MARILYN: We spent a lotta time together. He was nice.

KEITH: That's great. How long? A year?

MARILYN: Naw.

KEITH: A few months?

MARILYN: Three weeks, give or take.

KEITH: Oh.

MARILYN: I know. Maybe it wasn't a big deal for him—

KEITH: No.

MARILYN: Maybe he doesn't even think about me anymore.

KEITH: You can do a lot in three weeks.

MARILYN: Yeah, well, he said he'd take me away—to France or someplace like that.

KEITH: Does he have a castle or something?

MARILYN: No. I think we were just gonna stay in hotels.

KEITH: They're nice, too.

MARILYN: I was all ready to go. I packed up everything, sat on my bed. I waited for his car. But . . . well . . .

KEITH: Yeah.

MARILYN: Just one of those things, I guess. The worst part was having to unpack. So, I was watching—for their new video. *(Beat)* I'm in it.

KEITH: Really?

MARILYN: It's, like, a really small part.

KEITH: He must've really liked you.

MARILYN: I lie on this big brass fish.

KEITH: I mean, I'm sure they don't put any old—just anyone in their videos.

MARILYN: That's my part. I just lie there.

KEITH: I'll watch for it.

(Silence)

MARILYN: Do you think it'll ever happen again?

(Pause; over the course of the next speech, KEITH wanders about the room, nervously turning on lights and appliances as he goes)

KEITH: I . . . I don't know. I'm not the right person to ask. I know what you mean—one second, your life seems better than everyone else's. Then, you look again, and it's gone. You're in the middle of nowhere.

MARILYN: I know where I am. I just didn't like getting here.

KEITH: I . . . I did something really bad at school. A few things. I mean, the bad thing—I did it a few times.

MARILYN: Don't tell me. I don't wanna know.

KEITH: I didn't even think it was bad. I thought it was . . . an opportunity. Like I was living a very glamorous life. Status, girls, fame—more than anyone around me.

MARILYN: You thought your life was glamorous?

KEITH: I really wanted it to be. So, it was. Until last week. When I looked at Jill—and I couldn't face myself anymore.

MARILYN: Jill?

KEITH: Now I'm like you. Lost.

MARILYN: I'm not lost. I feel good.

KEITH: You're not guilty of anything.

MARILYN: I'm guilty of a lotta things. But I loved someone. Someone who played rock 'n' roll. I feel like I paid my dues. Like the slate is clean. *(Pause)* You love Jill?

KEITH: What's that got to do with—?

MARILYN: Then go down the mountain.

KEITH: What?

MARILYN: Go down. I think you oughta look for her, Keith.

KEITH: She's outside?

MARILYN: Keith . . . go . . .

*(*KEITH *exits onto the driveway)*

*(*MARILYN *sees he is gone. Then, she slowly walks out onto the balcony, climbs onto the railing, and sits there)*

(A pause, then HINSON *and* BARBARA *enter from the driveway)*

HINSON: Why'd Marilyn have to blow up the TV?

BARBARA: You were singing! Probably your voice—it shatters the electronics!

HINSON: Am I that good? Like that girl?

BARBARA: I cannot believe you!

HINSON: Fitzgerald? The one that sings? Zelda? Zelda?

BARBARA: Ella! Ella!

HINSON: The Ella Fitzgerald of real estate. *(He sings)* Aaaah . . .

BARBARA: Quiet! Before you shatter the lightbulbs!

HINSON: Lightbulbs? Hey, Barbara, what are you trying to do? Don't you know the value of electricity?

(HINSON *goes around the room, turning off all the appliances* KEITH *turned on*)

BARBARA: Me? How could I have been searching for Jill with you and turning on appliances at the same time?

HINSON: Who knows? You're just impossible to live with!

BARBARA: Sometimes, the idiocy . . .

HINSON: Or Marilyn. Did Marilyn turn these on? Looking for new things to blow up?

BARBARA: Marilyn?

HINSON: You need to keep her on a tighter leash, Barbara. Girl like that—you never know the trouble she can get into.

(BARBARA *spots* MARILYN *on the balcony*)

BARBARA: Marilyn!

HINSON: See what I mean?

BARBARA: Come down from there!

HINSON: The kind of example you set for your children?

BARBARA: Do you hear me?

HINSON: With a mother like you, it's a wonder they grew up at all.

BARBARA: Marilyn!

MARILYN: Ma, fuck off!

(*Pause*)

HINSON: Your family is just a chaos, Barbara.

BARBARA: She is in one her moods.

HINSON: Who can blame her? Her mother climbs up on a balcony, screams stupid things at her brother, turns on every electrical appliance she can get her hands on . . .

BARBARA: I didn't touch them!

HINSON: Marilyn? Hey—c'mon down, now. See these chairs? See what happened to—uh-uh—to Jill? You never know when your crazy mother might blow up another appliance. It's better to sit in the leather showpieces.

Marilyn? Marilyn? *(No response)* I can't undo twenty years of lousy mothering in a few seconds. You know, if she falls—this all goes on my insurance policy.

BARBARA: I try to change her, she does not listen.

HINSON: Is that your scheme? You going to get your three thousand for charm school from my insurance?

BARBARA: How can that be?

HINSON: I wouldn't put anything past you.

BARBARA: She would be dead! What is the use of sending her to charm school if she does not breathe?

HINSON: Well, I meant that you'd—

BARBARA: Sometimes, the idiocy.

HINSON: You'd spend it on yourself.

BARBARA: And where is Jill?

HINSON: I don't know. You know, Barbara, things were so peaceful around here before you showed up.

BARBARA: Do not rake over the past! What do we do now?

HINSON: Should we call the police? Where's Keith? Keith!

BARBRA: Perhaps Keith—he caused this mess.

HINSON: Barbara, look out there. It's obvious who has the problems in this family.

BARBARA: Jill— It is like she disappeared into thin air.

HINSON: She's Keith's student, you know. If this gets out, he'll probably get a demerit or something. Keith? Keith? *(HINSON exits into the house)*

(BARBARA approaches MARILYN on the balcony)

BARBARA: I am surprised. To see you sit out there. I did not think the topic of suicide interested you at all. *(Pause)* Perhaps you hate me now. Fine. I never expect anything more. I hated my mother, my children hate me, your children will hate you—it is all mother nature. *(Pause)* But understand—I was not always so interested in money. I was interested more in the things of God. In magic. In miracles. But too many years have passed. The only magic I see now is in phones without wires, televisions which hear you, and ovens that defrost the chicken in only three minutes. So, I must worship God—but I must believe my eyes as well. And if this is a sin, then when Judgment Day arrives and God holds up the eye of a needle, I will have to pluck a hair from my head and say, "This is the best I can do. This is the only part of me made to fit your plans."

MARILYN: Ma?

BARBARA: You speak to me? What is the occasion?

MARILYN: How come you do this to yourself?

BARBARA: What?

MARILYN: Make yourself suffer. You didn't used to, remember?

BARBARA: When? I have always been miserable and proud.

MARILYN: Think back. Way back.

BARBARA: Will you get off the balcony?

MARILYN: Like when you raised Uncle Hinson from the dead.

BARBARA: Who can remember? You were not even born yet.

MARILYN: But you told me. Remember? It was a snap. You wanted to do it, so you did.

BARBARA: I have told you too many tales before bed.

MARILYN: Well, now, I believe them.

BARBARA: Why are we even discussing this?

MARILYN: 'Cuz I met a boy.

BARBARA: Ah, some things do not change.

MARILYN: And he played rock 'n roll.

BARBARA: So, he probably does not attend church.

MARILYN: And, now, I believe you.

BARBARA: It is too late. I do not want you to believe me. I want you to marry Keith. (KEITH *enters the room, sits in the center of it, stares out the window)* Keith? Your father—he is looking for you.

(HINSON enters the room)

HINSON: Keith! There you are! Did you—Keith? There's a problem outside! Did you see? Your friend—uh-uh—Jill. *(KEITH slowly gets onto all fours, lowers his ear to the ground)* Keith? Keith! Get up from there!

BARBARA: I believe, he has seen her.

HINSON: He's not doing a thing! Keith? Why do you go and make yourself look ridiculous in front of your crazy aunt?

BARBARA: He tries to listen, as I once listened.

HINSON: What are you going on about?

BARBARA: You—you want to forget, but you cannot.

HINSON: Get off it, Barbara. We're living in the twentieth century.

BARBARA: He tries to listen, as mother once did.

HINSON: Mother used to make soap in the basement.

BARBARA: As father looked on.

HINSON: Keith, get up off the floor!

BARBARA: He can feel the desire in his bones. As I once did.

HINSON: I didn't send you to Yale so you could end up like this!

BARBARA: When I raised you from the dead.

HINSON: *(To BARBARA)* Stupid talk! God raised me! Not you! Look around—it's obvious! God saw fit to raise me up!

(KEITH rises to his knees, looks at HINSON)

KEITH: I can't hear a thing.

HINSON: Good, son. No one expects you to perform miracles. Now, get up—

KEITH: Listen to me—I slept with them.

HINSON: What? Who?

KEITH: My students.

HINSON: Yeah?

KEITH: Seventeen-, fourteen-year-old girls.

HINSON: Oh, son, that's not so good.

KEITH: It's sick! I'm sick!

HINSON: On the other hand, who could resist? In that turn-on place?

KEITH: Everyone! Everyone else resists!

HINSON: Why are you screaming? Listen—your father wouldn't have lasted a week.

KEITH: Neither did I.

HINSON: See? Like father, like son.

KEITH: Now, will you help me?

HINSON: Sure, son. Now, you go back there on Monday, and don't do it again. Simple.

KEITH: No— Help me bring back Jill.

HINSON: Jill? From where? We looked all over, but—

KEITH: From the dead.

(Pause)

HINSON: Son, your coo-coo aunt is watching.

KEITH: Do something!

HINSON: Just get up, we'll go to a nice restaurant—

KEITH: Dad! Listen! I wrote the headmaster a letter. I told him what I'd been doing.

(Pause)

HINSON: That you're making his debate team into a number one team, right?

KEITH: No—that I slept with some of my students.

HINSON: You—? Ah! I can't believe— Stupid!

KEITH: Now, will you please help me?

HINSON: Shut up! How could you do that? Ah! I just feel like boiling inside!

KEITH: I love Jill!

HINSON: So what? Sometimes, I think you're smart, then you just— Ah! Why'd you have to go do that dumbest of all dumb things?

KEITH: I wanted to tell the truth.

HINSON: So tell *me!* Don't tell—! You know what this'll do to your record?

KEITH: I don't care!

HINSON: You don't— Haven't I taught you anything? This is the kind of thing they string guys up for!

KEITH: I just want Jill back!

HINSON: You're all mixed up! Stupid! My own son! It makes me want to fry you!

(HINSON *starts to kick at* KEITH. KEITH *jumps up, grabs* HINSON, *gets him in a headlock, then wrestles his ear to the ground*)

KEITH: C'mon. You always talk about resurrection! OK—do it!

HINSON: You bum! Lizard! Hold your father's ear to the ground?

KEITH: It's in your annual report! You tell the story in church!

HINSON: I'll . . . I'll . . .

KEITH: You tell it to the *Wall Street Journal!*

HINSON: I'll shoot you! Where's my gun!

KEITH: You don't have a gun!

HINSON: I don't care! I'll shoot you with my bare hands!

KEITH: You went down to hell. You overcame death.

HINSON: That was back in 1948!

KEITH: Do it again!

HINSON. How can I? I'm not dead!

KEITH: Jill is! You never raised anyone from the dead but yourself!

HINSON: I have a generous heart! Ask anyone!

KEITH: Did you raise Mom?

HINSON: I tried.

KEITH: You left her to rot. While you became a baron. Well, this time . . .

HINSON: Ouch! I can't hear a thing!

KEITH: This time, you will. You're going to raise Jill. Because I love her. Like I loved Mom. Lots more than I love you. If you died, I'd stuff my ears with cotton. You could call from hell—it wouldn't be worth the effort.

HINSON: You think it's so easy, you do it!

KEITH: Bring her back! Bring them both back!

(HINSON *breaks free, grabs a golf club*)

HINSON: You bum! Cannibal! Hold your father's ear to the ground? That's a sin! A sin against God! Your father created you! He spit, and you were born! Your blood is my blood! Your face is my face! What I eat, you eat! What I think, you think! Like father, like son! And I can kill you!

(HINSON *tries to hit* KEITH; KEITH *sidesteps, grabs the golf club. They struggle.* KEITH *gets it away.* KEITH *brings the golf club over his head to strike, hesitates, and brings it down instead on a clock radio.* HINSON *snatches the golf club away, looks* KEITH *in the eye, smashes a VCR with it.* KEITH *and* HINSON *take turns during the next section smashing different appliances*)

(BARBARA *goes onto the balcony, stands next to* MARILYN)

BARBARA: What a waste. Men. You believe you can beat everything into submission. You are so busy, you forget the resurrection. You forget the dead. You forget the ones you love.

(KEITH *and* HINSON *continue smashing, as* BARBARA *puts her arm around* MARILYN. *They tell a story*)

I was a young girl when Hinson fell ill. He lay in a bed of white, in a room of white, with attendants all in white. But his eyes did not open.

MARILYN: And, so, to him, the world was black—all black.

BARBARA: Black from sins accumulated and left hidden.

MARILYN: Black from guns, and fistfights, and nights without love.

BARBARA: It was so sad to watch, because from beneath those closed eyes, from within that black world—

MARILYN: A single tear would find its way out, and roll down, down his cheek, down his pillow, down the side of the white bed, down to the ground.

BARBARA: Carrying with it all the regret for things unsaid, jobs left undone—the inability to move by the instructions of the heart.

MARILYN: The doctor came, drew the sheet up over Hinson's face.

BARBARA: And I was left alone. In this sea of white.

MARILYN: A white bed.

BARBARA: And white walls.

MARILYN: And Hinson, all in white.

BARBARA: His tears became my tears. Because he could no longer cry, I cried for him. And with the tears came the feelings behind them, the great anguish of a disobedient heart.

MARILYN: A heart that could not even obey itself.

BARBARA: I felt the weight of his disobedience.

MARILYN: Pulling on my shoulders, down inside my throat.

BARBARA: Making a great hole in my heart.

MARILYN: Growing, expanding, until it would soon devour everything inside—

BARBARA: And leave me empty, not even a shell.

MARILYN: Alone.

BARBARA: The sorrow pulled me to my knees—

MARILYN: And I crawled across the floor.

BARBARA: Cold, blind, and groping.

MARILYN: I listened.

BARBARA: Listened for a sound that would still the draft running through my body.

(MARILYN *stands upright on the ledge of the balcony*)

MARILYN: Then, I heard it. Far away.

BARBARA: In the distance—a heart beating.

MARILYN: And the sound was so full.

BARBARA: Like it could fit into the hole where my heart used to be.

MARILYN: So I clutched it.

BARBARA: I pulled and tugged and scraped—

MARILYN: Pulled that heart into the center of me. *(MARILYN extends her arms straight out into space)* I felt it enter me.

BARBARA: And everything fell into place.

MARILYN: It beat within me, and I could breathe once more in great, heaving sobs.

BARBARA: So I opened my eyes.

MARILYN: And I saw it—for the first and last time.

BARBARA: I saw my own face.

MARILYN: Sweating, panting, in ecstasy.

BARBARA: I saw myself in the act of love.

MARILYN: I closed my eyes and knew.

BARBARA: I was Hinson now.

MARILYN: For this moment, I was Hinson and I was drawing strength from the body of a woman. A woman who loved me. Who took my place. To bring me back from the dead.

(BARBARA gives MARILYN a gentle shove. She falls out into the night. But her body is stopped miraculously in midfall and extends out at a forty-five-degree angle from the ledge)

(At the same time, all the appliances in the house suddenly go off, leaving the room black and in an abrupt silence. All that is left is the light from the moon and stars)

MARILYN: Listen— Can you hear it? Behind every noise in the city, every sound we've learned to make, behind the clatter of our streets, the hum of turbines, the roar of electricity—behind all this, there is a constant voice. A voice which carries hope from beyond the grave. It speaks in a fine, clear tone about matters which take our eyes upward—away from things we can touch, away from love made small and powerless. It is a voice which lurks behind every move we make. To listen to it is to rage against the grave, we save our souls, we bring ourselves back from the dead.

(Even the stars FADE TO BLACK *for a moment)*

(Slowly, the lights in the house, in the sky, in Los Angeles, all flicker back on. JILL *is sitting on the balcony in the place of* MARILYN, *who is gone)*

KEITH: Jill? Jill?

*(*KEITH *rushes to the balcony, pulls* JILL *onto the landing)*

JILL: I'm OK.

KEITH: Are you all right?

JILL: I'm OK. *(Beat)* Do you love me?

KEITH: Yes. I do.

JILL: Then hold me.

(They embrace)

KEITH: I love you, it's just that . . . I couldn't bring you back from the dead.

JILL: Sssh.

KEITH: I tried, but—

JILL: Don't waste your breath. I love you, too. And I'm back, see?

HINSON: Barbara, where's your daughter? Marilyn?

*(*MARILYN *enters from the door to the driveway)*

MARILYN: Ma, can we go now?

BARBARA: I have been telling you to leave for hours.

MARILYN: All the TV's here are broken.

BARBARA: Now, it seems like years. *(To* HINSON*)* Never fear. I will return. And we will talk about money.

*(*BARBARA *exits.* MARILYN *starts to exit, as* JILL *gets up, moves toward her)*

MARILYN: *(to* JILL*)* You wanna come along?

JILL: Sure. Maybe we could grab a bite to eat, or something.

MARILYN: Yeah. Sounds good. C'mon.
(MARILYN *exits*)

(JILL *pauses, looks at Keith*)
JILL: I'll be back. Soon, OK? We'll go dancing tonight, how 'bout that.
KEITH: Sure. Why not?
JILL: Keith, it shouldn't be that hard.
KEITH: What?
JILL: To bring someone back from the dead. It should be something you could do twice before dinner and still have energy for dishes. With just a flick of the wrist. The turn of a sleeve. Like magic. But without magic. With just a look in the right direction.
(*She exits*)

(HINSON *and* KEITH *are left alone. Silence*)
HINSON: Quite a mess we made, huh, son?
KEITH: Yeah—we sure did.
HINSON: Don't let it get to you. That's what men—we're like that. We get together, have a little fun, break a few things—that's par for the course, right?
KEITH: Sure. I mean, it's not like we can't afford to replace this stuff.
HINSON: Hell, no. Not like the girls, huh? If they make a mess like this, they get hysterical.
KEITH: Yeah. Probably.
HINSON: What do you mean, "probably"? They can't get things out in the open. Not like us. A little aggression, hostility—we can get past it.
KEITH: Yeah.
HINSON: I mean, the world is rotten. Business is shady. That's human nature. We try to be good, but nothing's really going to change, we know that.
KEITH: Probably not.

HINSON: You know that. You don't waste your time think-ing about that crap stuff. That's why you'll go far.

KEITH: Yeah.

HINSON: Listen, son—you can stay here as long as you like. It's good to have you here. We'll find you a new job—no time flat. You want a car? I'll get you one. How 'bout a Benz. Any of your friends drive a Benz?

KEITH: Dad?

HINSON: What, son?

KEITH: Sssh . . .

(KEITH *gets down on all fours, puts his ear to the ground.* HINSON *hesitates. Then, he, too, puts his ear to the ground. They remain in this position, listening, as:*

(Lights FADE TO BLACK*)*

CURTAIN

1000 AIRPLANES ON THE ROOF

A Science Fiction Music-Drama

1000 Airplanes on the Roof is a science-fiction music-drama realized by Philip Glass, David Henry Hwang, and Jerome Sirlin. It was composed and directed by Mr. Glass, written by Mr. Hwang, with design and projections by Mr. Sirlin. This piece was commissioned by the Donau Festival Niederosterreich; The American Music Theater Festival, Philadelphia; and by Berlin, Cultural City of Europe—1988. It had its world premiere on July 15, 1988, at the Vienna International Airport in Hangar #3. *1000 Airplanes* was produced by Robert LoBianco and Jedidiah Wheeler, and performed by the Philip Glass Ensemble, with Rocco Sisto, Patrick O'Connell and Jodi Long alternately playing the role of "M." Kurt Munkascsi was sound designer; Michael Riesman provided musical direction.

Playwright's Note

1000 Airplanes on the Roof is a three-way collaboration between myself, Philip Glass, and Jerome Sirlin. The text printed here is a monologue designed to be read against a 90-minute Glass instrumental piece, performed by his ensemble. This is the original definition of *melodrama,* a familiar example of the form being "Peter and the Wolf." The third element in our collaboration is the "visual libretto" supplied by Jerome Sirlin—a series of constantly changing three-dimensional projections which provide the set for our character "M." The resulting effect might be compared to putting a live actor into a three-dimensional movie. Philip Glass' music for *1000 Airplanes on the Roof* is available on Virgin Records.

Part I

M.

1

There was once a day when I lived in the open. In a converted farmhouse, with curtains and plants in the window, and everything inside painted white. But such a place would be impossible for me now. It would be impossible to face again the white fields, with the snow blending as one into the white clouds above. And the wooden fence with the horses behind—the horses in their winter coats, steam rising out of their nostrils, too calm to belong to this frantic earth. Such a place would be impossible for me now. For now, I live in New York City.

2

Last night, my girlfriend and I broke up. Well, I guess she would say it's kind of a glorification to call her my "girlfriend." OK, we'd only been out on one date. But—I'd come to think of her as my girlfriend. I'd already pictured her, with her arms wrapped around me, my head muffled in her flesh, all other sounds dropping away. All except the beating of her heart, the blood pumping through her veins. And, in the sound of her life, I would drift off to sleep.

3

She came into the Copy Shop where I worked. When I saw her, when I took her order—it was music she was copying— when I took her order, something came over me, and I thought, this is my chance. She might help me escape. If I could just find another life, then my days of running would be over. And I wouldn't even need the City anymore, the City which anyway only betrays me and leaves me exposed, always alone, with what I fear most—the sound of my memories.

4

"Bodies moving. Many as one. A giant machine, breathing. Smell. Smell—and you will remember. The hands of a clock. Following the path of a star. Moving forward, then back, across, then over. Time bending. Fluid. Like any other object, moving freely in space. After length, width, and depth, the fourth dimension is time."

5

We walked all around the City. All around the City on our date. As we walked, I wanted to tell her things. I wanted to tell her that I had not been born and raised to work in a Copy Shop. That I'd once had an important job. Not that it's so easy to believe at this point, but I have pictures, and they tell me that I was once a lawyer. I hope that I defended the innocent against the guilty, but chances are—if we're to be honest—that probably wasn't the case. Maybe that's why I'm being punished now. I wanted to tell her this, but when I opened my mouth, the only words that came out were those of a man who had been born and raised to work in a Copy Shop. And, I realized that I'd been wearing this disguise for so long, it had seeped through my skin:

"I see your watch is telling the correct time."

"That building once killed a woman under construction."

"Have you ever drunk a lot of beer?"

"And over there is one of New York's premiere sex clubs."

6

"Are you some kind of psychopath?"

This is the question she asked me, as we walked by Macy's. I had to admit, I admired her forthrightness. I wasn't sure, however, what she meant by "some kind" of psychopath. Is there more than one kind? And, if so, am I expected to know which category I fall under? I wanted to use this as an opportunity to tell her the truth. No, I'm not a psychopath. But, yes, I am disturbed. No, I'm not cruel or dangerous. But, yes, I am on the run. But, of course, I said nothing like that. Of course, I said "Me? A psychopath? What are you talking about?" Which is, of course, exactly how a psychopath would answer.

7

I used to live in a converted farmhouse, far away from the City. But not so far that I didn't have a great deal of life in the City. I believe I had a family, and, I think that family loved me, and, what's even more unusual, I have the impression that I loved them back.

8

We reached the street where I live, and I figured I'd better cut my losses and say good night. But, then, to top it all off, to put the icing on the worst first date in history—my building started to disappear.

9

"Many moving as one. Collective intelligence."

"Pebbles. Dropped into the lake. Creating ripples. Each of which recapitulates the image of the entire lake."

"There is a small silver ball. The size of a BB. It is inserted into my—into my right nostril. Shoved upwards . . . into the cavity . . . on the far side of my eye. I wince. It hurts! It's pushing against the fleshy membrane. Breaking through . . ."

10

When the earth reappeared around me, I was far from my building, but, oh God, she was still standing beside me. My first thought was, pretend like nothing happened. Just walk her home, make conversation—I can't do that.

Her mouth opened, lips began to form around words. I felt horror, terrible horror, at whatever was about to come from her mouth. Whatever had happened, couldn't be worse than what she was going to say about it. So at last, I attempted a sensible act.

I ran.

11

I ran because something was happening in my head. Something inside, struggling to get out. Something pushing against my skull—a steady pressure, as if to pop the bone. I didn't want to scream, not in public. Not in the subway. If I screamed, people would stare. So, I held my head high . . . and I managed . . . to smile. Smiled as faces began to appear, in the gratings above the subway, in the nooks and crannies of the City. I struggled to smile, and there they were looking down . . . smiling at me. I ran into my apartment. Slammed the door, heard its comforting "thud," tore off all my clothes, and looked in the mirror. My body was glowing, my skin red like a briquette. I stared at my face, and a stranger stared back. A stranger—smiling. I remembered my doctor, telling me I have the organs of an eighty-year-old man. And, then—finally—I screamed.

12

I have wandered—from town to town. Boston, Detroit, Seattle, L.A. Always seeking the brighter lights. A city that doesn't go dark at night. What could fit the bill better than New York? But, still, my head aches, my joints burn.

Still, on bad days, the City disappears from around me. And it is as if I have returned to the farmhouse. I look up at the sky. And where stars should be washed out by the lights of New York, instead I see again the powder blue of the countryside, with streaks of clouds like the fingers of a hand, some white, others gray or pink—a hand reaching over the horizon. And then I barely remember. I barely remember that one day, many years ago, the skies split open. And from the hole where the sky had been, descended . . . a sound. A sound I fight to forget.

13

"Layers upon layers of mesh. Each layer, a screen, holding a memory. Some memories, easier to touch. These, put up front, on display. Behind them, others—of shame and violation and pain—these, left in obscure places, far back as possible. Yet their presence bleeds through. So that the viewer, casually perusing the collection, is disturbed, a chill runs through his body. For even as he gazes at the most ordinary of memories, he becomes aware of other images he is not supposed to see. In this way, the screens behind acquire a power greater than those in front. The room is saturated with the presence of things hidden."

14

I was afraid when I woke up this morning. Afraid to discover that last night had been more than a bad dream.

I wondered if I should call her. I . . . I don't even have her number. Maybe she'll come into the Copy Shop again. But, no, would anyone I could love ever visit a man like me again?

The Copy Shop! I had to get to work, where 150 people would surround me at 8 a.m., all waving sheets of paper, calling me "jerk" and "schmuck" and "asshole." The alarm was ringing. It was 7:45. I brought my hand down on the clock—

And time leaves me. I step temporarily outside its domain.

When my hand comes off the clock, it's 7:30. Seven in the— The sun is already starting to set. The day is lost. Did I go to work? I'm still in my pajamas. I have to call my boss. I pick up the phone—

And time leaves me. I step temporarily outside its domain. The hands on the clock become fluid. Running off the face like water.

The phone is dead. The curtain's descended on the day, bringing—night! Darkness! Again—I'm in the dark again! The clock reads 10:40 a.m. My head is pounding itself raw. I have to take a pill—any pill. I run to the bathroom, pull open the medicine cabinet—

And time leaves me. I step temporarily outside its domain. The metronome clicks, hums, sings an aria. And time, obedient, follows its lead.

The bottle is in pieces on the floor, pills and broken glass beneath my feet. I step over them all, hard, letting the shards puncture the soles of my feet, lodge themselves there, anything—to keep me here in this world. Where is the clock? Clock? What good is a clock? What does a clock do, but spit out random numbers? Time is a lottery. 10:10 p.m.

1:30 a.m. What day?

Twelve. Noon or midnight? Check the sky. The sky is—

Black, no—

Red, no—

Gray. What time is gray? Have years gone by? Are the people I once knew long gone, leaving me alone in this room?

15

All right, then! I surrender! I can no longer hold the universe at bay. There is a universe in my mind, struggling to make its way out. Memories slip between the cracks. The trickles become a torrent, carrying me away. At this moment, I've lost my job, I've lost any sense of a world beyond me. And, worst of all, I've lost the will even to hope—that her life, the beating of her heart, could drown out these sounds! What choice do I have? No place could be as alien as this world has become.

I've run everywhere to escape my memories, everywhere but into my mind itself.

Part II

16

I enter my mind. And there I find webs upon webs. What a mess! It's been neglected for so long—patterns, stretched, altered over a lifetime of denial. I have to start again. Piecing bit by bit. The fragments that float to the surface.

I feel like it's a matter of focus. If I could only twist my eyes around, like the lens of a camera. I could bring it all into focus. And I would find myself encased in a globe. A whole world, where the pieces finally fit together, each with their proper place. A world to fit the sound.

17

"A pendulum. Off-center. Swinging too far to one side."

"Galileo. Picking up the earth, pushing it slightly off-center, and, in so doing, setting into motion a series of dislocations, like dominoes falling, shooting our earth farther and farther toward the edge of the universe."

"The world we see in a mirror. Parallel to ours, yet precisely reversed. A world with its own rules, yet dependent on ours, as we on it, in order to see ourselves."

18

I hear a voice—no, not sound waves. Something in my head, speaking in the voice of my own conscience:

"It is better to forget. It is pointless to remember. No one will believe you. You will have spoken a heresy. You will be outcast."

I work against the voice, though it grows louder.

19

On that night, in that farmhouse, when a hole appeared in the sky. The hole appeared and a sound came down. And the sound made light. And the light made my skin glow. And there was no more need for horses, or snow, or the fingers of pink and gray in the sky. There was only sound, sound and light, light to see, and sound to . . . sound to touch.

20

"Distance. All space compressed onto the head of the pin. A pin at once infinitely small and infinitely large. Its size dependent on whether one stands at a level with it or looks down from above."

21

"Hives. Thousands of creatures working as one. It is impossible to determine whether these are many beings conforming to one, or one being split into many."

22

On the farm, I remember, there was a hive. A hive of bees, which the man would come several times a year to tend. Dressed in his canvas suit, a window for his eyes, like a spaceman. Like a spaceman, he would touch the hive, bloated, with the fury all round his head.

After the night the sky opened, I remember spending hours. Hours watching the hive. The buzzing growing louder and louder, until it filled my brain, circling round my head. Growing louder and louder, beacuse one day, after weeks of watching and listening, one day, I walked toward it. Not with the spaceman's uniform, but only my body, exposed and vulnerable as it is every day in the world. I walked up to the hive. Then, like an orb, I held it. And the pain that followed seemed to relieve me of all my questions. Until I woke up in a hospital bed. Covered with welts and blood. And so, looking no longer human, I rose up like an alien. I rose out of my bed. And I began to run.

23

I must return to the hive. In order to understand. But can I do it this time? Can I penetrate the swarms? This time, I must not lose consciousness. Or else I wake up again in a hospital bed, running.

24

"It is better to forget. It is pointless to remember . . . remember. You will have spoken a heresy. . . . a heresy. You will be outcast."

25

In a hive! These words were spoken in a hive! With hundreds of creatures! One night on my—no, *above—above*—my farm! The sky—the sky . . . one night . . .

26

The sky burst open, and the rains came down. The rains, like slivers of sound, surrounding me, falling onto my face, fusing into one whole thing, until I stood at the center of a solid pillar of sound. It pushed in on me, gently, like soft rubber, against my face and body. The sound was . . . as if, on the roof, there had been . . . a thousand airplanes.

27

There are visitors who travel across the universe. Why? I don't know. How? I think I know. They travel because they've come to understand the role of matter over the five dimensions. There are always two ways to travel—the hard way . . . and the easy way. The hard way is across space—the easy way is within space.

The lone Zen monk, sitting on a frozen hillside, outside a pavilion, has also mastered the easy way. He turns his eyes inward. And finds, there, an imprint of the universe. And, then, wherever he wants to be, he has already arrived.

Part III

28

How can I say it? Even to myself—without thinking I'm crazy? And, yet, if it is the truth . . . and I continue to deny it, in order to appear sane . . . isn't that true insanity?

29

When I was with her—my girlfriend—there was a moment. Just a moment, long before the building disappeared. It was the moment in the Copy Shop when I first saw her, and I asked, "You don't know me, but would you like to take a walk?" There was a moment, when she hesitated. And I thought, no, I've made a terrible mistake, I'm fraternizing with the customers, she's going to call the police, quick, look away, pretend you never said a thing.

30

But as those thoughts passed through my mind, I chanced for an instant to look into her eyes. And saw the stream of thoughts passing there. As I think she did mine. Because I saw something change. I saw her thinking, "No, this is ridiculous, I can't go with him, but, no, look at his eyes, he's thinking, like me, he's thinking, no, he couldn't be, but what if?, if there's even the possibility, then, yes, I've got to, yes, I must, try."

She had never really been my girlfriend. Except maybe for that instant. In that instant, we each saw ourselves in the eyes of another. And she said, "Yes."

The truth? The truth is the sound. The sound came for me in the night. The sky split open. Over a field, near a converted farmhouse.

The truth? Like a rape victim, afraid of the stares and the condemnation, I have tried to bury it. Hiding my head under blankets, clinging to nooks and crannies. Having buried the truth, I find only guilt remains.

The truth? What I know, I have to say. If only once. If only to myself. I have been visited by beings from other worlds. They come to earth and, on several occasions, they have taken me away.

31

And, then, an old feeling burrows up from beneath the pavement of my memory. Awakened. The sound. It's so real. How can it be—? It's as if I'm again—I'm in my apartment. Is it a memory? No, I'm again in that converted farmhouse. And the buildings—the City is gone. Something forms around me, taking shape . . . something impossible.

The sound. It's here. It's come for me again.

I stand up, and the air around me explodes into black dots. I grope for the window, and the shade drops down on its own power.

My chair rises up, bounces about, to some electrical dance, the rest of the furniture joins in! The ashtray jumps off the coffee table, and twirls like a top. The carpet rolls itself up, then springs back out again.

Pots and pans in the kitchen clatter against one another. And the television explodes with a loud "kaboom," the sound of the electricity, shorting out across the wires. All these sounds join hands, until they are a web around me, closing in. And the harmless sound waves, they are once again solid, once again my visitor . . . and I, once more, their prisoner. No more apartment. No more City. No more people. Gone, all gone. Only the sound. I see the sound. I taste the sound. And, so, absorbed into sound, I am taken along with it. We go where the waves travel, together, up.

32

And then, sound, solid, falls away. And I strain my eyes. To see.

33

I remember once, at work, I allowed my hand to move a pen across the page without my knowledge. By the time I became aware, it was too late. My hand had sketched a machine. Like a blueprint. Doodled to precision over five dimensions. I couldn't begin to understand what my hand had drawn. I only knew that looking at it, my breathing stopped. Very quickly, I tore up the paper. And burned the bits. The smoke and ashes filled my lungs, making me cough.

Now, my eyes see what my hand had remembered. The architecture of the visitors is built to precise specifications over five dimensions. Walls which are straight in the third dimension appear curved in the fourth. Rooms requiring twenty-seven steps to pace in the fourth dimension may demand half a day in the fifth. And there's always enough room for guests. Because each guest, arriving, adds to the room's total space exactly one person's perception of its area. And, departing, he subtracts precisely one view of the room from the room itself.

34

The room begins to buzz, as members of the hive arrive. The room grows bigger as they enter, now, all headed toward me. I know where I'm supposed to go. They are surrounding me. Touching me. I have become another part of the hive. My will submerged, I am carried along.

35

I'm naked. The light glints off the probe. The silver globe. Up—oh, God—up again—into my right nostril. The one that bleeds. My head starts to ache. I feel the flesh—behind my eye—stretched. My eye! It'll pop out of its socket! It's breaking! Something is breaking through!

36

And then, on my naked stomach, there is a warm glow. Something touching me. I open my eyes. It's him. How do I know it's a him? I don't. But it's him. The one that told me to smell—and remember.

He puts his hand on my stomach. While he manipulates the globe, with something like his fingers. There is only numbness, then I hear the squishy wetness as it penetrates my brain.

In the voice of my conscience, I ask, "What are you doing to me?"

In the voice of my conscience, he answers, "Smell. Smell . . . and you will remember."

I breathe, and the burning begins again. Flames engulfing my brain. What am I changing into?

37

I look into those eyes. I see my face, reflected. Its terror strikes me as silly, and so I start to laugh. And then, I breathe, causing the burning once again, but this time I ignore it. Because I'm seeing . . . behind my skin—into my temporal lobe—the seat of all consciousness. And there, at the top of his fingers, there is the silver globe, lodged deep up into my brain. In the voice of my conscience, he explains: "By this, we know you. And you know us."

"But why? Why do you travel this distance? And why are you interested in me?"

I breathe again. And, looking into his eyes, I see the globe grow larger. Until it covers the length of my body. I stand up as it opens for me. I get inside. Curl myself into a ball. It closes around me. Then shoots off into space. Across all the five dimensions.

38

I travel past rows of faces, each varying slightly from my own. My father's face, my grandfather's face, back generations, to before the time of humans, long-past faces bearing any resemblance to our own. Then, forward, faces yet to be born—my son, his child, their daughter, on and on, until those faces, as well, lose their familiar shapes and evolve into alien forms. I am following this line of faces, one transforming into another, until finally I am looking once again at him.

The globe is gone, I am back on the table. And I realize all this time, I have been looking into his face. Seeing in his eyes a mirror reflecting myself. And, all this time he has been looking into my eyes, and he, too, has seen himself.

Now, I understand why they travel. Why any of us ever feels the need to walk across a room toward another being whose heart beats and whose flesh smells of life.

We are all visitors. We all travel. We all ask questions. We all hope one day, looking into the eyes of another, to find part of an answer.

We all perceive.

39

After length, and width, and depth, and time, the fifth dimension is perception.

40

My nose. I know there'll be bleeding when I return home. There always is. But this time, I'll understand . . . and remember.

Part IV

41

There is a gray cloud hanging over New York. And flakes, tiny particles, illuminated by the rising sun, glowing as they fall. It looks like the earth has fallen into nuclear winter. A radio voice blares from someone's window. 7:15 a.m. The pavement is intact, steps beneath me are solid. Knock, knock. The radio says fires have broken out all over West Virginia, North Carolina, Kentucky, winds have blown the ashes thousands of miles to New York. 7:15 a.m. I head off—for work.

42

From out of the gray cloud, New York reappears. I remember all the details. And the fact that the City is fluid, that faces appear and disappear in its walls and gratings—it's not scary anymore. I know they're watching me. But now I'm watching them, too. In our familiarity, we've become distant equals.

I'm thinking about maybe buying another farmhouse. Of course, I'd have to make some money. I walk into the Copy Shop. And my boss asks me where I've been. For how long?

Four days?

43

Running my hand over my face. What is this? I have a beard. My clothes are unwashed. I'm still in my pajamas! God, I've soiled my pants front and back. My hands are covered with filth. I stink. "Where have I been?" For four days?

Four— You mean, I haven't eaten or drunk a thing in four—? My mouth closes, my throat . . . gags . . . Room explodes. Black dots. Converging.

44

When I wake up, I'm in . . . a spaceship? What is this? Strapped to a table? No, wait. The smells are different. No rotten leaves. This time . . . I smell . . . Listerine. I'm on earth. In a hospital. The doctor looks down from above. In a voice far removed from my conscience he asks, "Where have you been?"

Where have I been?

45

I've been on a spaceship. I've been in contact with the visitors. Several times they've abducted me. Only this time, I remembered. Their methods of travel. The patterns in their architecture. I looked into the face of one and saw my own, and he looked into mine . . . You see, it all started with this girl—

I can't stay that.

46

"It is better to forget. It is pointless to remember. No one will believe you. You will have spoken a heresy. You will be outcast."

47

To think that there are others who live, closer to the center of the universe, possessing a sophistication befitting their position. To think that we are only poor backwards cousins—no, no, no. Galileo died years ago, but humans, in our arrogance, still believe that the universe revolves around us.

"It is better to forget. It is pointless to remember. No one will believe you. You will have spoken a heresy. You will be outcast."

48

"Where have you been?" asks the doctor.

In the voice of my own conscience, I reply, "Four days? I've been sick. I bumped my head."

Upon saying the words, I begin at once to forget.
Like a tape run backward, visions of my memories are swallowed up, erased.

49

What I remember, couldn't possibly have happened.

Then, it must've been a dream.

I've had dreams before, that was no dream.

But it couldn't have happened.

Then, there's only one explanation—if it can't have happened, it didn't.

And my memories?

They're at odds with what happened. Are you crazy?

I'm not crazy!

Then you can't have such memories.

I don't. Whatever they were—I forget them.

50

The doctor finds my explanation incomplete. He says, "Lying here, you talked in your sleep. A fantastic story."

It . . . must be a dream, I reply.

"Yes. Probably. But I feel compelled to ask:

"Do you ever see faces above the subways?"

No, I do not.

"Have you ever been visited by beings from other worlds?"

I have not.

"You've never been afraid to return to a farmhouse?"

No.

"You've never touched a beehive?"

No.

"Has your apartment building ever disappeared before your eyes?"

It has not.

"Has the furniture in your apartment ever been visited by a paranormal experience?"

It has not.

"Has a sound appeared to you in the flesh?"

It has not.

"Has it ever imprisoned you?"

It has not.

"Do you understand the mechanics of the fourth and fifth dimensions?"

I do not.

"Do you even have any idea what they are?"

I do not.

"Have you ever studied Zen or any of the Eastern disciplines?"

I have not.

"Is there imprinted in your person a plan of the cosmos?"

There is not.

"Does the presence of a silver globe mean anything to you?"

It does not.

"Has your hand ever drawn, in its spare moments, machines beyond your comprehension?"

It has not.

"Have you ever seen any such machines?"

I have not.

"Do you remember a room smelling like rotting leaves?"

I do not.

"Do hives, such as those of bees and other insects, play a part in your memories?"

They do not.

"Did anyone ever ask you to remember?"

No one has asked that.

"Have you ever looked into the eyes of another, and there found answers?"

No.

"Have you ever seen yourself in the face of another?"

No.

"You've never crawled into any small globe?"

No.

"You've never followed a line of faces?"

No.

"You've never shot out across space?"

No.

"You've never been told to forget?"

No.

"You have nothing to forget?"

No.

"You're forgetting nothing?"

That is correct.

The doctor tells me I may return to the world. I will no longer tell stories which cannot be verified. I will wear clothes which are not soiled with myself. I will shave my face and dress in conservative colors. When I look out the door into the sky, I will see only the glow of neon.

51

I run home through the Soho streets, as the ground opens beneath my feet. I run home, away from the faces over the subways. It's a normal reaction. To be terrified.

I had a bad day. I was confused because I once lived on a farm. But, no longer. Now, I live in New York City. And the lights are always bright. And the people are always present. And my mind . . . my mind is calm. With, yet, with only . . . just a little pulse, a little throbbing some-place, hardly noticeable, behind my nostrils in the front of my brain. Just a minor thing.

The throbbing grows. It threatens to become a sound. There is a universe in my mind, struggling to break out. And I'm a normal man. A normal man, running.

THE END

EXCEPTIONAL PLAYS